Cracking the SAT Chemistry Subject Test

Cracking the SAT Chemistry Subject Test

THEODORE SILVER, M.D. AND
THE STAFF OF THE PRINCETON REVIEW

2005–2006 EDITION

RANDOM HOUSE, INC.
NEW YORK

www.PrincetonReview.com

The Independent Education Consultants Association recognizes The Princeton Review as a valuable resource for high school and college students applying to college and graduate school.

Princeton Review Publishing, L.L.C.
2315 Broadway
New York, NY 10024
E-mail: booksupport@review.com

ISBN: 0-375-76448-8

SAT is a registered trademark of the College Board.

Editor: Rachel Warren
Production Editor: Patricia Dublin
Production Coordinator: Ryan Tozzi

Manufactured in the United States of America.

9 8 7 6 5 4 3

2005–2006 Edition

ACKNOWLEDGMENTS

The author thanks John Bergdahl, Greta Blau, Cynthia Brantley, Sarah Brockett, Jessica Brockington, Joseph Cavallaro, Ji Sun Chang, Andrew Dunn, Leland Elliott, Alicia Ernst, Kristin Fayne-Mulroy, Paul Foglino, Effie Hadjiioannou, Julian Ham, Adam Hurwitz, Sung (Peter) Jung, Sara Kane, Jason Kantor, Chris Kensler, Martha Link, Illeny Maaza, Kim Magloire, Russell Murray, Jeff Nichols, John C. Pak, Dinica Quesada, Lisa M. Ruyter, Chris "short-hair" Scott, Ramsey Silberberg, Linda Tarleton, Chris Thomas, Thane Thomsen, Robert McCormack, P. J. Waters, and Chris Volpe.

Thanks also to Editor, Rachel Warren, Production Editor, Patricia Dublin, Production Coordinator, Ryan Tozzi, and Updater, Sandy Haberny.

Special thanks to Adam Robinson, who conceived of and perfected the Joe Bloggs approach to standardized tests and many of the successful techniques used by The Princeton Review.

CONTENTS

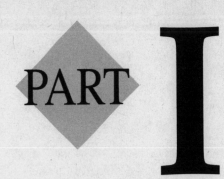

PART I

Orientation

1 Introduction

WHAT ARE THE SAT SUBJECT TESTS?

The SAT Subject Tests are a series of tests administered by the Educational Testing Service (ETS). Unlike the regular SAT, the SAT Subject Tests are designed to measure knowledge in very specific areas. About one-third of all colleges require that you take one or more of these tests in order to qualify for admissions; but even at colleges that do not require that you take them, administrators view student performances on the tests as an important factor that contributes to the decision to grant or withhold admission. Additionally, at some schools, a high score on one or more of the tests might enable you to "place out" of certain required college courses. For example, if you do well on the SAT Chemistry Subject Test, you might be exempt from fulfilling the science requirement at one or more of the schools to which you're applying!

WHICH SAT SUBJECT TESTS SHOULD I TAKE?

The colleges that do require you to take the SAT Subject Tests will expect you to take two or three of them. In order to find out which tests are required by the colleges to which you're applying, you can ask your guidance counselor, call the admissions office of the colleges, or check in college guidebooks. Alternately, you can visit the College Board website at **www.collegeboard.com** and use their college search engine to look up the colleges you're interested in; each school on this search engine has a profile in which this information is provided.

Once you find out which, if any, tests are required, part of your decision making is done. The next step is to find out which of the tests will show your particular strengths. After all, the SAT Subject Tests are given in a variety of subjects: Literature, U.S. History, World History, Biology, Chemistry, Physics, French, German, Spanish, Modern Hebrew, Italian, Latin, Japanese, Korean, Chinese, and English Language Proficiency. You should take the tests on which you think you'd score the highest. If you're fluent in Chinese, take the SAT Chinese Test. If, however, you're most comfortable in the world of moles, atoms, and titrations, take the SAT Chemistry Test—and read on.

When Are the Tests Offered, and How Do I Register for Them?

The SAT Subject Tests are administered in October, November, December, January, May, and June at test centers around the country. Since not all the tests are offered at each administration, be sure to check the dates and details on the College Board website carefully. You'll want to take the test on a date that's as close as possible to the end of your coursework in the subject. For example, if your chemistry course ends December 21, take the January test. If it ends in May, take the test in May or June—whichever date falls the soonest after your course has ended.

You can register for these tests either through the College Board website or through regular mail. To register by mail, ask your guidance counselor for the appropriate forms, which you'll need to mail in by the date listed on the College Board website—generally about five weeks before the test. You can register late, but late registration ends about four weeks prior to the test week and will cost you an additional $18. The costs of registering for individual tests vary; any language test with listening costs $12 and all of the other tests cost $8. In other words, taking the SAT Chemistry Subject Test will cost you less than going to the movies and is certain to be just as entertaining!

You'll need to arrive at the test center pretty early—by 8:15 A.M. Your first test will begin promptly at 8:30 A.M., and since each test is an hour long, if you take the maximum of the three tests that you're allowed to take at each sitting, you'll be done by 12:30 P.M. If you're taking just one or two tests, you can leave as soon as you've finished.

One final, but important, note—ETS allows you to change your mind about what test you'd like to take, *on* the test day. This means that if you aren't sure which test you'll feel more confident taking, you can study up until test day and then make your decision at the last moment.

How Is the Test Scored, and What Does the Score Mean?

As with the regular SAT, the SAT Subject Tests are scored on a scale from 200 to 800, where 200 is the lowest and 800 is the highest; the exception to this rule is the English Language Proficiency Test, which is scored on a scale from 901 to 999.

Subject tests that do not involve written responses (such as the SAT Chemistry) are graded by a computer. The computer simply adds up the number of questions you answered correctly and subtracts from this number one-quarter of the number of questions you answered incorrectly. (It doesn't count questions that you skipped either way.) This determines your raw test score. The raw score is then converted to a scaled score.

So, what's a good score on the SAT Chemistry? Well, a good score is one that falls in, or above, the range that the colleges you are interested in state as desirable. On the scale from 200 to 800, 500 is considered the average score of all test takers. If you score higher than this, your performance on the test is above average—if you score lower, then your performance is below average. Along with your regular score, you'll receive a percentile rank; this is another indication of how you fared in relation to all of the other test takers. If you receive a percentile ranking of 60 percent, that means that you scored higher than did 60 percent of test takers and lower than 40 percent of test takers. But keep in mind that even if your score is below average, or below the range that the schools of your choice list as being desirable for entrance, this doesn't necessarily mean that you won't get into these schools. Your scores on the SAT Subject Tests are not the only factor that goes into the admissions decision.

WHEN CAN I SEE MY TEST RESULTS?

About eight days after you sit for the test(s), you will be able to access your test scores over the phone for a fee of $8. A hard copy of your score report is then sent to you, as well as to your high school through regular mail approximately three to five weeks after the test date. How will colleges get your test results? Well, when you first register for the SAT Subject Tests, you're allowed to give the names of four schools to which you'd like your scores sent. If you want additional schools to receive your scores, you can request this through the College Board website, which will cost you $6.50 per request. You can also phone in a request, but this costs more: $10 for the phone call, plus $6.50 for the request.

Keep in mind that when you request additional copies of your scores to go to a school, the College Board automatically sends the results of ALL of the tests you've taken thus far—including previous scores for tests you may have taken more than once. In other words, it's all or nothing, as far as additional score reports go!

WHAT IS THE PRINCETON REVIEW?

The Princeton Review is a test-preparation company based in New York City, but we have offices across the country and abroad. We've developed the techniques you'll find in our books, courses, and online resources by analyzing actual tests and testing their effectiveness with our students. What makes our techniques unique is that they're based on the same techniques that the test writers use when they write the tests. We don't want you to waste your time with superfluous content; we'll give you only the information you need to get a great score. You'll also learn to avoid common test traps, think like the test writers, find answers to questions you're unsure of, and budget your time effectively. You need to do only two things: (1) learn chemistry the way the subject test tests it, and (2) approach the test strategically.

POINT 1: LEARN CHEMISTRY THE WAY THE SUBJECT TEST TESTS IT

ETS says that the SAT Chemistry Subject Test, among many other subjects, tests the concept of Gibbs free energy.

If you sat and read your chemistry textbook to prepare for this test, you'd read a whole lot of material relating to Gibbs free energy that definitely will *not* be tested. You'd see diagrams such as this.

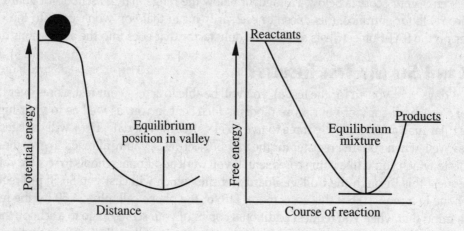

And you'd read text such as this.

> We may consider free-energy change in a spontaneous reaction much as we consider the potential energy change that accompanies the rolling of an ordinary ball down a hill. The ball is driven down the hill by the potential energy within a gravitational field. By analogy, the free energy within a chemical system decreases continuously over time . . . blah, blah, blah . . . ultimately reaching a minimum. When potential energy is at a minimum, the reaction reaches its equilibrium.
>
> We might best illustrate the concept by reference to the formation of ammonia from its elements hydrogen and . . . blah, blah, blah. . . . Imagine that a particular number of moles of nitrogen react with three times the number of hydrogen atoms. The formation of ammonia will not be complete because . . . blah, blah, blah. . . . An equilibrium will be attained by the system, and at equilibrium the reaction chamber will contain a mixture of . . . blah, blah, blah. . . . At that time there can be no additional spontaneous formation of ammonia because the system has reached a minimum state of free energy that . . . blah, blah, blah. . . . Free energy is a state function, and that is why. . . blah, blah, blah. . . .

The text would go on and on, intimidating and boring you but would offer nothing that raises your test score. You'd get so sick of it that you'd stop reading.

When we teach you about Gibbs free energy, we tell you exactly what you have to know to raise your test score. As we do that we give you opportunities to practice on realistic chemistry problems, to make sure you're with us at every step. The most important thing for you to remember about Gibbs free energy is that it is symbolized as ΔG, and that if ΔG is negative, the reaction proceeds spontaneously in the forward direction, but if it's positive, the reaction proceeds spontaneously in the reverse direction.

In other words, you need to associate:

$-\Delta G$ with: a reaction that proceeds spontaneously in the forward direction

$+\Delta G$ with: a reaction that proceeds spontaneously in the reverse direction

Now try to answer the following two questions:

<u>Directions:</u> Each set of lettered choices below refers to the numbered statements or formulas immediately following it. Select the one lettered choice that best fits each statement or formula and then fill in the corresponding oval on the answer sheet. A choice may be used once, more than once, or not at all in each set.

Questions 1–2

    (A) Heat of formation
    (B) Work
    (C) Entropy
    (D) Gibbs free energy
    (E) Enthalpy

1. Must be negative if reaction proceeds spontaneously in forward direction

2. Must be positive if reaction proceeds spontaneously in reverse direction

The answers are both D, and you know that simply by making the associations we talked about. The computer that grades your test doesn't care if you know why the answer is D; it just wants to see the D oval filled in on your answer sheet.

POINT 2: APPROACH THE TEST STRATEGICALLY

It isn't enough to study chemistry the way the SAT Chemistry Subject Test tests it, you must also study the questions themselves. You will need to understand the way they're designed and be familiar with certain techniques that systematically lead to correct answers.

When you sit down to take this test, you won't know the answers to all of the questions. But in Chapter 2 of this book, we'll show you ways to choose the correct answer even if you don't know it right away. We'll present eight strategies that will help you "outsmart" the SAT Chemistry Subject Test and its writers. Then, in Chapters 3 through 14, we'll show you over and over again how to use them.

Our strategies are powerful stuff. They teach you how to find the right answers logically and systematically—in much the same way that a detective solves a crime.

WHAT ABOUT PRACTICE AND PRACTICE TESTS?

This book is interactive. Over and over again you show us what you've learned. We don't put a long line of "drill questions" at the end of each chapter. Instead, we teach, and then we test—right away—with subject test–type questions. We check your progress page by page, paragraph by paragraph, and make sure you're with us every step of the way. If you're not, we help you figure out *why* you're not.

You might notice that our book cover is unlike most others. It doesn't promise you six, seven, or eight full-length practice tests. It would be easy for us to fill our pages with simulated test after simulated test, but testing yourself repeatedly with practice tests won't raise your score. You'll just prove that you can get the same score over and over again.

However, Chapters 15, 16, and 17 of this book are made up of three full-length tests, complete with explanations that are just like the real SAT Chemistry Subject Test. As you work your way through these tests, you'll become more comfortable with the way that ETS tests content, and when you sit down to take the real test on test day, you'll be more than prepared.

SHOULD I BUY PRACTICE MATERIAL FROM ETS?

It isn't a bad idea. If you want to take more than just the three tests in this book, the College Board publishes a book called *The Official Guide to the SAT II: Subject Tests*. Take the chemistry test that's in their book, and see how easy it is after you've worked through our book. It should be a piece of cake.

> For book updates, links to more information, and last-minute test changes, visit this book's online companion at www.PrincetonReview.com/cracking.

Test Strategies

CRACKING THE SAT CHEMISTRY

The SAT Chemistry Subject Test is made up of 85 multiple-choice questions, and you have one hour to answer them. You're not allowed to use a calculator on this test, but you won't need one. The test is divided into three sections: Parts A, B, and C, and each section is made up of a different type of question. Let's take a closer look at these parts.

PART A: CLASSIFICATION QUESTIONS

The first 20 to 25 questions you'll see on the exam fall under the category of what ETS calls Classification Questions. In this type of question, you'll see a list of five words or phrases lettered A through E, followed by three to five questions. But sometimes the questions aren't really questions; they're phrases. Your job is to match the phrase in the "question" with a word or phrase that appears in the list A through E. Forget about chemistry for a minute, and see how it works.

Directions: Each set of lettered choices below refers to the numbered statements or questions immediately following it. Select the one lettered choice that best fits each statement or answers each question and then fill in the corresponding oval on the answer sheet. A choice may be used once, more than once, or not at all in each set.

Questions 1–4

    (A) Red light
    (B) Swimming pool
    (C) Piano
    (D) Fire engine
    (E) Ocean liner

1. Musical instrument that involves keyboard outside and strings inside

2. Motor vehicle designed to assist in effort to extinguish flames

3. Sea vessel that carries passengers across large bodies of water

4. Water-filled pit designed for recreational or athletic activities

The answers, of course, are C, D, E, and B. Now let's move on and see what the questions in Part B look like.

PART B: RELATIONSHIP ANALYSIS QUESTIONS

The questions that make up Part B of the exam won't ask you to decide among choices A, B, C, D, or E. Relationship analysis questions consist of two statements with the word BECAUSE in-between them. You're supposed to figure out if the statements are true or false. If both are true, you're also expected to figure out whether the word BECAUSE belongs there. Once again, forget about chemistry for a second so we can show you how the questions work. The questions in part B of the exam are numbered in a peculiar manner. This section begins with the number 101, although there are only 85 questions in the whole test!

Directions: Each question below consists of two statements, I in the left-hand column and II in the right-hand column. For each question, determine whether statement I is true or false <u>and</u> whether statement II is true or false and fill in the corresponding T or F ovals on your answer sheet. <u>Fill in oval CE only if statement II is a correct explanation of statement I.</u>

	I		**II**
101.	If one takes a shower, one gets wet	BECAUSE	the shower head releases water that falls on the individual taking the shower.
102.	If one walks rapidly, one will be in motion	BECAUSE	automobiles burn gasoline.
103.	A boat will sink if it fills with water	BECAUSE	it is impossible for a boat to develop a leak.
104.	President Lincoln died of natural causes	BECAUSE	Lincoln was president during the Civil War.
105.	Omaha, Nebraska, is the capital of the United States	BECAUSE	Omaha is the largest city in the entire world.

Question 101 Both statements are true and the "because" belongs there. You get wet in a shower *because* the shower pours water on you.

Question 102 Both statements are true. If you walk, you move, and automobiles do burn gasoline. But the "because" doesn't belong there. A walker doesn't move *because* automobiles burn gasoline. The statements have nothing to do with one another.

Question 103 A boat will sink if it fills with water. That's true. But the second statement is false. Boats *can* develop leaks.

Question 104 The first statement is false. Lincoln was murdered. The second statement is true. He was president during the Civil War.

Question 105 Both statements are false. Omaha is not the capital of the United States, and it isn't the largest city in the world.

Now let's talk about the third and final section of the exam, Part C.

PART C: FIVE-CHOICE COMPLETION QUESTIONS

The question-type that makes up the majority of the test (40–50 questions) are ordinary looking multiple-choice questions such as the one below.

28. Which is the formula of a compound?
   (A) HCl
   (B) He
   (C) Cu
   (D) O_2
   (E) Br_2

Here, the answer is A. A **compound** is a chemical combination of two or more elements. (We'll talk more about that later.) This type of question is straightforward: You read the question and choose the answer choice that best answers the question.

Now that you know what kinds of questions you'll see on the SAT Chemistry Subject Test, let's talk about the strategies you can use to tackle these questions.

STRATEGY #1: STUDY THE RIGHT STUFF IN THE RIGHT WAY

One important strategy for preparing to take this exam is to study only the concepts that will be tested. In Chapters 3 through 14, we will take a look at all the subjects that are certain to appear on the test and explain them in a way that's specifically designed to help you answer the test questions.

What topics do we cover? Well, the same topics that the College Board lists on their website as being covered.

I. Structure of Matter (25% of the questions will be on this topic): atomic theory and structure, periodic relationships, chemical bonding and molecular structure, nuclear reactions

II.   States of Matter (15%): kinetic molecular theory of gases; gas laws; liquids, solids, and phase changes; solutions, concentration units, solubility, conductivity, and colligative properties

III. Reaction Types (14%): acids and bases, oxidation-reduction, and precipitation

IV.   Stoichiometry (12%): mole concept and Avogadro's number, empirical formula and molecular formulas, percent composition, stoichiometric formulas, and limiting reagents

V.   Equilibrium and Reaction Rates (7%): gas equilibria, ionic equilibria, Le Chatelier's principle, equilibrium expressions, rate of reaction

VI.   Thermodynamics (6%): energy changes in chemical reactions and physical properties; Hess's law; randomness

VII. Descriptive Chemistry (13%): physical and chemical properties of elements and their familiar compounds; chemical reactivity and products of chemical reactions; simple examples from organic chemistry and environmental chemistry

VIII. Laboratory (8%): equipment, measurements, procedures, observations, safety, calculations, and interpretations of results

As you can see, we do not include everything there is to know about chemistry, since your chemistry textbook does that. We just hope to strengthen and refresh your knowledge in the specific areas that will be important on the test.

STRATEGY #2: DO THE EASY ONES FIRST

In each of the three sections of the SAT Chemistry Subject Test, the easier questions tend to come first and the harder ones come later. When you begin each section, answer as many of the "easy" questions as you can, but when they start to become more difficult, go on to the next section and do the same. Once you've answered all of the relatively easy questions in all the sections, go back to each section and start answering the more difficult ones.

This strategy makes sense because all questions are worth the same amount; answering a hard question correctly won't get you more points than answering an easy one correctly. If there's a chance that you might not be able to get to every question on the exam in the 60 minutes you're given, make sure you at least answer the ones you're sure to get right, first!

You don't need to answer every question to get a good score on the SAT Chemistry. It's possible to leave 30 questions blank and still score near 600 if you do well on the questions you *do* answer.

STRATEGY #3: TAKE A GUESS!

As we told you in the last chapter, in calculating your "raw score" (from which it then calculates your scaled score), ETS does the following:

1. gives you one point for each question you answer correctly

2. deducts $\frac{1}{4}$ of a point for each question you answer incorrectly

3. doesn't count questions you didn't answer

Because ETS deducts one-quarter of a point for any question you answer incorrectly, you should definitely guess the answer to any question for which you can eliminate at least one of the five answer choices. If you can eliminate one answer choice and then take a guess, then you will have a one in four chance of choosing the correct answer. If you can eliminate two answer choices, your odds of choosing correctly go to one in three.

As you read Chapters 3 through 14 you'll see that all of our techniques and strategies teach you to eliminate wrong choices. After you've done that, use guessing to your advantage.

STRATEGY #4: MAKING ASSOCIATIONS (TYPE A, B, AND C QUESTIONS)

One helpful strategy for learning the key chemistry concepts that will show up on the test is to make associations between terms and concepts. What are we talking about? Well, let's forget chemistry, just to make the point. You may have learned in school that Teddy Roosevelt was a "trustbuster." You might not know what trusts are, how he busted them, why he wanted to bust them, or why anyone cares if trusts get busted. But if you learned to associate the name Teddy Roosevelt with the phrase "trustbuster," you would be able to answer a test question that looks like this.

- Theodore Roosevelt believed in

    (A) creating trusts
    (B) destroying trusts
    (C) making trusts larger
    (D) communism
    (E) socialistic economics

The association you learned to make—"Teddy Roosevelt" with "trustbuster"—allowed you to choose the correct answer: B.

This strategy will also be useful on the SAT Chemistry; many questions will test your ability to associate one word or phrase with another. For example, suppose you had no idea what was meant by "pH," "acid," or "base," and you had just learned to associate

pH less than 7 with: acid
pH greater than 7 with: base

You'd be able to answer a test question that looked like this:

- Which of the following solutions is most acidic?

  (A) A solution of phosphoric acid at pH 4
  (B) A solution of sodium hydroxide at pH 11
  (C) A solution of hydrochloric acid at pH 5
  (D) A solution of acetic acid at pH 6
  (E) A solution of aqueous ammonia at pH 9

Whatever else you know about acids and bases, you know that choice A is right because, among the listed solutions, it has the lowest pH.

Throughout our teaching of SAT Chemistry, we will show you what associations to make, how to make them, and how they will point you to the right answers on test day.

STRATEGY #5: AVOID THE CAMOUFLAGE TRAP (TYPE A AND C QUESTIONS)

In the questions seen in parts A and C on the exam, the test writers will sometimes try to make you fall into what we call the "camouflage trap."

To understand the camouflage trap, read the two sentences below.

1. In any dynamic chemical equilibrium, the removal of product will drive the equilibrium to the right and thus increase the concentration of product, while the concentration of reactants will decrease.

2. If a dynamic chemical equilibrium is subjected to withdrawal of product, the concentration of reactants will diminish, and the concentration of product will become greater.

These two statements mean exactly the same thing, but their wording is very different. Many of the words and phrases in statement 2 have the same meaning as those in statement 1, but they're disguised—they're camouflaged.

subjected to withdrawal of product	is camouflage for	the removal of product
concentration of product will become greater	is camouflage for	increase the concentration of product
concentration of reactants will diminish	is camouflage for	the concentration of reactants will decrease

So, What About It?

When you learn something, whether it's chemistry or anything else, you tend to learn it in certain particular phrases. For instance, maybe you think of an element as "a substance that cannot be broken into any simpler substance." Fine. But if you're too attached to that particular way of stating it, look what happens when you try to answer the question on the following page.

- Which of the following best describes the characteristics of an element?

    (A) It is capable of existing in relatively simple molecular forms.
    (B) It exists only in molar quantities.
    (C) It will always react with any other element.
    (D) It is a fundamental form of matter.
    (E) It is more reactive if the surrounding entropy is high.

If you're too attached to the way that you usually describe elements, you might not see the right answer although (a) you do know it, and (b) it's staring you in the face. The right answer to this question is D. To say that an element is a fundamental form of matter is, more or less, to say it can't be broken down into simpler substances. The words aren't the same, but the meaning is.

Many students who know what an element is might still not answer this question correctly. This is because they'll look quickly through the choices and not see anything they recognize—this throws them into "answer-choice panic," and they'll pick something that "sounds right"—something that has the word "simple" in it, such as choice A.

That's too bad. Students who do know the content sometimes choose the wrong answer simply because they fall for the camouflage trap.

Here's another example from a type C question. Suppose you know that: "The average kinetic energy of gas molecules is directly proportional to the absolute temperature of the gas." In other words, if you add heat to a sample of gas molecules, each molecule, on average, starts bouncing around faster than it did before. But you're accustomed to stating it this way:

> *The average kinetic energy of gas molecules is directly proportional to the absolute temperature of the gas.*

If you're married to that statement, what's going to happen when you see the question below?

- Which of the following is *always* increased by the addition of thermal energy to a sample of gas in a closed container?

    (A) Ideal gas constant
    (B) Average speed of gas molecules
    (C) Molecular weight of gas molecules
    (D) Volume of gas sample
    (E) Volatility

You know that increased heat increases average kinetic energy, but the answer has been camouflaged.

average speed of gas molecules	*is camouflage for*	average kinetic energy
addition of thermal energy	*is camouflage for*	increasing the temperature

Maybe you're not used to thinking of the "addition of thermal energy" resulting in an increase in temperature. When it comes to gases, you're also not accustomed to thinking of "average speed of gas molecules" as reflecting the average kinetic energy. Although you know your chemistry, you might not realize that the right answer to this question is B. You might decide to pick some crazy answer such as A or D. Why? Because you fell into the camouflage trap.

HERE'S THE GOOD NEWS: YOU CAN AVOID THE CAMOUFLAGE TRAP

To avoid the camouflage trap, keep some simple rules in mind.

- Remember that there's usually more than one way to say something.

- When you see a question that asks about a topic you've studied, don't fall apart just because the answer doesn't leap out at you right away.

- Relax. Realize that the right answer is probably camouflaged by words that are different from the ones you have in mind. Calmly search for them, and chances are, they *will* leap out at you.

In other words, keep an open mind. Don't expect test makers to use your words. Remember: The same concept or idea can be expressed in many different ways. Keep the concepts you know in mind, and don't get too attached to the words you use to express them.

ANOTHER WAY OUT OF THE CAMOUFLAGE TRAP:
TRANSLATE AND WORK BACKWARD

Suppose you *do* try to keep an open mind on a particular question, and it just doesn't seem to work; the right answer isn't coming to you, although you know your chemistry. For questions in Part A, here's what you can do: Look through all of the answer choices and restate them in your own words. Below, we've listed five possible answer choices you might see in Part A of the exam. Below each answer choice, we've included one way of restating the answer.

(A) ideal gas constant
It's the letter R in the equation PV = nRT. It equals about 0.082 $\frac{\text{L-atm}}{\text{mol-K}}$.

(B) average speed of gas molecules
It's the speed at which gas molecules are moving around in a tank or container—it has to do with how much energy they have. It goes up with higher temperature and down with lower temperature.

(C) molecular weight of gas molecules
It's the weight (expressed in amu) of a gas molecule.

(D) volume of gas sample
It's the space the gas sample takes up—equal to the size of the container.

(E) volatility
It has to do with how easily a liquid below its boiling point evaporates when it's sitting around.

Now look at each of the questions:

Questions 1–4

1. Is always increased by the addition of thermal energy to a sample of gas in a closed container

2. Can be related to the pressure of a gas sample by the ideal gas law

3. Property associated with vapor pressure

4. Depends on the formula of a gas but not its temperature

Read the questions carefully, one by one, and compare them to the answer choices that you've put into your own words.

1. Hopefully you realize that "thermal energy" means heat. Now, which of the answer choices (stated in your own words) has to do with a factor that's affected by the addition of heat? (B) does—it says that the average speed of gas molecules increases as heat (thermal energy) is added to the system and decreases as heat is taken away from a system. The answer to question 1 is (B).

2. If you know the ideal gas law (covered in Chapter 8), you would simply look among the answer choices for one of the variables from the equation, $PV = nRT$. In this equation, P = pressure, V = volume, n = number of moles of gas, R = the ideal gas constant, and T = temperature. Volume is the variable listed among the answer choices, so the correct answer is (D).

3. You should associate vapor pressure with the degree to which a liquid will evaporate at a temperature that's below its normal boiling point—and lo and behold, this is similar to how you've paraphrased choice (E): volatility. The answer is (E).

4. Read the question, and then look at the answer choices. Which of the choices, when stated in your words, mentions a characteristic of a gas that depends on its formula but not its temperature? Well, choice (C) looks like the most likely—the weight of a gas molecule does depend on its identity (formula) but not on its temperature. None of the other answer choices make any sense, so choose (C).

STRATEGY #6: AVOIDING THE TEMPTATION TRAP

Suppose we gave this question to a seven-year-old girl:

- Which of the following best expresses the effect of Gibbs free energy and the spontaneity of a chemical reaction?

    (A) When Gibbs free energy is negative, the reaction proceeds spontaneously in the forward direction.
    (B) When Gibbs free energy is negative, the reaction proceeds spontaneously in the reverse direction.
    (C) George Washington was the first president of the United States.
    (D) Gibbs free energy affects the spontaneity only of exothermic reactions.
    (E) Gibbs free energy affects the spontaneity only of endothermic reactions.

The child won't know what any of this means, but she *will* probably know that George Washington was the first president. So she'll choose C; it's something she knows. She fell into the "temptation trap." The test writer stuck something into the answer choices that was familiar to the student; it was so familiar that the student chose it although it has nothing to do with the question.

WHAT'S THAT GOT TO DO WITH ME AND THE SAT CHEMISTRY TEST?

A lot. The temptation trap usually rears its head on questions from Parts A and C of the exam. On the day you take the test, there will be many things you know and some that you don't know. When you meet up with a type C question that's stumping you, you might reach out and grab an answer choice that "sounds familiar" although it has nothing to do with the question.

Suppose you know that adding an acid to a base increases the hydrogen ion concentration of the solution. Now, look at this question.

- Which of the following will definitely occur if a quantity of acetic acid is added to a solution of potassium hydroxide at pH 11?

    (A) The number of free protons per liter of solution will increase.
    (B) Titration will tend to neutralize the solution.
    (C) The acetic acid will act as a weak base.
    (D) Acetate ion will precipitate out of solution.
    (E) The pH will remain constant.

The correct answer is A, but if the answer to this question doesn't leap right out at you, you might decide to make a dash for something you know. Choice B, by itself, is a true statement with which you might be familiar; titration between an acid and base does tend to neutralize a solution. You might say to yourself, quickly, quietly, and almost unconsciously: "I've heard that statement. It sounds right." But B is wrong because it doesn't answer the question.

HERE'S SOME MORE GOOD NEWS: YOU CAN AVOID THE TEMPTATION TRAP

The temptation and camouflage traps often work together. One choice tempts you, while the right answer is sitting there in camouflage.

When you find yourself ready to choose an answer because it sounds right, stop and look at the question again carefully. Then take another look at the answer choices to see if another of them, although in camouflage, is really a better answer to the question.

Let's think about the question we just looked at. We're adding an acid to a base. We know that we'll be lowering the pH of the solution—increasing the hydrogen ion concentration. Choice A says exactly that—in camouflage. Instead of referring to hydrogen ions, it refers to free protons. Instead of referring directly to concentration, or pH, it talks about increasing the number of protons per liter of solution. The right answer is A, and you knew it, but you might not have chosen it. Why? Because panic led you straight into the temptation trap. Don't let that happen!

STRATEGY #7: DIVIDE AND CONQUER

Let's take another look at the instructions to Part B.

<u>Directions:</u> Each question below consists of two statements, I in the left-hand column and II in the right-hand column. For each question, determine whether statement I is true or false <u>and</u> whether statement II is true or false and fill in the corresponding T or F ovals on your answer sheet. <u>Fill in oval CE only if statement II is a correct explanation of statement I.</u>

Now let's look at a question that has nothing to do with chemistry, to show how the divide and conquer strategy works.

<u>I</u>		<u>II</u>
101. All persons must breathe	BECAUSE	oxygen is necessary to human survival.

Here's what to do.

Step 1: Look at the first statement by itself and decide whether it's true or false. It's true. That means we fill in the oval marked T.

Step 2: Look at the second statement by itself. Is it true or false? It's true. That means we fill in the second oval marked T.

Step 3: Put the statements together, and join them with the "because," then decide if the sentence makes sense. "All persons must breathe *because* oxygen is necessary to human survival."

Does it make sense? Yes. So you would fill in the oval marked CE.

Try this question.

	I		II
102.	It is unlawful to drive while drunk	BECAUSE	most automobiles in the United States are powered by internal combustion engines.

Step 1: Look at statement I by itself. Is it true or false? It's true. We fill in the first oval marked T.

Step 2: Look at statement II by itself. Is it true or false? It's true. We fill in the second oval marked T.

Step 3: Now put them together. "It is unlawful to drive while drunk *because* most automobiles in the United States are powered by internal combustion engines."

Does it make sense? No. So we do not fill in the oval marked CE.

	I	II	CE
102	● ⓕ	● ⓕ	◯

Let's do another one.

	I		II
103.	All Americans are exactly alike in their beliefs	BECAUSE	no foreign country has ever made a valuable contribution to civilization.

Step 1: Look at statement I by itself. Is it true or false? It's false.

Step 2: Look at statement II by itself. Is it true or false? It's false.

	I	II	CE
103	ⓣ ●	ⓣ ●	◯

Notice that if either statement I or statement II is false, then there can be no cause-and-effect relationship, and you don't have to worry about filling in the CE oval.

When it comes to the divide and conquer strategy, use step 3 only if you determine that both statements are true.

LET'S GET GOING

In Chapters 3 through 14, we'll teach you chemistry with our own special tailored-to-the-subject-test method. All along the way we'll ask you subject test–type questions. Then we'll explain the answers, showing you how to use knowledge and strategy to earn a high score.

Some Basic Stuff

Some of the questions that appear early in each part of the SAT Chemistry Subject Test will ask about the basic properties of matter and how they're measured. In this chapter, we'll review some basic terms: *mass, volume, density, pressure, energy, temperature,* and *specific heat,* and we'll show you how to approach the sometimes scary looking questions that cover these topics, on the exam.

MASS

Think about a sample of any type of matter, whether it's a hunk of solid, a glass of liquid, or a container of gas. The **mass** of any of these samples refers to the amount of matter in the sample, while **matter** simply refers to anything that occupies space and has mass. So, what units are used to measure mass?

- grams (g)

Mass is measured in grams. One gram is nearly equal to the weight of a paper clip—for heavier samples it's often more convenient to use kilograms (1 kg = 1,000 grams), while for very small samples, it's convenient to use milligrams (1 mg = 1/1000 grams). For any particular substance, a sample of greater mass means a sample with more atoms or molecules in it. (For now, think of atoms and molecules as tiny pieces of matter. We'll talk more about them later.) Two different samples of the same substance that have different masses must be made up of different numbers of atoms or molecules; for example, ten water molecules have greater mass than seven water molecules. Eight carbon dioxide molecules have greater mass than four carbon dioxide molecules.

For the SAT Chemistry, there's nothing more you need to know about mass itself. It represents the quantity of matter that makes up a sample. It's usually measured in grams, kilograms, or milligrams.

VOLUME

Again, suppose we're thinking about a sample of matter—solid, liquid, or gas. When we say **volume**, we're talking about how much room the sample takes up in space. The SAT Chemistry usually measures volume in liters (L) or milliliters (ml; 1 ml = 1/1,000 L—also keep in mind that 1 ml = 1 cm^3, or cubic centimeter).

How a sample is measured depends on what state it's in—whether it is a solid, liquid, or gas. When the sample is a liquid, we can determine its volume by pouring it into a graduated cylinder or any other measuring flask.

If the sample is a solid, we can immerse it in a liquid and see how much liquid it displaces. In other words, we can compare the original volume of the liquid and the volume of the solid/liquid combination, knowing that the difference will be equal to the volume of the solid.

For samples of gas, the volume of the gas is always equal to the volume of its container, since a gas always expands to fill its container. How do we learn the volume of the container? Well, if the volume isn't marked on the container, we can just treat the container as a solid object and find out its volume by immersing it in a liquid.

DENSITY

The property of density is intrinsic to a substance; substances such as water, lead, carbon dioxide, or ethyl alcohol, for example, all have different densities. **Density** is a measure of the ratio of an object's mass to its volume.

Generally, if we say "water is heavy," we mean that water has a high density relative to other substances. Ten kilograms of water occupy a relatively small volume—about 10 L. When we say "feathers are light," we mean that feathers have a low density relative to other substances. Ten kilograms of feathers occupy a relatively large volume.

How do we measure density? We measure it in units that reflect mass per volume. That means we might measure it in g/L, or mg/L, or kg/ml, or any other combination that represents mass per volume. We calculate density using the following formula:

$$\text{Density} = \frac{\text{mass}}{\text{volume}}$$

If we say that substance X has a density of 2 g/ml, we're really saying that 1 ml of that substance has a mass of 2 g, which means that 2 ml have a mass of 4 g, that 10 ml have a mass of 20 g, and so on.

If another substance, substance Y, has a density of 1.75 g/ml, then its density is *less* than that of substance X. If we had samples of both substances X and Y, and the two samples were of equal volume, we'd find that sample X has greater mass than sample Y. Why? Because Y is less dense than X.

While gases always expand to fill their containers, this is not true of solids and liquids. A particular volume of some solid or liquid will always have the same mass at a given temperature (and thus a constant density), since mass is determined by the actual number of atoms or molecules present in a sample. But for a gas at a given temperature, mass does not necessarily vary with volume. We can change the volume of a gas sample, even while holding its temperature steady, simply by changing the size of its container. The number of atoms or molecules that make up the gas will remain the same, but the volume will change. This is shown in the illustration below.

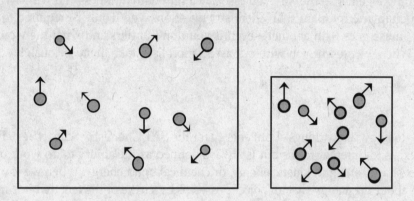

PRESSURE

When test writers say "pressure," they are usually talking about (1) the force that a sample of gas in a closed container exerts on the container walls, or (2) a solid or liquid standing in an environment and the force that a gas is exerting on the walls of the environment and everything in it—including the surface of the solid or liquid.

(1)   (2)

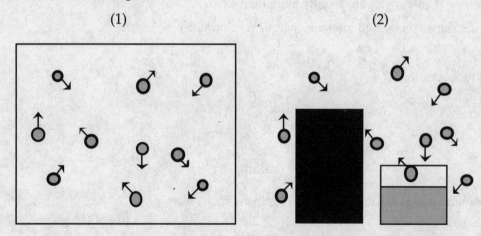

So, what units do we use to express pressure? A few. There are torr, millimeters of mercury (mmHg), and atmospheres (atm): 1 torr and 1 mmHg are equal, and 760 torr (or 760 mmHg) = 1 atm.

What instruments are used to measure pressure? The (1) barometer and the (2) manometer. Both the barometer and manometer involve the use of the liquid metal, mercury (Hg), to determine atmospheric pressure.

Learn to associate:	
Pressure with:	torr;
	mmHg;
	atm;
	barometer;
	manometer;
	standard pressure = 760 mmHg, 1 atm

When we say you should *associate* one thing with another, we mean you should remember to think of them as "going together"—the way you associate night with darkness and winter with cold. As we mentioned in Chapter 2, for many SAT Chemistry questions, you'll only be required to remember that one word or phrase goes with another—even if you don't understand what the words and phrases really mean. When we present you with our association lists, take them seriously!

ENERGY

You will have to know a few things about energy for the SAT Chemistry Subject Test. First, remember that **energy** exists in different forms but is always defined as the ability to do work or transfer heat. Energy can exist as heat, light, kinetic energy, or chemical bond energy. When we say kinetic energy, we're talking about the energy that an object possesses by virtue of the fact that it is moving. A moving bus, train, or car has kinetic energy. When we deal with chemistry, we're usually thinking about *molecules* that move; moving molecules have kinetic energy. The faster molecules move, the higher their kinetic energy.

What units are used to describe energy?

- calories (cal)
- joules (J) or kilojoules (kJ, which equals 1,000 J)

One calorie (1 cal) is equal to slightly more than 4 J.

What instrument is used to measure energy? A calorimeter.

Learn to associate:	
Energy with:	heat;
	light;
	chemical bond energy;
	kinetic energy;
	calorimeter
Kinetic energy with:	moving molecules;
	increased rate of movement = increased
	kinetic energy

TEMPERATURE AND SPECIFIC HEAT

What exactly is heat? When you touch something warm, you feel heat, but what is that? Technically, **heat** is defined as the flow of energy from a body at a higher temperature to one at a lower temperature. If a particular sample of a substance experiences an increase in temperature, then you can say that particular sample has experienced an increase in heat content. So what exactly does temperature measure? Temperature measures the average kinetic energy of molecules in a sample; as the molecules in a sample move more quickly, the temperature of that sample increases.

For certain substances, the addition of a large amount of heat will have only a small effect on their temperature, while for other substances, the addition of a small amount of heat will have a dramatic effect on their temperature. The **heat capacity** of a substance refers to the amount of heat it must absorb for its temperature to be raised 1°C. Different substances have different heat capacities, and the heat capacity of a substance is described by its specific heat. The **specific heat** of a substance is the heat capacity of 1 gram of the substance.

Here's an equation that puts together all of the terms we just reviewed.

$$q = mc\Delta T$$

In this equation, q equals heat, m equals mass, c equals specific heat, and ΔT represents the difference between final and initial temperatures. (The symbol "Δ" means change or difference.)

For example, it takes 1 calorie of heat to raise the temperature of 1 gram of water by 1°C. So we say that the specific heat of water is 1 cal/g–°C. The specific heat of carbon is 0.033 cal/g–°C, so it takes 0.033 calorie to raise the temperature of 1 gram of carbon by 1°C.

Now suppose you take 40 grams of water and 40 grams of carbon and add 200 calories of heat to each sample. Because water has a significantly higher specific heat than carbon, the input of the same amount of heat to both samples will result in a greater increase in temperature in the carbon sample, than in the sample of water. See the calculations below.

$$\Delta T = \frac{q}{mc}$$

$$\Delta T_{carbon} = \frac{(200 \text{ cal})}{(40g)\left(.033 \dfrac{cal}{g-°C}\right)} = 151.5 °C$$

$$\Delta T_{water} = \frac{(200 \text{ cal})}{(40g)\left(1 \dfrac{cal}{g-°C}\right)} = 5 °C$$

Carbon increases in temperature by 151.5°C, but water only increases in temperature by 5°C. Why? Because the specific heat of water is roughly 30 times that of carbon.

Similarly, if we have equal masses of water and carbon and we want to raise the temperature of each sample by the same amount, we'll have to put about 30 times more heat into the water than we have to put into the carbon.

We've been talking about temperature in °C, and when we think of specific heat, that's the right unit of temperature to use. But, for this test, you also need to know about another temperature scale:

degrees Kelvin (K). The Kelvin scale is also called the "absolute temperature" scale. How do you convert °C to K?

$$K = °C + 273$$
$$0 \text{ K} = -273°C$$
$$0°C = 273K$$

Learn to associate:

Temperature with:	°C and K; average kinetic energy
Specific heat with:	the amount of heat required to raise the temperature of 1 gram of a substance by 1°C; cal/g–°C

And remember, when it comes to heat content, temperature is a *reflection* of, but not a direct *measure* of, heat content. Heat content is **not** measured in °C. It's measured in calories, joules, or kilojoules.

HOW THE SAT CHEMISTRY SUBJECT TEST WILL TEST YOU ON ALL THIS

The SAT Chemistry test writers sometimes make their questions look more difficult than they are, by trying to catch you off guard and steer you off course. They might, for instance, use camouflage and temptation traps. Try the ten subject test–type questions that follow, keeping the techniques from Chapter 2 in mind.

QUESTION TYPE A

(A) Volume
(B) Temperature
(C) Density
(D) Pressure
(E) Mass

1. Is a quantity that allows one to calculate mass if density is known

2. Always varies with the number of molecules present in a sample of a particular substance

3. Can be expressed as kilograms per liter

4. Is a measure of the average kinetic energy of a substance's molecules

QUESTION TYPE B

Directions: Each question below consists of two statements, I in the left-hand column and II in the right-hand column. For each question, determine whether statement I is true or false <u>and</u> whether statement II is true or false and fill in the corresponding T or F ovals on your answer sheet. <u>Fill in oval CE only if statement II is a correct explanation of statement I.</u>

	I		II
103.	If the density of a solid substance and its volume are both known, mass can be calculated	BECAUSE	for any substance, the relationship between mass and volume varies directly with sample size.

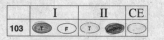

$$D = \frac{M}{V}$$
$$D \cdot V = M$$

104.	For any substance, solid, liquid, or gas, mass increases as volume increases	BECAUSE	density represents mass per volume.

$PV = PV$

$\dfrac{V}{T} = \dfrac{V}{T}$

as V ↑
but as temp

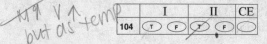

$$D = \frac{M}{V}$$

105.	If substances X and Y have specific heats of 0.2 cal/g–°C and 0.6 cal/g–°C, respectively, then 10 g of substance X has less heat content than 10 g of substance Y	BECAUSE	a substance with a relatively low specific heat will, when heated, experience less change in its temperature than a substance with a relatively high specific heat.

QUESTION TYPE C

26. Two solid objects are of equal volume, but object A has density = X, and object B has density = (0.5)(X).

Which of the following is true concerning objects A and B?

(A) Objects A and B are of equal density.
(B) Object B has twice the density of object A.
(C) Objects A and B are of equal mass.
(D) Object A has one half the mass of object B.
(E) Object A has twice the mass of object B.

33. The specific heat of a substance is approximately 0.5 cal/g–°C. If 30 calories of heat are absorbed by 15 g of the substance at 30°C, its temperature will become
    (A) 19°C
    (B) 32°C
    (C) 34°C
    (D) 60°C
    (E) 90°C

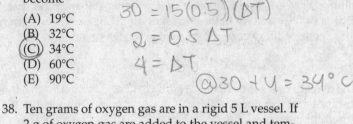

38. Ten grams of oxygen gas are in a rigid 5 L vessel. If 2 g of oxygen gas are added to the vessel and temperature is kept constant, which of the following characteristics of the gas will increase?
    I. Mass
    II. Density
    III. Pressure

    (A) I only
    (B) III only
    (C) I and II only
    (D) II and III only
    (E) I, II, and III

LET'S LOOK AT THE ANSWERS

Question 1: (A) If you chose "mass" or "density" just because those words appeared in the question, you fell for the temptation trap. The test writers wanted you to do this. To answer this question correctly, you have to think carefully about what the words mean, and you must not rush to an answer simply because an answer choice contains a word that reminds you of something.

Let's work through this. If you're given a sample of some substance, and you know the density of the substance, what additional information would allow you to calculate the mass? If you know its density, then you know the ratio of mass/volume. Therefore, if you were also provided with the sample's volume, you could figure out its mass. That's why A is right.

Question 2: (E) You're asked to determine which quantity or property always varies with the number of molecules in a given sample of a substance. You have the knowledge to answer this question, so don't let the wording throw you.

Think about what you know; mass is a measure of the quantity of matter. This means that for any sample of a particular substance, mass always varies with the number of molecules in the sample. More molecules of substance X have a greater mass than fewer molecules of substance X.

What about volume, temperature, density, and pressure? Volume, (A), is a measure of the space a sample occupies. The volume of a substance might vary as the number of molecules of that substance is varied, however, it does not *have* to change with the number of molecules. This is certainly true in the case of gases: a rigid container (with a fixed volume) may hold vastly different amounts of the same gas because gases are expandable and compressible.

Changing the amount of a substance will not raise its temperature (B). (C) By remembering the formula for density $(d = m/v)$ we see that the density of a substance will remain the same despite an increase or decrease in the mass of a substance, if the volume is changed in direct proportion to the change in mass. (D) The pressure exerted on a solid or liquid will remain the same, regardless of the number of molecules of the substance. The pressure of a gas in a closed container will change with an increase or decrease in mass, but if the volume of the container holding the gas is increased or decreased as the mass changes, the pressure will not change.

Question 3: (C) Kilograms are used to represent mass, and liters are used to represent volume. Mass/volume = density, so (C) is correct.

Question 4: (B) If you remembered to associate temperature with average kinetic energy, you knew that (B) was correct.

Question 103: (T, F) Divide and conquer! First examine each statement separately, and determine whether it's true or false.

Is the first statement true? Yes it is, although camouflage might at first prevent you from realizing that. But because

$$\text{density} = \frac{\text{mass}}{\text{volume}}$$

simple algebra allows you to calculate mass, if you know density and volume.

$$\text{mass} = (\text{density})(\text{volume})$$

Now look at statement II, and decide whether it's true or false. What does the statement mean? For a bigger piece of some substance, the relationship between mass and volume is different than it is for a smaller piece of that same substance. That's false. For any substance, the relationship between mass and volume is given by the density of the substance. For solids and liquids, density does not change with sample size.

Question 104: (F, T) Again, divide and conquer. Look at the first statement. Is it true? For solids and liquids, volume can increase somewhat by heating the substance, even while the mass remains constant. The volume of a constant amount of gas can also be increased by heating or cooling the gas, or by simply placing the gas in a larger container. Therefore, the statement is false.

Look at the second statement. Does density represent mass per volume? Yes, it does. The second statement is true. Since one of the statements is false, you leave the CE oval blank.

Question 105: (F, F) Divide and conquer. Since we do not know the temperature of X or Y, we cannot say which 10-g sample has more heat content, so statement I is false.

Consider statement II. A substance with a relatively low specific heat will undergo a relatively large temperature change upon the addition of heat, so statement II is false. Don't fill in the CE oval.

Question 26: (E) Don't even look at the answer options until you really understand the situation that's being described. You've got two objects. They occupy the same volume, but one has half the density of the other. Since

$$\text{density} = \frac{\text{mass}}{\text{volume}}$$

you know that this means that the object with less density has one half the mass of the object with greater density.

Object A has twice the density, so it should have twice the mass of an equal volume of object B. That's why E is right.

Question 33: (C) Remember $q = mc\Delta T$? Substituting the values into it gives

$$30 \text{ cal} = (15 \text{ g})(0.5 \text{ cal/g–°C}) \, \Delta T$$

Solve for ΔT, and you'll get 4°C. This is the increase in temperature. So if the substance was at 30°C, it's now at 34°C. That's choice C.

Question 38: (E) Adding more oxygen gas will certainly increase the mass of the gas sample; therefore, statement I is true.

Since density is the ratio of mass per volume, increasing the mass while maintaining the same volume will increase the density of the gas, so statement II is also true.

Pressure is a measure of the force per unit area with which gas molecules collide with the walls of the vessel. More gas occupying the same volume will mean more collisions and, therefore, greater pressure. So statements I, II, and III are true, and (E) is the answer.

Notice that even if you don't know if all of the statements are true, you can make a really good guess with just a little knowledge. Just knowing that statement I is true allows you to eliminate choices B and D, and by knowing that statement II is also true, you can rule out choice A. At this point, you have a 50 percent chance of choosing the right answer even if you know nothing about pressure!

PART II

Subject Review

4

Atoms: The Building Blocks of Matter

A solid understanding of atoms, which are the building blocks of matter, is critical for success on the SAT Chemistry Subject Test. Atoms and elements are the focus of this chapter.

ATOMS AND ELEMENTS

An **element** is any substance that cannot be broken down into a simpler substance by a chemical reaction.

Now, what exactly is an **atom**? Suppose you have a spoonful of some element—carbon, for instance. The smallest, tiniest, teeniest "piece" of carbon in the spoonful is one atom of carbon. Technically, an atom is the smallest particle of an element that still retains the chemical properties of that element.

Learn to associate:

Element with: can't be broken into anything simpler
without losing its identity

Atom with: smallest piece of any element

HOW AN ATOM IS MADE: PROTONS, NEUTRONS, AND ELECTRONS

At the center of every atom is a nucleus. What makes up the nucleus of an atom? Two things: **protons** and **neutrons**. Protons have a charge of +1, and neutrons have no charge at all—they are neutral. Because protons and neutrons comprise the nucleus of an atom, they are sometimes referred to as **nucleons**. What's outside the nucleus? **Electrons**; electrons have a charge of –1.

In an electronically neutral atom, the number of electrons is equal to the number of protons; the charges inside and outside the nucleus are balanced.

Sometimes it happens that an atom loses or gains one or more electrons. When that happens, the number of electrons outside the nucleus is not equal to the number of protons inside. The atom isn't electrically neutral anymore and has become an **ion**. If the atom loses one or more electrons, it has fewer negative charges than positive charges, so it is a positively charged ion, or **cation**. If the atom gains one or more electrons, it has more negative charges than positive charges. This is a negatively charged ion, or **anion**.

THE PERIODIC TABLE

When you sit down to take the SAT Chemistry Subject Test, you will be provided with a periodic table. On the periodic table, the vertical columns are called **groups**, and the horizontal rows are called **periods**. The symbols (such as H, Li, Be, etc.) represent elements.

PERIODIC TABLE OF THE ELEMENTS

1 **H** 1.0																	2 **He** 4.0
3 **Li** 6.9	4 **Be** 9.0											5 **B** 10.8	6 **C** 12.0	7 **N** 14.0	8 **O** 16.0	9 **F** 19.0	10 **Ne** 20.2
11 **Na** 23.0	12 **Mg** 24.3											13 **Al** 27.0	14 **Si** 28.1	15 **P** 31.0	16 **S** 32.1	17 **Cl** 35.5	18 **Ar** 39.9
19 **K** 39.1	20 **Ca** 40.1	21 **Sc** 45.0	22 **Ti** 47.9	23 **V** 50.9	24 **Cr** 52.0	25 **Mn** 54.9	26 **Fe** 55.8	27 **Co** 58.9	28 **Ni** 58.7	29 **Cu** 63.5	30 **Zn** 65.4	31 **Ga** 69.7	32 **Ge** 72.6	33 **As** 74.9	34 **Se** 79.0	35 **Br** 79.9	36 **Kr** 83.8
37 **Rb** 85.5	38 **Sr** 87.6	39 **Y** 88.9	40 **Zr** 91.2	41 **Nb** 92.9	42 **Mo** 95.9	43 **Tc** (98)	44 **Ru** 101.1	45 **Rh** 102.9	46 **Pd** 106.4	47 **Ag** 107.9	48 **Cd** 112.4	49 **In** 114.8	50 **Sn** 118.7	51 **Sb** 121.8	52 **Te** 127.6	53 **I** 126.9	54 **Xe** 131.3
55 **Cs** 132.9	56 **Ba** 137.3	57 **La*** 138.9	72 **Hf** 178.5	73 **Ta** 180.9	74 **W** 183.9	75 **Re** 186.2	76 **Os** 190.2	77 **Ir** 192.2	78 **Pt** 195.1	79 **Au** 197.0	80 **Hg** 200.6	81 **Tl** 204.4	82 **Pb** 207.2	83 **Bi** 209.0	84 **Po** (209)	85 **At** (210)	86 **Rn** (222)
87 **Fr** (223)	88 **Ra** 226.0	89 **Ac**† 227.0	104 **Unq** (261)	105 **Unp** (262)	106 **Unh** (263)	107 **Uns** (262)	108 **Uno** (265)	109 **Une** (267)									

	58 **Ce** 140.1	59 **Pr** 140.9	60 **Nd** 144.2	61 **Pm** (145)	62 **Sm** 150.4	63 **Eu** 152.0	64 **Gd** 157.3	65 **Tb** 158.9	66 **Dy** 162.5	67 **Ho** 164.9	68 **Er** 167.3	69 **Tm** 168.9	70 **Yb** 173.0	71 **Lu** 175.0
†	90 **Th** 232.0	91 **Pa** (231)	92 **U** 238.0	93 **Np** (237)	94 **Pu** (244)	95 **Am** (243)	96 **Cm** (247)	97 **Bk** (247)	98 **Cf** (251)	99 **Es** (252)	100 **Fm** (257)	101 **Md** (258)	102 **No** (259)	103 **Lr** (260)

For the SAT Chemistry, you have to know certain things about the elements and other information you see on the periodic table.

ATOMIC NUMBER

Look at any element on the periodic table. Above every element's symbol there is a whole number that represents the element's atomic number. The **atomic number** of an element tells you how many protons are in the nucleus of an atom of that element. The number of protons in the nucleus of an atom gives that atom its identity. Oxygen, for instance, has the atomic number 8; an atom of oxygen has 8 protons in its nucleus. If we take a proton away from an oxygen atom, it would have only 7 protons in its nucleus, and it wouldn't be oxygen anymore; it would be a nitrogen atom. Any atom with 7 protons in its nucleus is nitrogen.

What if an oxygen atom loses an electron but not a proton? Well, as long as the atom has 8 protons in it, it's still oxygen. If it has only 7 electrons, then it's a positively charged oxygen ion, and if it has 9 electrons, then it's a negatively charged oxygen ion. But as long as the atomic number—the number of protons in the nucleus—doesn't change, the element doesn't change either: It's still oxygen.

Mass Number, Isotopes, and Atomic Weight

We said before that the nucleus of an atom is made up of two types of subatomic particles: protons and neutrons. Protons have a positive charge, and neutrons are neutral. Another important point is that both protons and neutrons have mass, while electrons have practically no mass.

Protons and neutrons each have mass of roughly 1 atomic mass unit (amu), and an atom's **mass number** is equal to the sum of its protons and its neutrons.

Now, we've said that in an electronically neutral atom, the number of protons is equal to the number of electrons. But this says nothing about neutrons. Most carbon atoms, for instance, have 6 neutrons in their nuclei. A few have 8. All have 6 protons in their nuclei, so they all have the atomic number 6, and they're all carbon. But they can differ in number of neutrons.

If two atoms of the same element differ in the number of neutrons in their nuclei, they are said to be **isotopes**; a carbon atom that has 6 neutrons and a carbon atom that has 8 neutrons are isotopes.

Since an atom's mass number is equal to the sum of its protons and its neutrons, two different isotopes of the same element will have different mass numbers. For instance, the carbon atom that has 6 neutrons in its nucleus has a mass number of 6 protons + 6 neutrons = 12 amu. And, because its mass number is 12, we call it carbon-12. The carbon atom that has 8 neutrons in its nucleus has a mass number of 6 protons + 8 neutrons = 14 amu. And, because its mass number is 14, we call it carbon-14.

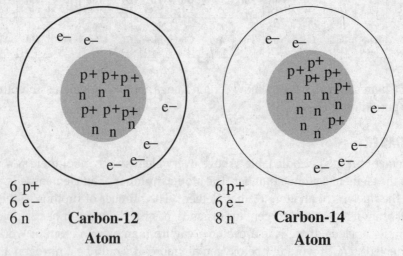

6 p+
6 e−
6 n   **Carbon-12**
          Atom

6 p+
6 e−
8 n   **Carbon-14**
          Atom

By the way, mass number doesn't appear on the periodic table. Why not? Because for any element, there's no such thing as one mass number. As we've just learned, different isotopes of the same element have different mass numbers.

However, chemists have figured out, roughly, the degree to which each isotope of each element tends to occur on the Earth. So, for each element, they've figured out an average mass number, which for each element represents the average of the mass numbers of all isotopes as they occur on the Earth. This average number is called the **atomic weight** of the element. The atomic weight of each element appears on the periodic table, just below the element's symbol. When we want to know the mass of an atom of a particular element, for practical purposes, we use the atomic weight that appears on the periodic table.

Learn to associate:

Neutrons with:
along with protons, make up the
nucleus of an atom;
electrical neutrality;
isotopes—two atoms of the same
element are isotopes if they differ
in their number of neutrons

Mass number with:
number of protons plus number of neutrons;
isotopes—two isotopes of an element
have different mass numbers because
they differ in number of neutrons

Atomic weight with:
average of mass numbers for all
isotopes of an element as they occur on
the Earth

Now try the questions below.

QUESTION TYPE A

(A) Atom
(B) Ion
(C) Neutron
(D) Proton
(E) Electron

4. The smallest representative particle of helium A

5. Gain or loss creates positively or negatively
charged ion, respectively E

6. Particle responsible for positive nuclear charge D

7. Isotopes of uranium always differ in their number
of this particle C

8. Their number in the nucleus determines an
element's atomic number D

QUESTION TYPE B

Directions: Each question below consists of two statements, I in the left-hand column and II in the right-hand column. For each question, determine whether statement I is true or false <u>and</u> whether statement II is true or false and fill in the corresponding T or F ovals on your answer sheet. <u>Fill in oval CE only if statement II is a correct explanation of statement I.</u>

	I		II

105.   The periodic table does   BECAUSE   a mass number can be assigned to one
          not report mass numbers   isotope of an element but not to an
                                                            element in general.

106.   Addition of an electron   BECAUSE   every electron carries a negative
          to an atom creates a   charge.
          positively charged ion

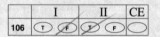

QUESTION TYPE C

27. Two different sodium atoms or ions may differ in all of the following ways EXCEPT

    (A) the number of electrons outside their nuclei
    (B) the overall charge they carry
    (C) their mass numbers
    (D) the number of neutrons in their nuclei
    (E) the number of protons in their nuclei

28. Two isotopes of the same element will always differ in

    (A) mass number but never in atomic number
    (B) atomic number but never in mass number
    (C) charge outside but never inside their nuclei
    (D) nuclear charge but never in overall charge
    (E) the number of electrons outside their nuclei but never in the number of neutrons inside their nuclei

LET'S LOOK AT THE ANSWERS

Question 4: (A) Helium is an element and the smallest piece of an element is an atom. That's why A is correct. An atom is the smallest particle of an element that still retains the properties of that element.

Question 5: (E) You know that every electron carries a charge of –1, and that an atom becomes a positively charged ion when it loses an electron(s), and a negatively charged ion when it gains an electron. That's why E is correct.

Question 6: (D) Which of the components of the nucleus—protons or neutrons—have a positive charge? Protons have a positive charge, while neutrons have no charge—they are electrically neutral. The answer is D.

Question 7: (C) Don't be fooled by the mention of uranium; it's just another element. You know that isotopes of the same element do not differ in their number of protons, may differ in their number of electrons, but *must* differ in their number of neutrons. That's why C is correct.

Question 8: (D) The atomic number of an element depends on the number of protons in that element's atoms, so the answer must be D.

Question 105: (T, T, CE) Divide and conquer! Evaluate the first statement without looking at the second, and decide whether it's true or false. It's true. The periodic table reports atomic weights but not mass numbers.

Now see if the second statement is true or false. Is it true that a mass number can be assigned only to a single isotope of an element but not to an element in general? Yes. Mass number = number of protons + number of neutrons. Different atoms of the same element may vary as to the number of neutrons they contain. That's what makes them isotopes.

Both statements are true. Now see if this sentence makes sense: "The periodic table does not report mass numbers because a mass number can be assigned to one isotope of an element but not to an element in general." It does, so fill in the oval marked CE.

Question 106: (F, T) Divide and conquer. Look at the first statement on its own, and decide whether it's true or false. Electrons are negatively charged, so if we add an electron to an atom it becomes a negatively charged ion. This statement is false.

Now look at the second statement; is it true? Yes. Electrons are negatively charged. The first statement is false, and the second is true. Do not fill in the CE oval.

Question 27: (E) You know the answer, so don't fall into the camouflage trap. The atomic number represents the number of protons in the nucleus, and it gives the atom its identity. Any sodium atom or ion must have, in its nucleus, the same number of protons as any other sodium atom, otherwise it isn't sodium.

A and B are both wrong because sodium ions can carry different charges, depending on how many electrons they've gained or lost. C and D are wrong because different isotopes of sodium will differ in the number of neutrons in the nucleus. That means their mass number will differ. But all sodium atoms or ions must have 11 protons in their nuclei. That's why E is correct.

Question 28: (A) You know what isotopes are—atoms of the same element that differ in their number of neutrons. Isotopes may also differ in their number of electrons. They must differ in their mass numbers since they have different numbers of neutrons. They can't differ in their number of protons, or they wouldn't be atoms of the same element. B, C, D, and E are incorrect, and A is correct.

Chemical Reactions and Stoichiometry

As you probably know from your chemistry class, a **chemical reaction** is simply a process that changes one or more substances into different substances. **Stoichiometry** describes the relationships between the amounts of substances consumed and produced in the course of chemical reactions.

THE WORLD OF MOLECULES

As we mentioned in Chapter 4, an atom is the smallest particle of an element. Atoms of one element often attract each other or atoms of a different element. If this attraction is strong enough, a chemical bond can result. Chemical bonds join two or more atoms into units called **molecules**. (We'll talk more about bonding in Chapter 7.)

Everybody knows the formula of water—it's H_2O. This formula tells us that, in a molecule of water, 2 hydrogen atoms and 1 oxygen atom are bonded together into a unit. An individual water molecule is the smallest unit of water that exists.

DIATOMIC MOLECULES

When a molecule consists of just two atoms (whether they are of identical or different elements), it's called a **diatomic molecule**. Some elements exist as diatomic molecules at room temperature and atmospheric pressure (1 atm). For example, oxygen in air exists in the form of O_2. There are seven important elements that exist as diatomic molecules: hydrogen (H_2), nitrogen (N_2), fluorine (F_2), oxygen (O_2), iodine (I_2), chlorine (Cl_2), and bromine (Br_2). Try to remember.

Oh, I Have Nice Closets For Brooms
O_2, I_2, H_2, N_2, Cl_2, F_2, Br_2

FORMULA WEIGHTS, EMPIRICAL FORMULAS, AND PERCENT COMPOSITION

For the SAT Chemistry, you'll need to know some simple atom-molecule math.

1. **Formula Weight:** For any molecule, we calculate the formula weight by adding up the atomic weights of all the atoms in the molecule. It's easy. Let's take hydrogen peroxide: H_2O_2. The molecule has:

   - 2 hydrogen atoms, and the atomic weight of hydrogen is 1 amu. That gives us 2(1) = 2.

   - 2 oxygen atoms, and the atomic weight of oxygen is 16 amu. That gives us 2(16) = 32.

     2 + 32 = 34.

So the formula weight for H_2O_2 is 34 amu.

Let's figure out the formula weight for sulfuric acid: H_2SO_4. The molecule has

   - 2 hydrogen atoms, and the atomic weight of hydrogen is 1 amu. That gives us 2(1) = 2.

   - 1 atom of sulfur, and the atomic weight of sulfur is 32 amu. That gives us 1(32) = 32.

   - 4 atoms of oxygen, and the atomic weight of oxygen is 16 amu. That gives us 4(16) = 64.

     2 + 32 + 64 = 98.

So the formula weight for H_2SO_4 is 98 amu.

2. **Empirical Formula:** An empirical formula shows the ratio of atoms within a molecule. For instance, we know that the molecular formula for hydrogen peroxide is H_2O_2; this tells us that, in a molecule of hydrogen peroxide, there's 1 hydrogen atom for every oxygen atom. The molecule contains hydrogen and oxygen atoms in a ratio of 1:1. Hydrogen peroxide's empirical formula, therefore, is HO.

To find an empirical formula from a molecular formula, first find the largest whole number by which all of the subscripts in the molecular formula are divisible, then divide each subscript by that number. In the case of H_2O_2, that number is 2. Dividing each subscript by 2, we get 1, so the empirical formula is HO.

Ethane has the molecular formula C_2H_6. So, what is its empirical formula? Take a look at the molecular formula. What's the largest whole number that goes evenly into 2 and 6? It's 2. We divide both subscripts by 2, and we get an empirical formula of CH_3.

How about water, H_2O? The largest whole number that will divide evenly into 2 and 1 is 1. So the empirical formula is the same as the molecular formula: H_2O.

3. **Percent Composition:** The test writers may ask you to determine the percent composition of a particular element within a molecule. Here's an example of a question you might see on the test: What is the percent of oxygen by mass in hydrogen peroxide, H_2O_2?

    In order to determine the percent composition of oxygen, you need to find the mass in amu of all of the oxygen atoms in the molecule and compare it to the total formula weight. As shown earlier, the two oxygen atoms in H_2O_2 each weigh 16 amu. So the mass due to oxygen is 2(16) or 32 amu. The formula weight of H_2O_2 is 34 amu. So the percent of oxygen by mass in H_2O_2 is $\frac{32}{34} \times 100\%$ or roughly 94%. That means the percent of hydrogen by mass in H_2O_2 is about 6%.

THE MOLE

What's a mole? It's a number, like a dozen or a gross. Dozen, as you know, means 12. Gross means 144. **Mole** means 6.02×10^{23}. The number 6.02×10^{23} is known as **Avogadro's number**.

We said earlier that atomic mass is measured in atomic mass units (amu); well, there are 6.02×10^{23} atomic mass units in 1 g. Think about what that means. If, for any element, we take a sample whose mass in grams is numerically equal to its atomic weight in amu, the sample has 1 mole of atoms in it. If we take a substance whose mass in grams is numerically equal to twice its atomic weight in amu, we have 2 moles of atoms. If we take a substance whose mass in grams is numerically equal to 3 times its atomic weight in amu, we have three moles of atoms. It's as simple as that.

For example, helium's atomic weight is 4 amu, so 4 g of helium contain 1 mole (6.02×10^{23}) of helium atoms, and 8 g of helium contain 2 moles of helium atoms. Carbon's atomic weight is 12 amu, so in 12 g of carbon there is 1 mole (6.02×10^{23}) of carbon atoms, and in 36 g of carbon there are 3 moles of carbon atoms. Got it?

How many moles of oxygen molecules are in 64 g of oxygen gas? Remember, oxygen is diatomic. Each O_2 molecule has a mass of roughly 2(16) or 32 amu, so 1 mole of O_2 molecules would have a mass of 32 g. Thus, in 64 g of oxygen gas, there are 2 moles of oxygen molecules. Now how many moles of oxygen atoms would be present in this 64 g sample? Each O_2 molecule is made up of 2 oxygen atoms, so if the sample contains 2 moles of oxygen molecules, it contains 4 moles of oxygen atoms.

CONVERTING MASS COMPOSITION TO EMPIRICAL FORMULA

Now that you know what an empirical formula is, we'll tell you how to figure out an empirical formula from the percent composition of a molecule. For example, the test writers might tell you that some unknown substance is made up of approximately 75% mercury and 25% chlorine, and they might ask you to take this percent composition and figure out the substance's empirical formula.

Here's how you do it.

- Imagine, first, that you have 100 g of the substance.

- If you have 100 g of the substance, and it's 75% mercury by mass, then you've got 75 g of mercury, right? Since the atomic weight of mercury is about 200 amu (which means that 1 mole of mercury atoms weighs 200 g), you've got $\frac{75}{200}$ mole = 0.375 moles of mercury atoms in a 100 g sample.

- If you have 100 g of the substance, and it's 25% chlorine by mass, then you've got 25 g of chlorine. Since the atomic weight of chlorine is about 35 amu (which means that 1 mole of chlorine atoms weighs 35 g), you've got $\frac{25}{35}$ = 0.700 moles of chlorine atoms in the 100 g sample. (Note: When finding moles of a diatomic element such as chlorine in a *compound*, use its atomic weight, *not* its formula weight in the calculation.)

- If you've got 0.375 moles of mercury atoms and 0.700 moles of chlorine atoms, then the ratio of chlorine to mercury atoms is $\frac{0.700}{0.375}$ (which is close to 2:1), which means the empirical formula is $HgCl_2$.

Now review everything we've told you about molecules and moles, and answer the following questions.

QUESTION TYPE A

(A) N_2O
(B) $C_6H_{12}O_6$
(C) SO_3
(D) NO
(E) N_2O_5

6. Is a diatomic molecule D

7. Has a formula weight of approximately 108 amu (E)

8. Has an empirical formula that is different from its molecular formula B

9. Composition is approximately 60% oxygen by mass C

QUESTION TYPE B

I   **II**

102. Chlorine is an   BECAUSE   chlorine exists as unbonded atoms at room
     element   temperature and atmospheric pressure.

	I		II		CE
102	T	F	T	F	

103. One mole of HBr   BECAUSE   the mass of a molecule of HBr is greater than
     has greater mass   the mass of a molecule of NO_2.
     than one mole of
     NO_2

	I		II		CE
103	T	F	T	F	

QUESTION TYPE C

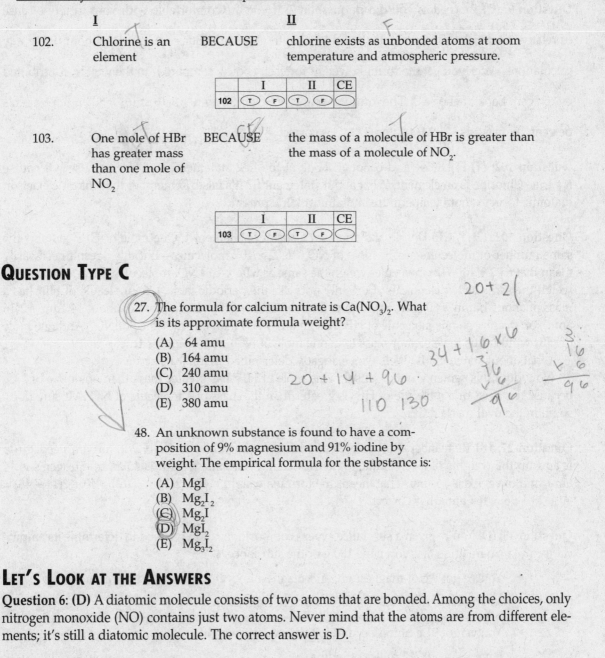

27. The formula for calcium nitrate is $Ca(NO_3)_2$. What
    is its approximate formula weight?

    (A) 64 amu
    (B) 164 amu
    (C) 240 amu
    (D) 310 amu
    (E) 380 amu

48. An unknown substance is found to have a com-
    position of 9% magnesium and 91% iodine by
    weight. The empirical formula for the substance is:

    (A) MgI
    (B) Mg_2I_2
    (C) Mg_2I
    (D) MgI_2
    (E) Mg_3I_2

LET'S LOOK AT THE ANSWERS

Question 6: (D) A diatomic molecule consists of two atoms that are bonded. Among the choices, only nitrogen monoxide (NO) contains just two atoms. Never mind that the atoms are from different elements; it's still a diatomic molecule. The correct answer is D.

Question 7: (E) First, eliminate the obvious wrong choices: By inspection you know that N_2O and NO are nowhere near 108 amu, so cross them out. Then you'll need to do some math. Use the periodic table to find the atomic weight of each element in the compounds. Then multiply this mass by the number of that kind of atom in the molecule. Add the mass contributions from each element to get the formula weight. When you do this for choice E, you'll get: 2(14 amu) + 5(16 amu) = 28 amu + 80 amu = 108 amu. E is your answer.

Question 8: (B) Look at the ratios between different types of atoms. If the ratio can be put in terms of smaller whole numbers, then the formula is *not* an empirical formula. Check out choice B. In this molecule the ratio of carbon to hydrogen to oxygen is 6:12:6. If we divide this ratio by 6 we'll get the simpler (though still equivalent) ratio of 1:2:1. So the empirical formula of $C_6H_{12}O_6$ is CH_2O. Since the molecular and empirical formulas differ, this must be the answer.

Question 9: (C) Proceed as you did in question 7. If you are comfortable with your intuitive sense of relative molecular weights, you should be able to eliminate choices A and E without doing any calculations. After you get the formula weight for each choice, compare it to the weight contributed by oxygen. Look at choice C. The formula weight of SO_3 is 32 amu + 3(16 amu) = 80 amu. Oxygen's percent, by mass, is $\frac{48}{80} \times 100\%$ or 60%. C is correct.

Question 102: (T, F) Divide and conquer! Look at the first statement. Is it true or false? Of course it's true. Chlorine is an element. What about statement II? It's false. Remember that chlorine exists in diatomic form at room temperature and atmospheric pressure.

Question 103: (T, T, CE) Divide and conquer. Consider statement I. One mole of HBr contains the same number of molecules as one mole of NO_2—6.02 × 10²³ molecules—but this doesn't necessarily mean that 6.02 × 10²³ HBr molecules weigh the same as 6.02 × 10²³ NO_2 molecules. Do ten paper clips weigh the same as ten elephants? Certainly not. Use the periodic table. One molecule of HBr has a mass of about 1 amu + 80 amu, or 81 amu. One molecule of NO_2 has a mass of about 14 amu + 2(16 amu), or 46 amu, so one molecule of HBr has greater mass than one molecule of NO_2. And one mole of HBr would thus have greater mass than one mole of NO_2. Statement I is true.

What about statement II? Well, we've already determined that it's also true.

Now does this sentence make sense? "One mole of HBr has greater mass than one mole of NO_2 because the mass of a molecule of HBr is greater than the mass of a molecule of NO_2." It sure does, so fill in the oval marked CE.

Question 27: (B) Remember that to calculate the formula weight of $Ca(NO_3)_2$, all you need to do is add up the weights of its constituent atoms. Calcium's atomic weight is 40 amu, nitrogen's is 14 amu, and oxygen's is 16 amu. That means the formula weight = 40 + 2(14 + 3(16)) = 40 + 2(14 + 48) = 40 + 28 + 96 = 164 amu. B is correct.

Question 48: (D) You're given a substance's mass composition, and you need to determine its empirical formula. So imagine that you have 100 g of the substance.

- You've got 9 g of magnesium, and magnesium's atomic weight is 24 amu, so you have $\frac{9}{24}$ = 0.375 moles of magnesium atoms.

- You've got 91 g of iodine, and iodine's atomic weight is 127 amu, so you have $\frac{91}{127}$ = 0.717 moles of iodine.

- The ratio of iodine atoms to magnesium atoms is $\frac{0.717}{0.375}$, which is very close to 2:1.

This means that the empirical formula of the substance is MgI_2, and that's why D is correct.

CHEMICAL REACTIONS—HOW MOLECULES ARE FORMED, BROKEN DOWN, AND RE-FORMED

In the course of a chemical reaction, the bonds that hold together the atoms that make up the reactants break. The free atoms then form new bonds with one another to form new molecules—the products of the reaction. Take a look at the chemical reaction below:

$$C_3H_8(g) + 5O_2(g) \rightarrow 4H_2O(l) + 3CO_2(g)$$

What does this equation tell us? Well, two things. On a molecular level, this equation says that 1 molecule of propane (C_3H_8) and 5 molecules of oxygen react to form 4 molecules of water and 3 molecules of carbon dioxide. It also tells us that 1 mole of C_3H_8 reacts with 5 moles of O_2 to form 4 moles of H_2O and 3 moles of CO_2. This equation also indicates the state of each reactant and product: (s) means solid, (l) means liquid, and (g) means gas.

CHEMICAL EQUATIONS MUST BE BALANCED

Look again at the chemical equation we just presented:

$$C_3H_8(g) + 5O_2(g) \rightarrow 4H_2O(l) + 3CO_2(g)$$

This is a balanced equation. How can you tell? For each element on the left side of the equation, multiply the molecular coefficient by the element's subscript. (Any number that doesn't appear is assumed to be 1.) For oxygen, in $5O_2$, there are $5 \times 2 = 10$ oxygen atoms. Now do the same for the right side of the equation. In $4H_2O$, there are $4 \times 1 = 4$ oxygen atoms. In $3CO_2$, there are $3 \times 2 = 6$ oxygen atoms. So there are $4 + 6 = 10$ oxygen atoms on the right side, and since there are also 10 oxygen atoms on the left side, oxygen is balanced. Now check to see that carbon and hydrogen are also balanced. They are. There are 3 carbons on the left and 3 carbons on the right. There are 8 hydrogens on the left and 8 hydrogens on the right. For each element in a balanced equation, the total number of atoms on the left must equal the total number on the right.

On the SAT Chemistry Subject Test, you may see up to five questions that will show you unbalanced equations and ask you to balance them. Here's what those will look like.

$$\ldots C_2H_4(g) + \ldots O_2(g) \rightarrow \ldots CO_2(g) + \ldots H_2O(l)$$

When the equation above is balanced and all coefficients are reduced to lowest whole-number terms, which of the following would be the coefficient for CO_2?

(A) 1
(B) 2
(C) 4
(D) 5
(E) 6

Fortunately, these questions are easy to answer if you use the "plug-in" balancing strategy. Start with choice A, and put the number 1 in front of CO_2. (Don't be afraid to write in your test booklet as much as you want. Your test booklet belongs to you, and nobody cares what you write in it; only your answer sheet is scored.) By adding a 1 in front of CO_2, we end up with 1 carbon on the right. Yet, we have at least 2 carbons on the left, so we know that 1 is not the answer.

Let's try choice B. Put a 2 in front of CO_2, and see what happens. We have 2 carbons on the right and 2 on the left. Good. We have 4 hydrogens on the left, so let's try putting a 2 in front of the H_2O. That gives us a total of 6 oxygens on the right and 2 on the left. Let's put a 3 in front of O_2 on the left so we have a total of 6 oxygens on the left.

Now we have 2 carbons on the right and the left, 4 hydrogens on the right and the left, and 6 oxygens on the right and the left. The equation is balanced, and B is correct. So, every time a question asks you to balance an equation, use the plugging-in strategy. It can't fail.

STOICHIOMETRY

Sometimes SAT Chemistry questions will ask you to determine how much product is formed or reactant is consumed in the course of a chemical reaction. These are stoichiometry questions. When you begin a stoichiometry problem, always remember to work from a balanced equation. The coefficients in front of each species indicate the molar ratio between the species. Consider the reaction between ammonia gas and oxygen, which yields nitrogen monoxide and water.

$$4NH_3(g) + 5O_2(g) \rightarrow 4NO(g) + 6H_2O(l)$$

This equation tells us that:

- For every 4 moles of ammonia consumed, 5 moles of oxygen are also consumed.

- For every 5 moles of oxygen consumed, 6 moles of water are produced.

- For every 4 moles of ammonia consumed, 4 moles of nitrogen monoxide are produced. In other words, the molar ratio of ammonia consumption to nitrogen monoxide production is 1:1.

How do you put these molar ratios to use? Take a look: If 2 moles of ammonia are consumed, how many moles of water are produced?

From the balanced equation, we see that for every 4 moles of ammonia that are consumed, 6 moles of water are produced. So the ratio of ammonia to water is 4:6 or 2:3. So 2 moles of ammonia will react completely to produce 3 moles of water.

Remember that reactants combine according to their mole ratio. So if we combine two reactants that are not in their correct stoichiometric mole ratio, one reactant will be consumed first. When this happens, the excess reactant will remain unreacted.

Consider this question: If 34 g of ammonia and 32 g of oxygen are combined, how many grams of nitrogen monoxide will be produced?

The formula weight of NH_3 is 17 amu; 1 mole of NH_3 has a mass of 17 g and 2 moles have a mass of 34 g. This means that we have 2 moles of ammonia. How many moles of oxygen do we have? Since the formula weight of O_2 is 32 amu, 1 mole of O_2 has a mass of 32 g. So our actual mole ratio of ammonia to oxygen is 2:1. However, from the balanced equation given earlier in this section, we see that the ratio of ammonia consumption to oxygen consumption is 4:5. In keeping with this stoichiometric ratio, 2 moles of ammonia would react with 2.5 moles of oxygen—but we have only 1 mole of oxygen. We will run out of oxygen before all 2 moles of ammonia have reacted and so oxygen acts as the **limiting reagent**. Once the limiting reagent has been consumed, the reaction will no longer proceed. So we know that 1 mole of oxygen actually reacts, and since 4 moles of nitrogen monoxide are produced for every 5 moles of oxygen that react, $\frac{4}{5}$ moles, or 0.8 moles, of nitrogen monoxide is produced when 1 mole of oxygen reacts. Finally, the formula weight of NO is 30 amu, so 1 mole of NO has a mass of 30 g. The mass of 0.8 mole of NO is (0.8 mole)(30g/mole), or 24 g.

THERMODYNAMICS

ENTROPY

One of the most important things to remember about thermodynamics is that low-energy states are more stable than high-energy states. That's such a fundamental principle that we'll ask you to repeat it. Fill in the blank lines:

_____ energy states are more stable than _____ energy states.

Fundamentally, the universe prefers low-energy states, and also fundamentally, it tends toward disorder. When we talk about disorder, we use the term **entropy**, which is symbolized by S. Everything tends toward maximum entropy. When we talk about a chemical reaction and the difference between entropy of the products and entropy of the reactants, we use the symbol ΔS. If ΔS is negative, the reaction has lost entropy; the products are more "orderly" than the reactants. If ΔS is positive, the reaction has gained entropy; the products are less "orderly" than the reactants.

For the SAT Chemistry, when you see the word entropy, think "disorder," and realize that because the universe is lazy, it tends toward maximum entropy. All things in the universe are more stable when they're in (1) states of low energy and (2) states of high entropy. DON'T FORGET THESE TWO THINGS.

Learn to associate:	
Entropy with:	disorder; randomness
Stability with:	low energy; high entropy

ENTHALPY

Because the universe tends toward low energy, chemical reactions that release energy—reactions that set energy free—are favored in the universe. When we talk about the energy states of reactants or products, we use the term **enthalpy**, which is symbolized by H. High enthalpy means high energy state, and low enthalpy means low energy state. So, the universe likes reactions in which the enthalpy decreases—reactions in which ΔH (the change in enthalpy that occurs in the course of a reaction) is negative. These reactions are said to be **exothermic**, and they result in the release of energy in the form of heat. If, however, the enthalpy of the products is greater than the enthalpy of the reactants, then ΔH is positive and the reaction is said to be **endothermic**. Endothermic reactions require the input of energy in order to take place.

> **Learn to associate:**
>
> | Exothermic with: | ΔH is negative, enthalpy decreases |
> | Endothermic with: | ΔH is positive, enthalpy increases |

Heat of Formation

Another term you should be familiar with for the test is heat of formation. A compound's **heat of formation** is the amount of heat that's released or absorbed when one mole of the compound is formed from its elements. When we talk about heat of formation, we use the same symbol we use for enthalpy change but we put a subscript "f" on it: ΔH_f. Let's consider the heat of formation of gaseous carbon dioxide, CO_2):

$$C(s) + O_2(g) \rightarrow CO_2(g); \Delta H_f = -393 \text{ kJ/mol}$$

The fact that the heat of formation is negative means that heat is released during this reaction; this is an exothermic reaction. When 1 mole of CO_2 (g) is formed from its elements ($C(s)$ and $O_2(g)$), 393 kJ of energy are released.

For all elements, the heat of formation is zero: C, Ni, Cl_2, O_2, H_2, and N_2—or any other elemental atom or molecule—all have a heat of formation value of zero. Remember this for the exam!

For this test, you'll also need to keep in mind that for any reaction, the heats of formation of all the products minus the heats of formation of all the reactants is equal to ΔH_f *for the whole reaction.* The test writers might show you a reaction and give you heats of formation for all of the reactants and products. Then they'll ask you to figure out ΔH_f for the whole reaction.

That's simple to do, you just add up the heats of formation for all of the products and then all of the reactants, multiplying each by its coefficient from the balanced equation, and you've got ΔH_f for the reaction. Remember: ΔH_f (reaction) = ΔH_f (products) – ΔH_f (reactants) and the heats of formation of all elements are zero. Look at this reaction:

$$C_6H_{12}O_6(s) + 6O_2(g) \rightarrow 6CO_2(g) + 6H_2O(l)$$

Suppose you're told that the heat of formation for:

- $C_6H_{12}O_6(s)$ is –1,273 kJ/mol
- $H_2O(l)$ is –286 kJ/mol
- $CO_2(g)$ is –393 kJ/mol

(ΔH_f for $O_2(g)$, of course, is 0.)
ΔH_f for the whole reaction is equal to:

$$\Delta H_f(\text{products}) - \Delta H_f(\text{reactants})$$

So:

$\Delta H_f(\text{products}) = 6(-393) + 6(-286) = -4{,}074 \text{ kJ}$

$\Delta H_f(\text{reactants}) = -1{,}273 \text{ kJ} + 0\text{kJ} = -1{,}273\text{kJ}$

So, ΔH for the whole reaction = $(-4{,}074) - (-1{,}273) = -2{,}801$ kJ. ΔH for the whole reaction is negative, which means the reaction is exothermic.

This principle also applies to reactions that occur in more than one step. **Hess's law** says that if a reaction is carried out in a series of steps, ΔH for the reaction will be equal to the sum of the enthalpy changes for the individual steps. Overall, ΔH is independent of the number of steps or the pathway the reaction follows.

SPONTANEITY AND GIBBS FREE ENERGY

A **spontaneous reaction** is one that will occur at a given temperature without the input of energy. Strangely enough, however, sometimes endothermic reactions (which require the input of energy in order to take place) occur spontaneously. Why? Because, as we said, the universe likes entropy—disorder. If a particular reaction is endothermic (ΔH is positive) but creates greater disorder (ΔS is also positive), and the disorder the reaction creates exceeds the energy it requires, then the reaction may occur spontaneously although it's endothermic. Similarly, if a reaction creates order instead of disorder, it may occur spontaneously as long as it's exothermic, and the negative enthalpy change exceeds the negative entropy change.

What determines whether a reaction will or won't occur spontaneously? The combination of ΔH and ΔS. This combination of ΔH and ΔS is called Gibbs free energy, and is symbolized by ΔG. The actual formula for determining ΔG is $\Delta G = \Delta H - T\Delta S$ (where T is temperature, measured in degrees Kelvin). Remember the following points about Gibb's free energy:

- If ΔG for the reaction is negative, then that reaction occurs spontaneously in the forward direction.

- If ΔG for the reaction is positive, then that reaction occurs spontaneously at that temperature in the reverse direction.

- If ΔG for the reaction is 0, then the reaction is in equilibrium. (We'll discuss equilibrium later.)

Learn to associate:	
Gibbs free energy, ΔG, with:	combination of enthalpy change (ΔH) and entropy change (ΔS)
Negative ΔG with:	the reaction is spontaneous in the forward direction
Positive ΔG with:	the reaction is spontaneous in the reverse direction

Review everything we've talked about in this chapter, and then answer the following set of questions.

QUESTION TYPE A

(A) Gibbs free energy
(B) Heat of formation
(C) Enthalpy change
(D) Entropy
(E) Kinetic energy

6. Value that determines whether reaction is spontaneous

7. Quantity that determines whether reaction is exothermic or endothermic

8. Indicates the degree of disorder of a system

QUESTION TYPE B

Directions: Each question below consists of two statements, I in the left-hand column and II in the right-hand column. For each question, determine whether statement I is true or false <u>and</u> whether statement II is true or false and fill in the corresponding T or F ovals on your answer sheet. <u>Fill in oval CE only if statement II is a correct explanation of statement I.</u>

I | | II

105.   If a reaction is exothermic   BECAUSE   the universe favors a negative
it always proceeds   enthalpy change.
spontaneously

	I		II		CE
105	T	F	T	F	

106.   Ice melting is an   BECAUSE   heat must be absorbed by ice if it
endothermic process   is to melt.

	I		II		CE
106	T	F	T	F	

QUESTION TYPE C

28. $\ldots C_2H_4(g) + \ldots O_2(g) \rightarrow \ldots CO_2(g) + \ldots H_2O(l)$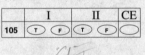

If the equation for the reaction above is balanced using the smallest possible whole-number coefficients, then the coefficient for oxygen gas is

(A) 1
(B) 2
(C) 3
(D) 4
(E) 5

50. $2Na(s) + Cl_2(g) \rightarrow 2NaCl(s) + 822$ kJ

How much heat is released by the above reaction if 0.5 mole of sodium reacts completely with chlorine?

(A) 205 kJ
(B) 411 kJ
(C) 822 kJ
(D) 1,644 kJ
(E) 3,288 kJ

56. $2Al(s) + Fe_2O_3(s) \rightarrow Al_2O_3(s) + 2Fe(s)$

If 80 grams of Al and 80 grams of Fe_2O_3 are combined, what is the maximum number of moles of Fe that can be produced?

(A) 0.5
(B) 1
(C) 2
(D) 3
(E) 4

LET'S LOOK AT THE ANSWERS

Question 6: (A) You know to associate Gibbs free energy with the spontaneity of reactions—that alone is enough to tell you which answer choice is correct. But if you want to take it further, remember that a reaction is spontaneous if the overall combination of enthalpy change—energy change—and entropy change is energetically adequate. Even an endothermic reaction—a reaction in which energy is consumed—can proceed spontaneously if it's accompanied by a large enough increase in entropy.

Question 7: (C) You should associate enthalpy with the words "exothermic" and "endothermic." Exothermic reactions release energy (which the universe tends to like), while endothermic reactions consume energy (which the universe tends to dislike). If, in the course of the reaction, the enthalpy change is negative, the reaction is exothermic. If it's positive, the reaction is endothermic. That's why C is correct.

Question 8: (D) Remember to always associate entropy with disorder. That's what it measures, and that's why D is correct.

Question 105: (F, T) Divide and conquer! Look at the first statement on its own. Is it true? No. The fact that a reaction is exothermic does not necessarily mean that it's spontaneous. The first statement is false.

Does the universe favor a negative enthalpy change? Yes. Generally speaking, it likes exothermic reactions. So the first statement is false and the second is true.

Question 106: (T, T, CE) Divide and conquer. Evaluate the first statement by itself. Is it true or false? It's true! In order for ice to melt, it must absorb heat. Melting involves a net absorption of heat energy because bonds between water molecules must be broken in order for melting to occur; it is an endothermic process.

What about statement II? Your own experience tells you that this is true. Ice must absorb heat in order to melt. Now put both statements together: "Ice melting is an endothermic process because heat must be absorbed by ice if it is to melt." Does it make sense? Absolutely. So fill in the CE oval.

Question 28: (C) Starting with A, let's plug in choices. If the coefficient for O_2 is 1, then there are two oxygen atoms on the left. Since we are starting with 3 oxygen atoms on the right, this number is too small. Try B. If the coefficient for O_2 is 2, we get 4 oxygen atoms on the left. Putting a 2 in front of H_2O gives us 4 oxygen atoms on the right. However, now we cannot balance carbon without upsetting the oxygen balance. So B is also wrong. What about C? If the coefficient for O_2 is 3, then we have 6 oxygen atoms on the left. Putting a 2 in front of CO_2 and H_2O gives 6 oxygen atoms on the right. So far, so good. Notice that putting a "1" in front of C_2H_4 puts carbon and hydrogen in balance, so the answer is C.

Question 50: (A) Notice that the consumption of 2 moles of Na releases 822 kJ of heat. What happens if only 0.5 mole of Na is consumed? Since 0.5 is only 25% of 2, only 25% of 822 kJ of heat will be released. As you can see, choice A is about one quarter of 822 kJ, so the correct answer is A.

Question 56: (B) When information about more than one reactant is given, brace yourself for a limiting reactant question. The stoichiometric mole ratio of Al to Fe_2O_3 is 2:1. The atomic weight of 1 aluminum atom is roughly 27 amu, which means that 1 mole of Al has a mass of about 27 g, so 80 g of Al represents nearly 3 moles. The formula weight of Fe_2O_3 is 160 g, so we have approximately 0.5 mole of Fe_2O_3. We've calculated that the actual mole ratio of Al to Fe_2O_3 is roughly 3:0.5 (or 6:1). This means that Fe_2O_3 is the limiting reagent. Notice from the balanced equation that for every 1 mole of Fe_2O_3 consumed, 2 moles of Fe are produced. If 0.5 moles of Fe_2O_3 is consumed, then 1 mole of Fe is produced. The correct answer is B.

Electron Configurations and Radioactivity

Chemical reactions involve interactions between the electrons of atoms. To understand how and why atoms react, we need to know something about electron configurations—the arrangement of electrons in atoms. Radioactivity involves changes that occur within an atom's nucleus.

ORBITALS

QUANTUM THEORY AND THE HEISENBERG PRINCIPLE

Niels Bohr thought electrons orbited the nucleus the way planets orbit the sun; he proposed the Bohr model of the atom, which was later proved to be incorrect. For the SAT Chemistry Subject Test, you have to know that electrons do *not* circle the nucleus as planets circle the sun. Electrons do not orbit. Instead, they exist in things called **orbitals**.

Just as a room is a region in a house in which a person may be found, an orbital is a region in an atom where an electron may be found. Rooms come in a variety of sizes and shapes and so do orbitals. A collection of orbitals with roughly similar sizes constitutes an **energy shell**. Electrons that are farther from the nucleus have greater energy than those that are closer, so electrons in the orbitals of larger energy shells have greater energy than those in the orbitals of smaller energy shells. Each energy shell is designated by a whole number, so we have the 1st (smallest energy shell), 2nd, 3rd, and so on.

Shape is another important characteristic of orbitals. There are four significant types of orbital shapes. Orbitals that have the same shape in a given energy shell comprise a **subshell**. An *s* subshell always consists of one spherical orbital; a *p* subshell always consists of three dumbbell-shaped orbitals, and the *d* and *f* subshells contain five and seven oddly-shaped orbitals, respectively. Any orbital, regardless of size and shape, can hold a maximum of two electrons.

But what's an orbital? The test writers expect you to associate the word orbital with something called a "probability function." An orbital describes the "likelihood that an electron will be found in a particular location." Another important concept to know for the test is the **Heisenberg principle**. What's the Heisenberg principle? Well, simply put, it means this: It is impossible to know both the position and the momentum of an electron at the same time.

Learn to associate:

Bohr model with:	the incorrect idea that electrons orbit the nucleus in true orbits, as planets orbit the sun
Electron orbitals with:	probability function; quantum theory; Heisenberg principle
Heisenberg principle with:	the fact that electrons are located in orbitals, not orbits; the fact that one cannot know an electron's position and momentum at the same time

DE BROGLIE'S HYPOTHESIS

For this test, all you need to know about Louis De Broglie is that he postulated that matter could have the properties of a wave. He extended this to say that electrons can be thought of as behaving similarly to waves of electromagnetic radiation.

Learn to associate:

De Broglie's hypothesis with:	the idea that matter (including electrons) can be thought of as having the properties of both a wave and a particle

ELECTRON CONFIGURATIONS

For the SAT Chemistry, you'll have to be able to figure out electron configurations. Here's how.

1. The test will give you a periodic table. First, draw these brackets on it.

PERIODIC TABLE OF THE ELEMENTS

┌s subshell area┐   ⟨ p subshell area ⟩
  1A   8A

	1A	2A						B groups						3A	4A	5A	6A	7A	8A
1	1 H 1.0																		2 He 4.0
2	3 Li 6.9	4 Be 9.0											5 B 10.8	6 C 12.0	7 N 14.0	8 O 16.0	9 F 19.0	10 Ne 20.2
3	11 Na 23.0	12 Mg 24.3						d subshell area					13 Al 27.0	14 Si 28.1	15 P 31.0	16 S 32.1	17 Cl 35.5	18 Ar 39.9
4	19 K 39.1	20 Ca 40.1	21 Sc 45.0	22 Ti 47.9	23 V 50.9	24 Cr 52.0	25 Mn 54.9	26 Fe 55.8	27 Co 58.9	28 Ni 58.7	29 Cu 63.5	30 Zn 65.4	31 Ga 69.7	32 Ge 72.6	33 As 74.9	34 Se 79.0	35 Br 79.9	36 Kr 83.8
5	37 Rb 85.5	38 Sr 87.6	39 Y 88.9	40 Zr 91.2	41 Nb 92.9	42 Mo 95.9	43 Tc (98)	44 Ru 101.1	45 Rh 102.9	46 Pd 106.4	47 Ag 107.9	48 Cd 112.4	49 In 114.8	50 Sn 118.7	51 Sb 121.8	52 Te 127.6	53 I 126.9	54 Xe 131.3
6	55 Cs 132.9	56 Ba 137.3	57 La* 138.9	72 Hf 178.5	73 Ta 180.9	74 W 183.9	75 Re 186.2	76 Os 190.2	77 Ir 192.2	78 Pt 195.1	79 Au 197.0	80 Hg 200.6	81 Tl 204.4	82 Pb 207.2	83 Bi 209.0	84 Po (209)	85 At (210)	86 Rn (222)
7	87 Fr (223)	88 Ra 226.0	89 Ac† 227.0	104 Unq (261)	105 Unp (262)	106 Unh (263)	107 Uns (262)	108 Uno (265)	109 Une (267)									

*	58 Ce 140.1	59 Pr 140.9	60 Nd 144.2	61 Pm (145)	62 Sm 150.4	63 Eu 152.0	64 Gd 157.3	65 Tb 158.9	66 Dy 162.5	67 Ho 164.9	68 Er 167.3	69 Tm 168.9	70 Yb 173.0	71 Lu 175.0
†	90 Th 232.0	91 Pa (231)	92 U 238.0	93 Np (237)	94 Pu (244)	95 Am (243)	96 Cm (247)	97 Bk (247)	98 Cf (251)	99 Es (252)	100 Fm (257)	101 Md (258)	102 No (259)	103 Lr (260)

⟨————————— f subshell area —————————⟩

2. Each period (horizontal row) of the periodic table corresponds to an energy shell. For example, atoms of carbon, C, (row **2**) have outer electrons in the **2nd** energy shell; atoms of sodium, Na, (row **3**) have outer electrons in the **3rd** energy shell, and so on.

3. When writing electron configurations, and determining which subshells to fill, be aware of what area and row the element is in. Then remember:

   • An element in the *s* area of row *n* has outer electrons in the **n**s subshell.

   • An element in the *p* area of row *n* has outer electrons in the **n**p subshell.

   • An element in the *d* area of row *n* has outer electrons in the **(n − 1)**d subshell.

   • An element in the *f* area of row *n* has outer electrons in the **(n − 2)**f subshell.

How does this work? Consider an atom of phosphorus, P, (row 3). It's in the p area, so its outer electrons are in the $3p$ subshell. What about an atom of nickel, Ni, (row 4)? It's in the d area. That means its outer electrons go into the $(4-1)$ d or $3d$ subshell.

Let's put it all together and try writing the electron configuration for an atom of fluorine. Where do we start? At hydrogen, of course. It's in the s area of row 1. Hydrogen has an electron in its $1s$ subshell. Although helium looks like it is in the p area, it is actually part of the $1s$ area. Now we have 2 electrons in the lone orbital of the $1s$ subshell. Since no orbital can hold 3 electrons, we need to go to a different (higher energy) subshell for the next addition. Follow the numbers to lithium and then beryllium; they're in the s area of row 2 and fill the $2s$ subshell and keep going. Starting with boron and continuing through fluorine, we are in the p area of row 2. Boron atoms have 1 electron in the $2p$ subshell, carbon atoms have 2, and so on—up to fluorine, which has 5 electrons in its $2p$ subshell. This makes the electron configuration of a fluorine atom $1s^2\,2s^2\,2p^5$. The superscripts indicate the number of electrons occupying a particular subshell. Adding these superscripts gives the total number of electrons in a species. Since fluorine has the atomic number 9, we expect fluorine atoms to have 9 electrons. Add the superscripts from fluorine's electron configuration: $2 + 2 + 5 = 9$. This can serve as a check on your work or as a quick way to eliminate incorrect choices on an electron configuration question.

Finding the electron configuration of ions follows the same rules as for atoms but with one additional step. Suppose we need the electron configuration of the fluoride ion, F^-. First, find the electron configuration for the atom. That would be $1s^2 2s^2 2p^5$. Now, how does F^- differ from the neutral F atom? It has 1 extra electron. So add 1 electron to the electron configuration. Thus, the electron configuration of F^- is $1s^2 2s^2 2p^6$ (the same as that of a neon atom). If we were dealing with positive ions, we would find the atomic electron configuration and then remove one or more electrons.

Now, what about the f subshell, which you might remember learning about in school? For the test you don't have to know much about it. Just remember this: If an element has an atomic number greater than 57, some of its electrons are in the f subshell, which is another way of saying they're in f orbitals. So, element number 76, osmium (Os), has electrons in the f subshell, as do gold (Au), samarium (Sm), and terbium (Tb).

One more thing. In this section, we've described something called the **Aufbau principle**, which states that a subshell is completely filled before electrons are placed in the next higher one. But there are some exceptions to this principle that are worth mentioning. First, since completely filled and half-filled d subshells give extra stability to an atom, Cr and Cu violate the Aufbau principle and promote a $4s$ electron to the $3d$ orbital. Second, hybrid orbitals, which we will talk about in the next chapter, also violate the Aufbau principle by mixing orbitals of different energy levels.

THE STABLE OCTET

Look at element 10, neon (Ne). Its electron configuration is $1s^2\,2s^2\,2p^6$. Neon's configuration has one 1 subshell and two 2 subshells. It has no 3 subshells or 4 subshells, so the two 2 subshells (indicating the 2nd subshell) constitute its outermost shell.

Now take a look at neon's outermost shell: $1s^2\mathbf{2s^2\,2p^6}$. Count the electrons in this shell: $2 + 6 = 8$. The fact that neon has 8 electrons in its outermost shell means that it has a stable octet; 8 electrons.

Examine element number 18, argon (Ar), and look especially at its outermost shell, which is the 3rd shell: $1s^2\,2s^2\,2p^6\,\mathbf{3s^2 3p^6}$. Argon, too, has a stable octet. That is, it has 8 electrons in its outermost shell. The same is true for

- krypton (Kr): $1s^2\, 2s^2\, 2p^6\, 3s^2\, 3p^6 4s^2\, 3d^{10}\, 4p^6$
- xenon (Xe): $1s^2 2s^2\, 2p^6\, 3s^2\, 3p^6\, 4s^2\, 3d^{10}\, 4p^6\, 5s^2\, 4d^{10}\, 5p^6$
- radon (Rn): $1s^2\, 2s^2\, 2p^6\, 3s^2\, 3p^6\, 4s^2\, 3d^{10}\, 4p^6\, 5s^2\, 4d^{10}\, 5p^6\, 6s^2\, 4f^{10}\, 5d^{10}\, 6p^6$

All of the elements with stable octets are called **noble gases** or **inert gases**. They're very stable. They don't like to react with anything or change themselves in any way. They're very happy the way they are. Why? Because atoms are happiest with 8 electrons in their outermost shell. Helium [He, atomic number 2] is also very stable. It, too, is an inert gas although it has only 2 electrons in its outermost shell.

By the way, the electrons in an atom's outermost shell are called **valence electrons**. So another way of saying "stable octet" is to say "8 valence electrons." All of the noble gases have 8 valence electrons. Beryllium, however, (Be, atomic number 4)—$1s^2 2s^2$—has 2 valence electrons. Oxygen—$1s^2 2s^2 2p^4$—has 6 valence electrons.

Learn to associate:

Valence electrons with:	number of electrons in outermost energy shell
Stable octet with:	8 valence electrons; very stable atom or ion; noble gases

Now review the material on electrons, electron configurations, and the stable octet, and try these questions.

Question Type A

(A) Bohr model
(B) De Broglie's hypothesis
(C) Heisenberg principle
(D) Quantum theory
(E) Atomic theory

9. Provides that all matter may be considered as a wave   B

10. Views electrons in true orbits around nucleus   A

11. Considers that one cannot know position and velocity of electron at same moment   C

QUESTION TYPE B

Directions: Each question below consists of two statements, I in the left-hand column and II in the right-hand column. For each question, determine whether statement I is true or false and whether statement II is true or false and fill in the corresponding T or F ovals on your answer sheet. Fill in oval CE only if statement II is a correct explanation of statement I.

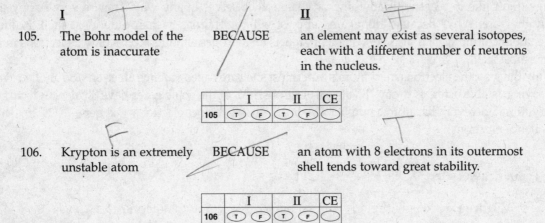

	I		II
105.	The Bohr model of the atom is inaccurate	BECAUSE	an element may exist as several isotopes, each with a different number of neutrons in the nucleus.

	I	II	CE
105	Ⓣ Ⓕ	Ⓣ Ⓕ	⬭

	I		II
106.	Krypton is an extremely unstable atom	BECAUSE	an atom with 8 electrons in its outermost shell tends toward great stability.

	I	II	CE
106	Ⓣ Ⓕ	Ⓣ Ⓕ	⬭

QUESTION TYPE C

31. The electron configuration $1s^2 2s^2 2p^6 3s^2 3p^6 4s^2 3d^7$ represents an atom of the element

(A) Br
(B) Co
(C) Cd
(D) Ga
(E) Mg

32. The electron configuration for an atom of the element Tc is

(A) $1s^2 2s^2 2p^6 3s^2 3p^6 3d^{10} 4s^2 4p^5 5s^2 5p^6$
(B) $1s^2 2s^2 2p^6 3s^2 3p^6 3d^{10} 4s^2 4p^3 5s^2 4d^5$
(C) $1s^2 2s^2 2p^6 3s^2 3p^6 3d^{10} 4s^2 4p^3$
(D) $1s^2 2s^2 2p^6 3s^2 3p^6 3d^{15}$
(E) $1s^2 2s^2 2p^6 3s^2 3p^6 3d^{10} 4s^2 4p^6 5s^2 4d^5$

33. A neutral species whose electron configuration is $1s^2 2s^2 2p^6 3s^2 3p^6 3d^{10} 4s^2 4p^6 4d^{10} 5s^2 5p^6$ is

(A) highly reactive
(B) a positively charged ion
(C) a noble gas
(D) a transition metal
(E) a lanthanide element

LET'S LOOK AT THE ANSWERS

Question 9: (B) You may be tempted to pick E, but don't. Atomic theory is associated with a fellow named Dalton and says that all elements are composed of atoms. For this test, you're not expected to fully understand the De Broglie hypothesis; you're just supposed to associate it with the idea that matter can be conceived of as waves, and waves can be conceived of as matter. So B is correct.

Question 10: (A) You learned that Bohr incorrectly believed that electrons circled the nucleus in orbits, the way planets circle the sun. So A is correct.

Question 11: (C) For this test, you need not completely understand the Heisenberg principle; you only need to associate it with the idea that one cannot, at any one moment, know both an electron's position and momentum. So C is correct.

Question 105: (T, T) Divide and conquer! Evaluate the first statement on its own, and decide whether it's true or false. Is it true that according to the Bohr model electrons circle the nucleus in true orbits? Yes, it is.

Now, look at the second statement by itself. Is it true? Yes. Now let's find out if the sentence makes sense. "The Bohr model of the atom is inaccurate because an element may exist as several isotopes each with a different number of neutrons in the nucleus." The second part of the statement has nothing to do with the first. Both statements are true, but they have nothing to do with each other, so do not fill in the CE oval.

Question 106: (F, T) Evaluate the first statement by itself, and decide whether it's true or false. Is it true that krypton is an unstable atom? No, that isn't true. Krypton is a very stable atom. Why? Because it has a full octet in its outermost shell.

Now look at the second statement. Is it true or false? It's true: Atoms with 8 electrons in their outermost shell are stable. The first statement is false, and the second is true.

Question 31: (B) Here you're given the configuration and asked to identify the element. The easiest way to solve this problem is to add up the electrons in the configuration; you'll find that their sum is 27. Since the question asks about an *atom*, and not an *ion*, this means the answer is Co, which has the atomic number 27. The correct answer is B.

Question 32: (E) Here you're given the element and asked to identify the electron configuration. Follow the steps we showed you for writing electron configurations, and you'll see that E is correct. If you had trouble writing the electron configuration, you could also have arrived at the answer by testing each answer choice. See which answer choices have superscripts that add up to the atomic number of Tc, which is 43. Then eliminate the other answer choices, and take your best guess.

Question 33: (C) Do it the easy way: Count up the superscripts. They add up to 54. Look on the periodic table, and you'll see that element 54 is xenon. Xenon, as you can see from the table, is a noble gas.

RADIOACTIVITY AND HALF-LIVES

Atomic nuclei, as you know, are made of protons and neutrons. In some atoms, the combination of protons and neutrons makes the nucleus unstable. These atoms will decay—on their own—spontaneously. As they decay, they emit high-energy radioactive particles. Radioactive particles include alpha (α) particles, beta (β) particles, and gamma (γ) rays. If you think about it, the process of radioactive decay makes sense: A radioactive nucleus is trying to become more stable; greater stability means lower energy, so the radioactive nucleus wants to lose energy.

As a radioactive atom decays—emitting α or β particles and γ rays—its identity changes, and it becomes either: (1) another isotope of the element it originally was or (2) another element entirely. Some nuclei are stable and some are unstable; the unstable ones have a tendency to break apart, and they are said to be **radioactive**.

Why are some nuclei unstable? For this test, you only have to know that the instability has something to do with the combination of neutrons and protons. Some combinations of neutrons and protons just don't get along well, and they try to solve this problem by undergoing nuclear decay. When you think of radioactivity, think this: When an unstable nucleus undergoes nuclear decay, it's radioactive, and it gives off radioactivity. A **Geiger counter** is used to detect and measure radioactive particles.

You should know about four kinds of radioactive decay.

RADIOACTIVE DECAY TYPE 1: ALPHA DECAY

An alpha particle is made up of 2 protons and 2 neutrons. When a nucleus gives off an alpha particle, its atomic number is reduced by 2 and its mass number is reduced by 4. Since the atomic number changes, it actually turns into a different element. After all, the atomic number is the basis of an atom's identity.

Another thing about alpha particles: Since an alpha particle consists of 2 protons and 2 neutrons, it's actually the same thing as a helium-4 nucleus, and it's often symbolized that way—$_2^4\text{He}$. The 4 represents the mass number, and the 2 represents the atomic number (number of protons). To sum up alpha decay:

- an alpha particle is emitted

- the atomic number decreases by 2; the mass number decreases by 4

RADIOACTIVE DECAY TYPE 2: BETA DECAY

Sometimes a nucleus becomes more stable through beta decay, in which it reduces its neutron to proton ratio by taking a neutron and turning it into a proton. In these cases, the atomic number goes up by 1, since there's an extra proton, but the mass number remains the same. (It lost a neutron, but it gained a proton, so there is no net change in the mass number.) When an atom undergoes beta decay, it emits a beta particle; a beta particle is identical to an electron and is symbolized as $_{-1}^{0}\text{e}$. To sum up beta decay:

- a neutron is converted to a proton

- a beta particle (an electron) is emitted

- the atomic number increases by 1, but the mass number stays the same

RADIOACTIVE DECAY TYPE 3: POSITRON EMISSION

Sometimes, when a nucleus can become more stable by increasing its neutron to proton ratio, it takes a proton and converts it to a neutron. The result of this is that the atomic number decreases by 1, and the mass number remains the same; this type of radioactive decay is known as positron emission. When a nucleus undergoes positron emission, it emits a positron. What is a positron? Well, it's a positively charged particle, but it isn't a proton. It has the same mass as an electron, but it carries a positive charge. A positron is symbolized as $_1^0 e$. To sum up positron emission:

- a proton is converted to a neutron
- a positron is emitted
- the atomic number decreases by 1, and mass number stays the same

RADIOACTIVE DECAY TYPE 4: GAMMA DECAY

We should also mention gamma rays, which are a form of electromagnetic radiation. Radioactive nuclei often emit gamma rays; these are high-energy particles with the symbol $_0^0 \gamma$, together with alpha particles, beta particles, or positrons. When nuclei emit alpha or beta particles, they are sometimes left in a high energy state, but when they emit gamma rays, they become stable.

HALF-LIFE

For the SAT Chemistry, you should know everything we just said about radioactive decay, and you should also know about the *rate* of radioactive decay. The rate of radioactive decay of a substance is called its **half-life**. For example, if we start with 1,000 g of a radioactive substance, and its half-life is 1 year, then

- after 1 year we'll have 500 g of the original sample left.
- after another year we'll have 250 g of the original sample left.
- after another year we'll have 125 g of the original sample left.
- after another year we'll have 62.5 g of the original sample left.
- after another year we'll have 31.25 g of the original sample left.
- after another year we'll have 15.625 g of the original sample left.

And so on. That's how half-lives work.

> **Learn to associate:**
>
> **Radioactive decay with:**   unstable nuclei;
> spontaneous process;
> emission of α and β particles, positrons,
>   and γ rays;
> half-lives;
> alteration of atom's identity

Now review everything we've said about radioactive decay and half-lives, and try the questions on the following pages.

QUESTION TYPE A

(A) Alpha decay
(B) Beta decay
(C) Positron emission
(D) Gamma decay
(E) Electron capture

14. Often accompanies other radioactive processes

15. Causes an atom to reduce its atomic number by 2 and its mass number by 4

16. Occurs when a neutron is converted into a proton in a nucleus

QUESTION TYPE B

Directions: Each question below consists of two statements, I in the left-hand column and II in the right-hand column. For each question, determine whether statement I is true or false and whether statement II is true or false and fill in the corresponding T or F ovals on your answer sheet. Fill in oval CE only if statement II is a correct explanation of statement I.

| | I | | | II | |

107. Radioactive elements can emit alpha particles, beta particles, and gamma rays   BECAUSE   radioactive elements have extremely stable nuclei.

	I	II	CE
107	(T) (F)	(T) (F)	()

108. If a radioactive sample with a half-life of 40 years decays for 80 years, 25% of the original sample will remain   BECAUSE   one half of 100% is 50%, and one half of 50% is 25%.

	I	II	CE
108	(T) (F)	(T) (F)	()

QUESTION TYPE C

$$^{222}_{86}Rn \rightarrow \, ^{218}_{84}Po + \, ^{4}_{2}He$$

39. The radioactive decay shown above is an example of

(A) positron emission
(B) gamma ray emission
(C) alpha decay
(D) beta decay
(E) ionization

$$^{131}_{53}I \rightarrow {}^{131}_{54}Xe + {}^{0}_{-1}e$$

40. The radioactive decay shown above is an
    example of

    (A) positron emission
    (B) gamma ray emission
    (C) alpha decay
    (D) beta decay
    (E) ionization

LET'S LOOK AT THE ANSWERS

Question 14: (D) As we said earlier, the emission of gamma rays generally accompanies other forms of radioactive decay. So D is right.

Question 15: (A) In order for its atomic number to be reduced by 2, an atom must lose 2 protons. In order for its mass to be reduced by 4, it must also lose a total of 4 nucleons (protons or neutrons). The atom loses 2 protons and 2 neutrons. That's the description of alpha decay, so A is correct.

Question 16: (B) Beta decay—which involves the emission of an electron—converts a neutron into a proton. Positron emission and electron capture (a decay process that you don't need to know for the test) convert a proton into a neutron. Beta decay is the correct answer; that's choice B.

Question 107: (T, F) Divide and conquer. The first statement is true. The second statement is false.

Question 108: (T, T, CE) Divide and conquer. The first statement is true: If an element decays for one half-life, half of the original sample remains. If it decays for two half-lives, one quarter of the original sample remains. The second statement is also true. Does the whole sentence make sense? Yes. So fill in the CE oval.

Question 39: (C) In this problem, an atom of Rn (radon) with an atomic number of 86 and a mass number of 222 undergoes a change. What happens to it? All of a sudden it's a different element, Po (polonium), with an atomic number of 84 and a mass number of 218. It lost two protons and 2 neutrons. The Rn atom has undergone alpha decay. In fact, you can see that an alpha particle—helium-4 nucleus—has been emitted as a part of the whole process. We're dealing with alpha decay, and C is correct.

Question 40: (D) To begin with, you can see that an electron has been emitted, so that's one way to know, right away, that we're dealing with beta decay. You can also see that the atom of I (iodine) has turned into something else—xenon—because its atomic number increased from 53 to 54. But its mass number stayed the same, so it looks as if a neutron was turned into a proton. That's beta decay, and D is correct.

7

The Periodic Table and Bonding

When you sit down to take the SAT Chemistry Subject Test, the periodic table may well be your best friend. Why? Well, first, it is one of the few tools you'll be allowed to use on test day. Second, it can help you answer quite a few different types of test questions. We just saw how to use the periodic table to figure out an atom's electron configuration, and we'll now take a look at how it can help you predict how atoms will bond.

THE PERIODIC TABLE

PERIODIC TABLE OF THE ELEMENTS

┌ s subshell area ┐ ———— p subshell area ————

1A																	8A
1 **H** 1.0	2A											3A	4A	5A	6A	7A	**2** **He** 4.0
3 **Li** 6.9	**4** **Be** 9.0				B groups							**5** **B** 10.8	**6** **C** 12.0	**7** **N** 14.0	**8** **O** 16.0	**9** **F** 19.0	**10** **Ne** 20.2
11 **Na** 23.0	**12** **Mg** 24.3	d subshell area										**13** **Al** 27.0	**14** **Si** 28.1	**15** **P** 31.0	**16** **S** 32.1	**17** **Cl** 35.5	**18** **Ar** 39.9

Period 1 = H, He; Period 2 = Li...Ne; Period 3 = Na...Ar

	1A	2A												3A	4A	5A	6A	7A	8A

Row 4:
19 **K** 39.1	**20** **Ca** 40.1	**21** **Sc** 45.0	**22** **Ti** 47.9	**23** **V** 50.9	**24** **Cr** 52.0	**25** **Mn** 54.9	**26** **Fe** 55.8	**27** **Co** 58.9	**28** **Ni** 58.7	**29** **Cu** 63.5	**30** **Zn** 65.4	**31** **Ga** 69.7	**32** **Ge** 72.6	**33** **As** 74.9	**34** **Se** 79.0	**35** **Br** 79.9	**36** **Kr** 83.8

Row 5:
37 **Rb** 85.5	**38** **Sr** 87.6	**39** **Y** 88.9	**40** **Zr** 91.2	**41** **Nb** 92.9	**42** **Mo** 95.9	**43** **Tc** (98)	**44** **Ru** 101.1	**45** **Rh** 102.9	**46** **Pd** 106.4	**47** **Ag** 107.9	**48** **Cd** 112.4	**49** **In** 114.8	**50** **Sn** 118.7	**51** **Sb** 121.8	**52** **Te** 127.6	**53** **I** 126.9	**54** **Xe** 131.3

Row 6:
55 **Cs** 132.9	**56** **Ba** 137.3	**57** **La*** 138.9	**72** **Hf** 178.5	**73** **Ta** 180.9	**74** **W** 183.9	**75** **Re** 186.2	**76** **Os** 190.2	**77** **Ir** 192.2	**78** **Pt** 195.1	**79** **Au** 197.0	**80** **Hg** 200.6	**81** **Tl** 204.4	**82** **Pb** 207.2	**83** **Bi** 209.0	**84** **Po** (209)	**85** **At** (210)	**86** **Rn** (222)

Row 7:
87 **Fr** (223)	**88** **Ra** 226.0	**89** **Ac**† 227.0	**104** **Unq** (261)	**105** **Unp** (262)	**106** **Unh** (263)	**107** **Uns** (262)	**108** **Uno** (265)	**109** **Une** (267)

* Lanthanide series:

58 **Ce** 140.1	**59** **Pr** 140.9	**60** **Nd** 144.2	**61** **Pm** (145)	**62** **Sm** 150.4	**63** **Eu** 152.0	**64** **Gd** 157.3	**65** **Tb** 158.9	**66** **Dy** 162.5	**67** **Ho** 164.9	**68** **Er** 167.3	**69** **Tm** 168.9	**70** **Yb** 173.0	**71** **Lu** 175.0

† Actinide series:

90 **Th** 232.0	**91** **Pa** (231)	**92** **U** 238.0	**93** **Np** (237)	**94** **Pu** (244)	**95** **Am** (243)	**96** **Cm** (247)	**97** **Bk** (247)	**98** **Cf** (251)	**99** **Es** (252)	**100** **Fm** (257)	**101** **Md** (258)	**102** **No** (259)	**103** **Lr** (260)

———— f subshell area ————

We've already seen that elements are arranged on the periodic table from left to right in order of increasing atomic number (except, of course, for the *f* area elements, which are alone at the bottom). We've also noted that the periodic table can be divided into four regions: the *s*, *p*, *d*, and *f* areas. By arranging elements in both of these ways, two important themes emerge.

1. Elements in the same period (horizontal row), have electrons in the same energy shells.

2. Elements in the same group (vertical column), generally have similar chemical and physical properties.

Let's look at these ideas a little more closely, one at a time.

The first period on the table consists of just hydrogen and helium. Both of these elements have electrons in the 1st energy shell. Since the 1st energy shell consists of 1 1*s* orbital, it can hold only 2 electrons, so the third element, lithium (Li) has an electron in the 2nd energy shell. So do Be, B, C, N, O, F, and Ne. These elements make up the 2nd period, and their 2nd energy shells are filled. Third-period elements from sodium (Na) to argon (Ar) fill up the 3rd energy shell. Now, you may ask: what about elements in the *d* area, such as iron (Fe)? Doesn't iron have valence electrons in the 3*d* subshell of the *third* energy shell? Well, it does, but iron also has 2 electrons the 4*s* subshell. It's an element in the 4th period, and it has electrons in its 4th energy shell.

CHEMICAL FAMILIES

Valence electrons are the most important electrons in an atom because they can participate in chemical bonds. Since chemical reactions involve bond breaking and bond making, the behavior of valence electrons is responsible for all the chemical reactions you see, from the souring of milk to the burning of rocket fuel. Thus, it makes sense that if two elements have atoms with the same number of valence electrons, they will react similarly. And in general, this is true. We mentioned that all of the atoms of elements (except helium) in the extreme right-hand column of the periodic table (the noble gases) have 8 valence electrons. Do they have similar reactivities? Yes. These elements (including helium) are all very unreactive and are said to be part of the noble gas *family*. A **family** is a collection of elements from the same vertical group that have similar chemical properties. Not surprisingly, the members of a particular family all have the same number of valence electrons.

There are other important families of elements. The atoms of elements in the extreme left-hand group on the periodic table all have 1 valence electron (in an *s* subshell). With the exception of hydrogen, these elements—from lithium (Li) to francium (Fr)—also have much in common. Chemically, they are all extremely reactive. (A piece of potassium, for example, will produce a violent reaction if placed into water.) Physically, they are shiny, grayish-white metals. However, they melt more easily than the metals you're used to seeing such as iron or copper. They also tend to have lower densities than the more common metals. The elements in the first column, from lithium (Li) to francium (Fr), are placed in the family of **alkali metals**.

The elements of the group to the right of the alkali metals, from beryllium (Be) to radium (Ra), constitute another family—the **alkaline earth metals**. The alkaline earth metals have 2 valence electrons. They are less reactive than the alkali metals but more reactive than common metals such as iron and copper. They look a lot like alkali metals; because of their highly reactive nature, elements of the alkali and alkaline earth families are collectively known as the **active metals**.

The group of elements alongside the noble gases make up another important family of elements—the **halogens**. All of the halogens are very reactive. These elements are quite physically distinct from one another: fluorine (F) and chlorine (Cl) are greenish-yellow, toxic gases; bromine (Br) is a brown liquid at room temperature; and iodine (I) is a grayish-purple solid. So what makes these elements a family? They all have 7 valence electrons, so they all have similar chemical properties.

All of the groups on the periodic table groups are indicated by a combination of a number and a letter. For instance, the alkali metals group is designated 1A. The alkaline earth metals group is 2A. The groups in the *d* area all have a designation that ends in a B. To the right of the *d* area, designations ending in A resume. The group containing aluminum is 3A, and so on up to 7A (the halogens) and 8A (the noble gases). Notice that for the A groups, the number represents the number of valence electrons possessed by elements in that group. So a lithium atom (1A) has 1 valence electron, a carbon atom (4A) has 4 valence electrons, and an iodine atom (7A) has 7 valence electrons.

METALS, NONMETALS, AND SEMIMETALS

All elements can be classified as being either a **metal**, **nonmetal**, or **semimetal** (also referred to as a **metalloid**). Let's start by talking about metals. **Metals** share certain physical characteristics. They are usually shiny and are good conductors of heat and electricity. Many metals are **malleable**, which means they can be hammered into thin sheets such as aluminum foil. Metals are also often **ductile**, which means that they can form wires. (Copper, for example, is ductile.) With the exception of mercury (a liquid), all metals are solid at room temperature. While these characteristics are noteworthy, however, there is one chemical characteristic that, above all else, makes an element a metal. Metals tend to give up electrons when they bond. Roughly 75 percent of the elements are considered to be metals, and metals can be further divided into **active** and **transition metals**. The reactive metals of the *s* area are classified as active, while the rest are classified as transition metals. Transition metals are quite different from active metals. They are generally harder, more difficult to melt, and less reactive than active metals. Transition metals include those elements in the *d* and *f* areas. Many of the elements that come to mind when we think of metals are transition metals such as iron, copper, gold, and silver. Many compounds that contain a transition metal are intensely colored. For instance, many copper compounds (but not the element itself) are blue.

Nonmetals are elements that tend to *gain* or *share* electrons when they bond. This distinguishes them from metals. Nonmetals are usually poor conductors of heat and electricity and some such as sulfur (S) and phosphorus (P) are solids at room temperature. Unlike metals, they are dull, brittle, and melt easily (although diamond, which is composed of the nonmetal carbon, is an exception to these rules). A few nonmetals, such as oxygen (O) and fluorine (F), are gases. The nonmetal bromine (Br) is a liquid at room temperature. As you can see, the physical properties of nonmetals vary considerably.

Semimetals, or **metalloids**, have some of the physical characteristics of both metals and nonmetals. For instance, silicon (Si) is shiny like a metal but brittle like a nonmetal. Appropriately enough, semimetals lay in-between metals and nonmetals on the periodic table.

The diagram below summarizes key families and regions on the periodic table.

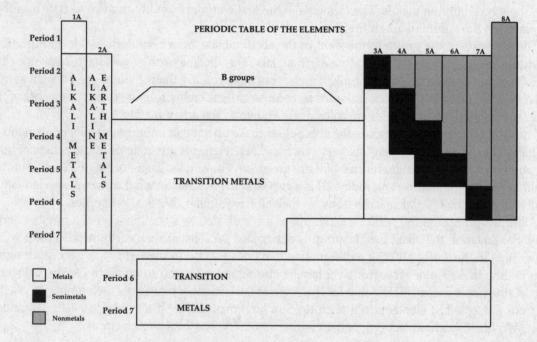

SOME IMPORTANT PERIODIC TRENDS

For the SAT Chemistry, you'll need to know about four important trends seen in the periodic table.

1. **Ionization Energy:** Because the atomic nucleus contains protons, nuclei are positively charged; the attraction between opposite charges is what keeps the negatively charged electrons in their orbitals. In order for an electron to be extracted from an atom (which creates a positively charged ion), energy must be expended. For any atom, the amount of energy required to remove an electron from an atom is called the **ionization energy**. As you move from left to right across the periodic table, ionization energy generally increases; it gets much harder to remove an electron from the atom. As you move from top to bottom through a column (group), ionization energy decreases.

    Also, it is much harder to remove each successive electron from an atom; the energy required to remove an inner (nonvalence) electron from an atom is incredibly high because these electrons are very strongly attracted to the atom's nucleus. For the exam, remember that **ionization energy increases from left to right across the periodic table, as you move up through a group.**

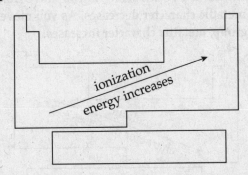

2. **Electronegativity:** An atom's **electronegativity** value refers to the amount of "pull" that an atom's nucleus exerts on another atom's electrons when it is involved in a bond. Atoms of different elements typically have different electronegativities. **As you move across the periodic table from left to right, electronegativity increases. As you move down a column (group) on the periodic table, electronegativity decreases.**

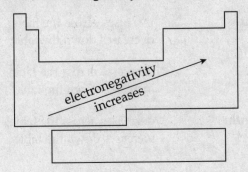

3. **Atomic Radius:** We can think of an atom as being roughly spherical, with the nucleus at the center of the sphere. Electrons move about in orbitals within the sphere. Every atomic sphere has a radius, which is known as **atomic radius**—the distance from its center to the edge. The larger the atom, the greater its radius. **As you move across the periodic table from left to right, atomic radius decreases. As you move down a group, atomic radius increases.**

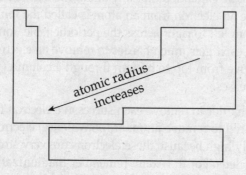

4. **Metallic Character:** **Metallic character** is a measure of how easily an atom gives up electrons to form a positive ion. **As you move from left to right across a period, metallic character decreases. As you move from top to bottom down a group, metallic character increases.**

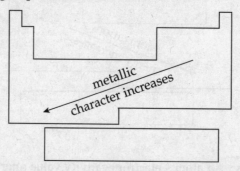

Learn to associate:

Ionization energy with:	increases across the table; decreases down the table
Electronegativity with:	increases across the table; decreases down the table
Atomic radius with:	decreases across the table; increases down the table
Metallic character with:	decreases across the table; increases down the table

Review what we've said about the periodic table, and tackle these questions:

QUESTION TYPE A

(A) Na
(B) Ca
(C) Mn
(D) F
(E) Ne

11. Is an alkaline earth metal *B*

12. Regularly forms bonds by receiving electrons *D*

13. Has the greatest difference between its first and
    second ionization energies *A*

QUESTION TYPE B

<u>Directions:</u> Each question below consists of two statements, I in the left-hand column and II in the
right-hand column. For each question, determine whether statement I is true or false <u>and</u> whether
statement II is true or false and fill in the corresponding ovals on your answer sheet. <u>Fill in oval CE
only if statement II is a correct explanation of statement I.</u>

I   **II**

109.   Only an atom's valence   BECAUSE   an atom's inner electrons are
       electrons can participate in   held too tightly to be shared or
       bonding   transferred.

T   *CE*   *T*

110.   Potassium has greater   BECAUSE   potassium has a higher melting
       metallic character than iron   point than iron.

T   *F*

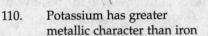

QUESTION TYPE C

39. Which of the following metals is most reactive?

(A) Sodium, Na
(B) Magnesium, Mg
(C) Copper, Cu
(D) Gold, Au
(E) Chlorine, Cl

42. All of the following are true regarding nickel, Ni,
    EXCEPT:

(A) It is malleable.
(B) It is ductile.
(C) It is lustrous.
(D) It is an insulator.
(E) It forms colored compounds.

51. Which of the following represents an ordering of the period 4 elements bromine (Br), calcium (Ca), krypton (Kr), and potassium (K) by increasing atomic size?

(A) K, Kr, Ca, Br
(B) K, Ca, Br, Kr
(C) Kr, Br, Ca, K
(D) Ca, K, Br, Kr
(E) Br, Kr, Ca, K

LET'S LOOK AT THE ANSWERS

Question 11: (B) Remember that the group 2A elements are alkaline earth metals. Calcium (Ca) is in this family, so B is correct.

Question 12: (D) Metals bond by *losing* valence, electrons, so eliminate A, B, and C. This leaves us with fluorine and neon. They're both nonmetals; however, neon is a noble gas, so it generally does not form bonds. Fluorine does. D is the answer.

Question 13: (A) The first ionization of an element refers to the amount of energy needed to remove one electron from an atom. The second ionization energy refers to the removal of a second electron. What kind of electrons are hardest to remove from an atom? Inner shell electrons. So the correct answer should be an element whose atoms have only 1 valence electron. Why? Because removing a second electron from such an atom would involve removing an inner shell electron and thus take an enormous amount of energy. So which of the choices has atoms with 1 valence electron? Think group 1A elements. Sodium is one of those, and A is correct.

Question 109: (T, T, CE) Time to divide and conquer. Is the first statement true or false? It's true. What about statement II? It's also true. Inner shell electrons are held more closely to the positive nucleus than are valence electrons; inner shell electrons are held too strongly to be useful in bonding.

Let's see if the whole sentence makes sense: "Only an atom's valence electrons can participate in bonding because an atom's inner shell electrons are held too tightly to be shared or transferred." It certainly does, so fill in CE oval.

Question 110: (T, F) Consider statement I. Does potassium have greater metallic character than iron? Remember that metallic character involves the ease with which an element's atoms can give up electrons. Potassium is much more reactive than iron and thus can be expected to give up its electrons much more readily, so potassium does have greater metallic character, and statement I is true.

Look at the second statement. Is it true or false? It's false. Potassium is an active metal, and active metals tend to have lower melting points than transition metals such as iron.

Question 39: (A) Don't be fooled by choice E. Chlorine is very reactive, but it isn't a metal. Recall that the alkali metals are the most reactive metals. Sodium is a member of the alkali metal family, so A is correct.

Question 42: (D) Nickel is a transition metal, so we can expect it to be malleable, ductile, and lustrous (shiny). As is true of many transition metals, nickel compounds are intensely colored (usually a bright green), so eliminate A, B, C, and E. That leaves D. Nickel is a conductor of heat (and electricity), not an insulator. Pick D.

Question 51: (C) Remember the periodic table trends. As you move from left to right within a period, atoms get smaller. So the smallest atom of a period 4 element is krypton (Kr). Eliminate any choice that does not start with Kr; that makes C the correct answer.

CHEMICAL BONDING

Not surprisingly, the SAT Chemistry Subject Test will want you to know something about bonding—how atoms join to form molecular or ionic compounds.

You'll need to remember, first of all, that bonding usually occurs because every atom in the bond would like to end up with 8 electrons (a stable octet) in its outermost shell.

There are three main types of bonds.

1. ionic bonds

2. covalent bonds (and polar covalent bonds)

3. metallic bonds

THE IONIC BOND

When an atom in a bond gives up 1 or more electrons to the atom it bonds with, an ionic bond is formed. Ionic bonds generally form between atoms that differ significantly in their electronegativity values. The atom that gives up the electron becomes a positively charged ion, and the one that accepts the electron becomes a negatively charged ion. The positively charged atom attracts the negatively charged atom, and this draws the two atoms together and results in the release of energy. One term you should be familiar with for the test is **lattice energy**—the lattice (binding) energy of an ionic solid is a measure of the energy required to completely separate a mole of a solid ionic compound into its separate ions. So, the higher the lattice energy, the stronger the ionic bond.

Now let's look at an example of an ionic bond. When sodium (Na) bonds with chlorine (Cl), the sodium atom gives up its outermost electron to become Na+ and the chlorine atom receives it to become Cl–. The Na+ ion has 8 electrons in its outermost shell. (Its electron configuration looks like neon's.)

But what about chlorine? Having *gained* an electron, chlorine also ends up with 8 electrons in its outermost shell. Its electron configuration looks like argon's. The bond that results creates sodium chloride: NaCl. The attraction between a positive charge and a negative charge is called an **electrostatic force**; this force is very strong. The strength of an ionic bond gives ionic compounds their high melting points, hardness, and other physical properties.

For this test, think: **When a metal and nonmetal bond, the result is an ionic bond, in which the atoms are held together by an electrostatic attraction between a positive and a negative ion.**

When an active metal and nonmetal bond, it is easy to predict the empirical formula of the resulting ionic compound. For example, suppose calcium and fluorine atoms bond. Since we have a metal and a nonmetal, these atoms will form an ionic compound. Now, ionic compounds consist of ions, but what ions will be involved? Calcium atoms have 2 valence electrons, and since calcium is a metal, it will give up its valence electrons to achieve a stable octet. It gives up 2 electrons to form a Ca^{2+} ion when it bonds. Conversely, fluorine atoms have 7 valence electrons. Since fluorine is a nonmetal, it will achieve an octet by gaining electrons. So each fluorine atom gains 1 electron (from calcium) to form a F^- ion. To get the empirical formula of calcium fluoride, begin by writing the cation and anion (in that order) next to each other: $Ca^{2+}\ F^-$. Now drop the "+" and "–" signs: Ca^2F^1. Finally, take the number next to the metal, and write it as the subscript of the nonmetal and vice versa to get the subscript for the metal. Thus, the empirical formula of calcium fluoride is Ca_1F_2, which we write CaF_2. If magnesium and oxygen were to bond, we would get the ions Mg^{2+} and O^{2-}. This would make the empirical formula of magnesium oxide Mg_2O_2, which reduces to MgO.

Substances that are held together by ionic bonds are solids at room temperature and atmospheric pressure. Ionic solids are characterized by their hardness, brittleness, and high melting points. Although ions are charge carriers, ionic solids cannot conduct electricity because their ions have very restricted movement. However, if an ionic solid is melted, its ions are freer to move, and the substance can conduct electricity.

THE COVALENT BOND

When two nonmetals (or atoms with similar electronegativities) bond, the result is a covalent bond. In a covalent bond, two atoms *share* electrons. By sharing electrons, each atom can achieve a stable octet. In fact, atoms form covalent bonds simply because it's a way for them to obtain a stable octet.

Look how two oxygen atoms bond to form a molecule of O_2. The dots signify oxygen's 6 valence electrons.

$$\ddot{O}: \; :\ddot{O}$$

Now, if each atom could somehow acquire two more electrons, it would have a stable octet. So what happens?

Each atom donates a pair of electrons, and the shared pairs are attracted to the nuclei of both atoms. In a sense, each atom has 8 valence electrons instead of 6. Each atom is happy. The sharing keeps the atoms together because each atom now has a stable octet.

$$\ddot{O} :: \ddot{O}$$

THE POLAR COVALENT BOND

The two oxygen atoms that we just looked at form a bond and share their electrons equally. But sometimes in a covalent bond, one atom tends to hog the electrons. It still shares them with the other atom, but it tends to keep the electrons for more than its fair share of the time. This hogging of the electrons is a result of one atom having a greater electronegativity value than the other. (Remember that electronegativity increases as we move from left to right across a period and decreases as we move from top to bottom in a column.)

Think about a water molecule. It's made of 2 hydrogen atoms and 1 oxygen atom. Each hydrogen atom has 1 valence electron, which it shares with oxygen. The oxygen atom donates 2 electrons to be shared with the hydrogen atoms. Then what happens? Basically, each hydrogen atom acquires an electron and has a configuration like helium's (which is very stable), and the oxygen atom acquires 2 electrons and has an electron configuration like neon's (an octet).

So a water molecule can be represented as follows:

$$H : \ddot{O} : H$$

But oxygen's electronegativity is greater than hydrogen's. Oxygen "hogs" the electrons it shares with hydrogen, and the shared electrons spend more time around the oxygen than they do around the hydrogen. The result? Each hydrogen atom has a partial positive charge, while the oxygen atom has a partial negative charge.

When, in a covalent bond, certain atoms have a partial positive charge and others have a partial negative charge, we say that the covalent bond is polar. This type of bond is called a **polar covalent bond**.

And what causes a polar covalent bond? A difference in electronegativity between bonded atoms causes it.

THE METALLIC BOND

As you've probably guessed, a metallic bond results when two metals bond. For example, the copper atoms that make up a copper wire are joined by metallic bonds. In metallic bonding, the metal atoms donate valence electrons to become cations. These valence electrons are not directly transferred to another atom as they are in ionic bonding. Instead, they move about freely throughout the sample, producing an attractive force that keeps the metal cations in place. Often the behavior of these free electrons is referred to as a "sea of mobile electrons." Because of the motions of the free electrons, metals are characteristically good conductors of electricity and heat.

Learn to associate:

		Examples
Ionic bond with:	exchange of electrons to form stable octet; bond between a metal and nonmetal	$NaCl$, CaF_2
Covalent bond with:	sharing of electrons to form stable octet; bond between nonmetals	Cl_2, N_2
Polar covalent bond with:	unequal sharing of electrons to form stable octet	H_2O, NH_3
Metallic bond with:	sea of mobile electrons; bond between metals	Cu, Ag

SINGLE, DOUBLE, AND TRIPLE BONDS

So far, we've considered covalent bonds in which one pair of electrons is shared between two atoms; these types of bonds are also called **single bonds**. In the structural formula of a compound, a single bond is represented by a single line. For example, water has two single bonds.

$$H-\overset{\cdot\cdot}{\underset{\cdot\cdot}{O}}-H$$

But more than one pair of electrons can be shared between atoms in a covalent bond. If two pairs of electrons are shared, the bond is called a **double bond**. If three pairs of electrons are shared, it is a **triple bond**. In general, as more pairs of electrons are shared between atoms, the bond gets stronger and the distance between bonded nuclei gets shorter. The oxygen molecule we looked at earlier contains a double bond. It is represented by a double line, as follows:

$$\overset{\cdot\cdot}{\underset{\cdot\cdot}{O}}=\overset{\cdot\cdot}{\underset{\cdot\cdot}{O}}$$

As you might expect, a triple bond such as the one that's present in hydrogen cyanide is represented by a triple line. Take a look.

$$H-C \equiv N:$$

PREDICTING Δ*H* USING BOND ENERGIES

Naturally, different bonds have different strengths. For instance, the bond between a carbon atom and an oxygen atom is stronger than the bond between two chlorine atoms. When a bond is relatively strong, we say its bond energy is high. **Bond energy** refers to the amount of energy it takes to break a bond. Since a C–O bond is harder to break than a Cl–Cl bond, the C–O bond has higher bond energy than the Cl–Cl bond.

Chemical reactions involve the breaking of bonds in the reactants (which requires energy) and the formation of new bonds to make products (which releases energy). If we know which bonds are to be made and which are to be broken, and we know their respective bond energies, we can estimate Δ*H* for the reaction.

Suppose we need to estimate Δ*H* for the reaction $H_2 + Br_2 \rightarrow 2HBr$, given the following bond energies:

$$H–H \text{ bond: } 436 \text{ kJ/mol}$$
$$Br–Br \text{ bond: } 193 \text{ kJ/mol}$$
$$H–Br \text{ bond: } 366 \text{ kJ/mol}$$

In converting H_2 and Br_2 to products, we must break 1 mole of H–H bonds and 1 mole of Br–Br bonds. This will require (1 mole) (436 kJ/mol) + (1 mole) (193 kJ/mol) = 629 kJ of energy. Since we form 2 moles of H–Br bonds, this releases (2 moles) (366 kJ/mol) = 732 kJ of energy. The enthalpy change for the reaction, Δ*H*, is equal to the net energy change, which is 629 kJ – 732 kJ = –103 kJ. If 1 mole of H_2 and 1 mole of Br_2 react to form 2 moles of HBr, the reaction should release 103 kJ. (A positive Δ*H* indicates a net absorbance of energy.)

MOLECULAR SHAPES

Some questions on the SAT Chemistry might ask you about the shapes of molecules. Although we can represent molecules in two dimensions on paper, they are actually three-dimensional. If you are given a molecular formula and asked to determine its shape, follow these preliminary steps:

- Assume the first atom in the formula is the central atom of the structure (unless it is hydrogen, which is never a central atom).

- Using dots to indicate the valence electrons of each atom, surround the central atom with the others, trying to give each atom an octet. Remember hydrogen needs only 2, not 8, valence electrons to be satisfied. It is important to realize that electrons shared between two atoms count toward the total for both.

Completing steps 1 and 2 will give you the structural formula of a molecule. To determine the *shape* of the molecule, you must consider the number of sites in which valence electron pairs surround the central atom. Since electrons all have the same negative charge, they repel each other. The valence electron sites will arrange themselves around the central atom to be as far from each other as possible. There are two types of electron pair sites: those that contain electron pairs in a bond and those that contain unbonded electron pairs (also called **lone pairs**). The number of total electron pair sites and number of lone pairs will dictate the molecule's shape.

Suppose we have a molecule of carbon tetrachloride, CCl_4. The structural formula of CCl_4 is as follows:

Focus on the central carbon atom. It has four sites at which it is surrounded by electron pairs. How can these four sites be situated as far from each other as possible around the central carbon atom? You might be tempted to say that they should be 90° apart from each other, as the structural formula shows. But that's thinking in two dimensions, not three. The four sites can actually be 109° apart if they arrange themselves in a tetrahedron (a symmetrical, four-sided figure):

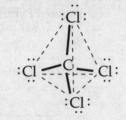

This molecular geometry is called **tetrahedral**.

A slightly different situation arises in a molecule of ammonia, NH_3. Ammonia's structural formula is as follows:

In ammonia, there are four distinct electron pair sites around the central atom of nitrogen. Three of these sites involve bonded pairs of electrons, and one involves a lone pair. These four sites arrange themselves in a tetrahedral geometry around nitrogen. *However, when you attempt to determine molecular shape, look only at the central atom and its surrounding atoms.* Ammonia looks as follows:

The molecular shape you see is not exactly a tetrahedron, it's more of a pyramid. This molecular geometry is known as **trigonal pyramidal**.

Now look at water's molecular structure.

$$H-\overset{\cdot\cdot}{\underset{\cdot\cdot}{O}}-H$$

Water has four electron pair sites around the central oxygen atom. However, two of them are lone pairs, so water's molecular geometry is as follows:

It's another variant of the tetrahedron, but with two corners occupied by electron pairs. This molecular geometry is known as **bent**. The angle between O–H bonds is about 105°.

The central molecule need not have four electron pair sites. If it has two, the molecular geometry will be **linear**, with 180° between bonds. If it has three electron pair sites (and no lone pairs) the sites will be 120° apart and the molecular geometry is **trigonal planar**. **Planar** means that the molecule is flat or two-dimensional. If there are three sites and one is a lone pair, the shape resembles that of the water molecule and is also called bent.

SUMMARY OF MOLECULAR SHAPES

Number of Electron Pair Sites Around Central Atom	Number of Lone Pairs Around Central Atom	Shape	Bond Angles with Central Atom*	Example
4	0	Tetrahedral	109.5°	CCl_4
4	1	Trigonal Pyramidal	approx. 107°	NH_3
4	2	Bent	approx. 107°	H_2O
3	0	Trigonal Planar	120°	NO_3^-
3	1	Bent	approx. 116°	SO_2
2	0	Linear	180°	CO_2

*assuming atoms of the same element surround the central atom

You should also be aware of two elements that violate the octet rule. Beryllium (Be) atoms are stable with 4 valence electrons. When beryllium is the central atom, the molecule is linear. Boron (B) atoms strive to gain 6 valence electrons. When boron acts as the central atom in a molecule, the shape is generally trigonal planar.

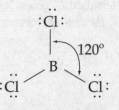

180°

:F — Be — F:

beryllium difluoride
(linear)

borontrichloride
(trigonal planar)

MOLECULES CAN ALSO BE POLAR OR NONPOLAR

We talked earlier about covalent bonds being polar or nonpolar, depending on the electronegativity difference between the bonded atoms. Well, *molecules* can also be polar or nonpolar. How can you tell if a molecule is polar or nonpolar? If the molecule is diatomic it's easy: Any diatomic molecule that has a polar bond is polar, for example CO. Any diatomic molecule that has a nonpolar bond is nonpolar, for example, all elemental diametric molecules, such as Cl_2, N_2, and O_2, are nonpolar. Otherwise there will be some electronegativity difference that makes the bond, and thus the molecule, polar. Molecules that consist of three or more atoms are generally polar unless the following condition is met: If the central atom has no lone pairs <u>and</u> is surrounded by atoms of one element, then the molecule will be nonpolar, for example, CO_2. In these cases, the individual bond polarities cancel each other out. So it's possible for a molecule to contain polar bonds but, itself, be nonpolar. Methane is an example of this.

The individual polarities from each C–H bond cancel each other out, making CH_4 nonpolar. Also note that methane satisfies our condition for being nonpolar: The carbon central atom has no lone pairs and is surrounded by atoms of one element (in this case, hydrogen).

Look back over what we've discussed since the last question set, and then try to answer the following questions.

QUESTION TYPE A

(A) Hydrogen gas, H_2
(B) Carbon monoxide, CO
(C) Potassium, K
(D) Aluminum oxide, Al_2O_3
(E) Bromine, Br_2

14. Substance held together by metallic bonds

15. Substance held together by ionic bonds

16. Consists of polar molecules

QUESTION TYPE B

Directions: Each question below consists of two statements, I in the left-hand column and II in the right-hand column. For each question, determine whether statement I is true or false and whether statement II is true or false and fill in the corresponding T or F ovals on your answer sheet. Fill in oval CE only if statement II is a correct explanation of statement I.

I		**II**
105. Some covalent bonds are polar in nature	BECAUSE	atoms of different electronegativities are unequal in the degree to which they attract electrons.

	I	II	CE
105	ⓣ ⓕ	ⓣ ⓕ	◯

| 106. Most atoms are less stable in the bonded state than in the unbonded state | BECAUSE | both ionic and covalent bonds fail to provide the participating atoms with a stable electron configuration. |

	I	II	CE
106	ⓣ ⓕ	ⓣ ⓕ	◯

QUESTION TYPE C

56. How many single bonds are in a molecule of carbon dioxide, CO_2?

(A) None
(B) One
(C) Two
(D) Three
(E) Four

60. The geometry of a molecule of SO_2 is

(A) linear
(B) bent
(C) trigonal planar
(D) trigonal pyramidal
(E) tetrahedral

63. What is the approximate ΔH for the reaction $CH_4 + Cl_2 \rightarrow CH_3Cl + HCl$ given the following bond energies:

C–H bond = 410 kJ/mol
C–Cl bond = 330 kJ/mol
Cl–Cl bond = 240 kJ/mol
H–Cl bond = 430 kJ/mol

(A) +270 kJ
(B) +110 kJ
(C) +70 kJ
(D) –70 kJ
(E) –110 kJ

LET'S LOOK AT THE ANSWERS

Question 14: (C) Metals are held together by metallic bonds. Potassium is the only pure metal listed; therefore, C is the correct answer.

Question 15: (D) Ionic compounds possess ionic bonds. How can you spot an ionic compound by looking at formulas? Easily; just find a compound composed of a metal and a nonmetal. Choices A, B, and E are substances composed solely of nonmetals. Choice C represents a purely metallic substance. Aluminum oxide consists of Al^{3+} ions from the metal aluminum and O^{2-} ions from the nonmetal oxygen, so D is the correct answer.

Question 16: (B) A polar molecule must contain polar covalent bonds. Of the choices, only A, B, and E involve covalent bonding. However, A and E involve diatomic molecules consisting of one element; we know that these molecules will contain nonpolar covalent bonds, since their atoms won't differ in electronegativity. Carbon monoxide molecules contain different nonmetals, and thus polar covalent bonds. That's why B is correct.

Question 105: (T, T, CE) Divide and conquer! Look at the first statement on its own and decide whether it's true or false. It's true. Look at the second statement by itself. It's true. We know that atoms have different electronegativities.

Let's see if the whole sentence makes sense. "Some covalent bonds are polar in nature because atoms of different electronegativities are unequal in the degree to which they attract electrons." Does that make sense? What makes a polar covalent bond polar? One of the atoms in the bond hogs the shared electrons; one atom has a higher electronegativity than the other. The sentence makes sense, so fill in oval CE.

Question 106: (F, F) Divide and conquer. Look at the first statement by itself. Is it true? No! We know that most atoms form bonds because they would like to achieve a stable octet.

What about the second statement? It's false. Ionic and covalent bonding *do* provide atoms with a stable configuration—the configuration that resembles a stable octet.

Question 56: (A) A carbon atom has 4 valence electrons, and an oxygen atom has 6. Using carbon as the central atom and arranging the atoms to give them octets yields

$$\ddot{O}::C::\ddot{O} \quad \text{or} \quad \ddot{O}=C=\ddot{O}$$

Notice that the carbon dioxide molecule consists of 2 double bonds, but no single bonds. The answer is A.

Question 60: (B) Determine the structure of SO_2. Sulfur is the central atom, and each atom has 6 valence electrons. Arranging them all so that they have octets gives you

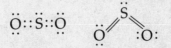

Notice that there are three electron pair sites around the central sulfur atom (a double or triple bond only counts as one site), one of which is a lone pair. This will result in a bent shape, so B is correct.

Question 63: (E) In the course of this reaction, 4 moles of C–H bonds and 1 mole of Cl–Cl bonds are broken. So 4(410kJ) + 240kJ, or 1880kJ, are needed to break these bonds. The reaction produces 1 mole of C–Cl bonds, 1 mole of H–Cl bonds, and 3 moles of C–H bonds. So 330 kJ + 430 + 3(410kJ), or 1990kJ, of energy is released by bond making. The net change, which is roughly equal to ΔH, is 1880kJ – 1990kJ = –110kJ. Therefore, this reaction is exothermic, and the correct answer is E.

which means that it will make up 20% of the total pressure. So if you're told that the total pressure within the container is 500 torr, you know that

- oxygen's partial pressure is (0.20)(500) = 100 torr
- hydrogen's partial pressure is (0.30)(500) = 150 torr
- nitrogen's partial pressure is (0.50)(500) = 250 torr

  100 + 150 + 250 = 500 torr

PARTIAL VOLUMES

In the same way that you can use the molar ratio to determine the partial pressure of a gas in a mixture, you can also determine the partial volume at standard temperature and pressure (STP). Using the ideal gas equation, $PV = nRT$, you can calculate that, at STP, 1 mole of a gas occupies a volume of 22.4 L. But this value does not apply only to ideal gases—it's also the accepted molar volume for *any* gas at STP. This means that, at STP, the molar ratio in a gaseous mixture will be directly proportional to the volume ratio, in a total volume of 22.4 L. For example, you can use the following formula to relate the molar ratio of gas A in a mixture of many gases to its partial volume in that mixture:

$$\frac{\text{\# of moles of gas A}}{\text{\# of total moles of gas}} = \frac{\text{volume of gas A at STP}}{22.4 \text{ L}}$$

If you know the ideal gas equation ($PV = nRT$) and what you've just learned about partial pressures, you'll be in good shape when the test asks you about gases.

Now try these.

QUESTION TYPE A

(A) Ideal gas constant
(B) Celsius temperature
(C) Kelvin temperature
(D) Partial pressure
(E) Volume

10. Is inversely proportional to moles of gas, when other variables are held constant

11. Sum for each gas in a mixture yields total for that mixture

12. Is a measure of average kinetic energy of gas molecules in a closed container used in the ideal gas equation

QUESTION TYPE B

Directions: Each question below consists of two statements, I in the left-hand column and II in the right-hand column. For each question, determine whether statement I is true or false and whether statement II is true or false and fill in the corresponding T or F ovals on your answer sheet. Fill in oval CE only if statement II is a correct explanation of statement I.

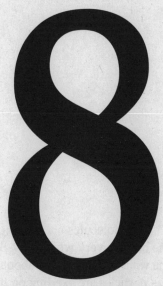

Gases, Liquids, and Solids

While the last few chapters have focused on atoms and molecules, the building blocks of matter, this chapter focuses on the three states of matter: gases, liquids, and solids.

GASES

Theoretically, all matter becomes gaseous if its temperature exceeds its boiling point, no matter how high or low that boiling point may be. For the SAT Chemistry Subject Test, you should be familiar with certain characteristics and properties of gases.

Let's start by looking at these gas molecules moving around in a box.

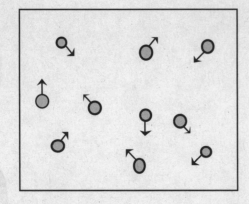

The molecules are moving, banging and bumping against one another and against the walls of the box in every which way. Because they bang into the walls of the box, they create pressure against the walls. When we talk about pressure, in relation to gases, we're talking about the amount of force the gas particles are exerting on the walls of their container, per unit area of the container. As we've said before, we measure pressure in torr or in millimeters of mercury (mmHg) or atmospheres (atm). Each of these units represents a unit of force per area, and 760 torr = 760 mmHg = 1 atm.

All of the gases you'll see on the SAT Chemistry are assumed to be ideal gases. An **ideal gas** satisfies these conditions.

- Its molecules do not attract or repel each other.

- Its molecules occupy an insignificant volume compared to the volume of the container holding the gas.

No gas ever acts completely as an ideal gas. In real gases, molecules attract each other slightly, which causes them to strike the walls of their container with slightly less force than ideal gases. However, most gases (especially lighter ones such as hydrogen and helium) under typical temperatures and pressures act enough as an ideal gas to make the concept useful.

In order to succeed on this test, you've got to know the relationships that exist among the temperature, volume, and pressure of an ideal gas.

1. **Pressure and Temperature:** Suppose we start with a 3 L sample of gas at 200 K and a pressure of 900 torr. If we raise the temperature to 400 K without changing the volume of the container, what will happen? Because we doubled the temperature, the pressure will double too—to 1,800 torr. In other words, if volume doesn't change, then pressure is directly proportional to the temperature in degrees K.

   Why is that? The increased temperature provides the gas molecules with more heat, which is converted to kinetic energy, which means, basically, movement. The molecules start moving faster, and if they're moving faster, they're hitting the walls of the container harder, and that increases the pressure.

   The technical term for this phenomenon is **kinetic molecular theory**, which states that the kinetic energy of a gas molecule increases proportionally with temperature in degrees K.

2. **Pressure and Volume:** Now suppose we start with the same 3 L sample of gas at 200 K and 900 torr. Imagine that, without changing the temperature, we suddenly increase the size of the container to 6 L. We've doubled the volume of the gas, and we haven't changed the temperature. What happens to the pressure of the system? It goes down by one half, to 450 torr. Here's why. The gas molecules have just as much kinetic energy as they had before, but they've got twice the volume in which to move around. Thus, gas molecules will hit the container walls less often, exerting half as much pressure.

   So remember, when there's no change in temperature, volume and pressure are inversely proportional. Triple the volume, and you'll cut the pressure to one third of its original value. Cut the volume by one half, and you'll double the pressure.

MAKING GASES EVEN SIMPLER: THE IDEAL GAS EQUATION

The relationship among pressure, volume, amount (moles), and temperature of an ideal gas is given by the **ideal gas equation**, $PV = nRT$.

$$PV = nRT$$

P	=	pressure in atm (mmHg or torr)
V	=	volume in liters
n	=	number of moles of gas particles in the container
R	=	the ideal gas constant
T	=	temperature in Kelvin

On this exam, the ideal gas equation is practically all you need to answer questions about gases.

Let's start by talking about R—the ideal gas constant, which is equal to 0.082 $\frac{L-atm}{mol-K}$ (you don't have to remember that number for the test).

From looking at the equation, you can see that P is inversely proportional to V. P and V are both directly proportional to T and to n. Here's another way to look at it. When you think about the ideal gas equation, think

- Values on the *same* side of the equation are *inversely* proportional to each other when the other variables are held constant.

- Values on *opposite* sides of the equation are *directly* proportional to one another when the other variables are held constant.

MORE ABOUT GASES: PARTIAL PRESSURES

If you have a container filled with more than one gas, each gas exerts a pressure. The pressu[re] one gas within the container is called its partial pressure, and all of the partial pressures create the total pressure inside the container.

When the test writers tell you about a container that has different gases in it, they mig[ht] figure out the partial pressure for one of them. Let's say there are 100 moles of gas in a[...] moles of oxygen, 30 moles of hydrogen, and 50 moles of nitrogen. Oxygen makes up [...]

	I	II

109. If an ideal gas is located in a closed container and temperature is increased, the average speed of the molecules will always increase as well   BECAUSE   for an ideal gas, temperature and moles of gas are inversely proportional.

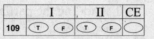

110. For an ideal gas, pressure and volume have no relationship   BECAUSE   according to the ideal gas law, temperature and volume are directly proportional when other variables are held constant.

QUESTION TYPE C

61. Four grams of helium are in a sealed, 2-L container. If helium were a true ideal gas, how would its behavior differ from its actual behavior?

(A) Its molecules would attract each other.
(B) Its molecules would repel one another.
(C) Its molecules would be in continuous motion.
(D) It would exert more pressure on the container walls.
(E) It would exert less pressure on the container walls.

62. A closed mixture of helium, hydrogen, and carbon dioxide gases are at a pressure of 1,200 torr in a 4-L container. There are a total of 24 moles of gas molecules in the container. If the helium concentration is 2 moles/L and the hydrogen concentration is 1.5 moles/L, which of the following expresses the approximate partial pressure of the carbon dioxide in torr?

(A) $\dfrac{1}{24} \times 1200$ torr

(B) $\dfrac{2}{24} \times 1200$ torr

(C) $\dfrac{3}{24} \times 1200$ torr

(D) $\dfrac{10}{24} \times 1200$ torr

(E) $\dfrac{14}{24} \times 1200$ torr

LET'S LOOK AT THE ANSWERS

Question 10: (C) Remember that values that are on the same side of the ideal gas equation are inversely proportional. In $PV = nRT$, both R and T (Kelvin temperature) are on the same side as n (moles of gas). Since R (ideal gas constant) cannot change with a change in moles, the answer must be C.

Question 11: (D) In a mixture of gases, each fills the container, so E cannot be right. It doesn't make sense to add the gases' temperatures to get a total temperature, so B and C are eliminated. That leaves us with A and D. The ideal gas constant is not something that could be summed up for each gas either, so the answer is D. Remember that adding the partial pressures of a mixture gives you the total pressure of the system.

Question 12: (C) Don't forget that temperature is a measure of average kinetic energy and that for ideal gases, Kelvin temperature increases in proportion to changes in kinetic energy. C is correct.

Question 109: (T, T) It's time to divide and conquer. What do you think of the first statement by itself? It's true; it describes kinetic molecular theory.

The second statement is also true; you know this from the ideal gas law: $PV = nRT$. Temperature and pressure are on opposite sides of the equation, so they're directly proportional when other variables are constant.

Let's see if the whole sentence makes sense. "If an ideal gas is located in a closed container and temperature is increased, the average speed of the molecules will always increase as well because for an ideal gas, temperature and moles of gas are inversely proportional.

The sentence does not make sense. Both halves are true, but when they're put together the statement makes no sense. Do not fill in the CE oval.

Question 110: (F, T) Divide and conquer. The first statement is false: pressure and volume *do* have a relationship: $PV = nRT$.

Now, what about the second statement? It's true. Look at the ideal gas law: $PV = nRT$. Temperature and volume are on opposite sides of the equation, so they're directly proportional when other variables are constant. The first statement is false, and the second is true.

Question 61: (D) Don't fall into the temptation trap. In an ideal gas there is *no* attraction or repulsion between molecules, so eliminate A and B. Gas molecules are in continuous motion in both ideal and nonideal gases, so eliminate C. In a real gas, molecules will slightly attract each other. As a result, gas molecules strike the container walls with less force. Less force means lower pressure. So pressure is less in the real situation as compared to the ideal. That's why D is correct.

Question 62: (D) This is a partial pressure question. You know that the total pressure of the system is 1,200 torr, and you know that each gas contributes to the total pressure by exerting a partial pressure.

There are a total of 24 moles of gases in the container. The helium concentration is 2 moles/L. We've got 4 L total, so there are $2 \times 4 = 8$ moles of helium molecules in the mixture. Hydrogen's concentration is 1.5 moles/L, so we've got $1.5 \times 4 = 6$ moles of hydrogen molecules. $8 + 6 = 14$. Since the total number of moles of molecules—for all 3 gases—is 24, there must be 10 moles of carbon dioxide molecules in the mixture.

If there are 10 moles of carbon dioxide molecules and 24 moles of molecules total, carbon dioxide's mole fraction $= \dfrac{10}{24}$. Total pressure = 1,200 torr, and carbon dioxide's pressure is therefore $\dfrac{10}{24} \times 1,200$ torr. D is correct.

INTERMOLECULAR FORCES

At this point in our study of the states of matter, we will stop to look more closely at the attractive forces that exist between molecules. These **intermolecular forces** are responsible for many of the physical properties of matter such as boiling point. Intermolecular forces are typically due to the attraction between the positively-charged portion of one molecule and the negatively charged portion of a nearby molecule. In a sample of water, the partial negative pole (δ–) of one molecule is attracted to the partial positive pole (δ+) of another as follows:

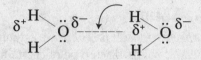

These forces of attraction are present between molecules throughout the water sample, holding it together.

The attractive forces that exist between water molecules (shown above) are a special type of intermolecular force called **hydrogen bonds**. Hydrogen bonds occur between the hydrogen atom of one water molecule—when it's bonded to a highly electronegative atom such as nitrogen (N), oxygen (O), or fluorine (F)—and an N, O, or F atom of a nearby molecule. Hydrogen bonds are stronger than most other examples of intermolecular attraction. However, even the strongest intermolecular force is far weaker than a covalent or ionic bond.

SOLIDS, LIQUIDS, AND GASES

The relationship between a substance's average kinetic energy and the strength of its intermolecular forces is responsible for determining if the substance will be a solid, a liquid, or a gas. In a solid, a substance's intermolecular forces are much stronger than the average kinetic energy of its molecules. As a result, molecules are restricted in their ability to move about. These strong intermolecular forces permit molecules to merely vibrate in place. This gives a solid its definite size and shape.

In a liquid, intermolecular forces are still more significant than the kinetic energy of molecules. However, molecules in a liquid have enough kinetic energy to move past each other. This allows for the liquid's ability to flow. Despite being able to move about, molecules in a liquid are still confined within the sample.

The relationship between intermolecular forces and molecular kinetic energies is vastly different in a gas. Molecules in a gas are so energetic that they easily overcome intermolecular attraction. Gas molecules spread about to fill the volume of whatever container they are in.

So when you boil water, what really happens? Adding heat to the water increases the kinetic energy of water molecules. At the boiling point, molecules have become energetic enough to overcome the intermolecular forces between H_2O molecules. This allows them to enter the gaseous phase. When steam condenses into water, the opposite occurs. Molecules lose energy to the point that intermolecular forces become significant, bringing them close together and limiting their movement. Notice that changes of state involve intermolecular forces and not covalent bonds.

What's a Network Solid?

For the SAT Chemistry Subject Test, you may need to know about something called a network solid. No, it has nothing to do with television. **Network solids** are covalently bonded substances that do not consist of individual molecules. Instead they consist of atoms joined to form molecules that attract each other through intermolecular forces. So, in a sense, the substance is one giant molecule. For this reason, network solids are sometimes called macromolecular substances. Since covalent bonds are much stronger than intermolecular forces, network solids are extremely hard to melt. Diamond (pure carbon network) and quartz (SiO_2 network) are both examples of network solids.

Properties of Crystalline Solids

Keep in mind that not all solids are network solids: There are actually four types of crystalline solids: ionic, network, molecular, and metallic solids. Each type of crystalline solid is held together in a different way, which means each has unique properties. The table below summarizes some aspects of these solids that you should know for the SAT Chemistry.

Crystal Type	Force Holding Units Together	Examples	Melting Point	Hardness	Electrical Conductivity
Ionic	Electrostatic attraction	LiF, NaCl	High	Hard, brittle	Only molten or aqueous solution
Covalent Network	Shared electrons	Diamond	Very high	Very hard	None
Molecular	H-bonding, dipole-dipole, dispersion forces	H_2O, HCl, He	Low	Soft	None
Metallic	Electrostatic attraction between cations and sea of electrons	Na, Fe, Cu, etc.	Variable	Malleable	High

Do I Need to Know About Hydrates?

Yes, but they're nothing you can't handle. A **hydrate** (or hydrated salt) is an ionic substance in which water molecules bind to the ions in a fixed ratio. For example, in copper sulfate pentahydrate the ratio is given by the formula: $CuSO_4 \cdot 5H_2O$. Anytime you see " $\cdot H_2O$" in a formula, you're looking at a hydrate. You might need to determine the percent composition of water in the hydrate (called its **water of hydration**). If you do, you simply multiply the molecular weight of water (18 amu) by the coefficient that precedes H_2O in the formula. For example, for a unit of $CuSO_4 \cdot 5H_2O$, the formula weight is approximately $64 + 32 + (4)(16) + 5(18) = 250$ amu. The percentage of water in the hydrate is about $\frac{90}{250} \times 100\%$ or 36%.

PHASE CHANGES

We refer to the condition of being a solid, liquid, or gas as being in a particular **state** or **phase**. Whether a substance is in one phase or another depends on temperature and pressure. H_2O, for instance, turns from solid to liquid or from liquid to solid at 0°C and 1 atm. It turns from liquid to gas or gas to liquid at 100° C and 1 atm.

When a substance turns from solid to liquid, we say it **melts**. When it moves in the reverse direction—from liquid to solid—we say it **freezes**. So when we think of H_2O at 1 atm we say 0°C is the **melting point** or **freezing point**: the temperature at which it melts or freezes. When a substance turns from liquid to gas it **vaporizes**, and when it goes from gas to liquid it **condenses**. When we think of H_2O at 1 atm we say 100°C is the boiling point, which means, generally, the temperature at which it vaporizes or condenses.

You should also be aware of **sublimation**. This is the process in which a solid turns directly into a gas. Dry ice (solid carbon dioxide) does this when it is exposed to room temperature.

THE PHASE CHANGE DIAGRAM

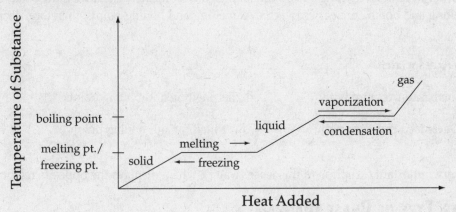

Above, we've shown the phase change diagram for some substance at some pressure. You might very well see a phase change diagram on the SAT Chemistry, so you should understand what information they might give you. Starting from the lower left, we see that, as heat is added to the substance, its temperature rises. Moving left to right, we reach the first plateau; that's the substance's freezing/melting point. Notice that the curve is flat for a little while as the substance passes its melting point. In other words, to move from a solid to liquid phase, we add heat—but for a while the temperature of the substance doesn't change. The heat energy absorbed is used to move the substance from one phase to the next. The amount of heat that it takes a substance to just move from solid to liquid phase—to just pass through its melting point—is called the **heat of fusion**. For H_2O at 1 atm, the heat of fusion is 80 cal/g; this means that it takes 80 calories to change 1 g of H_2O from 0°C in the solid phase (ice) to 0°C in the liquid phase (water).

After the substance melts, if we continue to add heat, the temperature increases until the substance reaches its boiling point. At the boiling point, the substance doesn't change temperature despite the continued addition of heat. The absorbed heat is used to move the substance from the liquid phase to the gaseous phase. The amount of energy that must be added to move the substance from liquid to gaseous phase is called the substance's **heat of vaporization** or **heat of condensation**. For H_2O at 1 atm, the heat of vaporization is 540 cal/g; it takes 540 calories to change 1 g of H_2O from 100°C in the liquid phase (water) to 100°C in the gaseous phase (steam).

Look again at the phase change diagram. This time start at the right, and move to the left.

PHASE CHANGE AND PRESSURE

You know that if we add heat to a solid, the temperature of the solid moves toward the melting point. If we add heat to a liquid, the temperature of the liquid increases until it reaches the boiling point. One interesting phenomenon that you should be aware of for the SAT Chemistry is that, under higher pressure, it's harder for solids to melt, and it's harder for liquids to vaporize. However, if we reduce the pressure of the surrounding environment, we lower a substance's melting and boiling points. Reduced pressure makes it easier for solids to melt and liquids to vaporize.

How come? Just imagine pressure as something that's pushing down on the solid or liquid, tending to prevent its molecules from moving around. If we increase that downward push, melting and boiling are harder to achieve; melting and boiling points, therefore, increase. If we reduce that downward push, melting and boiling are easier to achieve; melting and boiling points, therefore, decrease.

Learn to associate:

Increased pressure with: higher melting and boiling points

Decreased pressure with: lower melting and boiling points

One very important exception to this is ice (water), which displays the opposite relationship.

ANOTHER TYPE OF PHASE DIAGRAM

We mentioned that whether a particular substance is a solid, liquid, or gas depends on both its pressure and temperature. The relationship among pressure, temperature, and phase can be neatly shown in the following type of phase diagram, which is a graph of pressure versus temperature:

Phase Diagram for Substance X

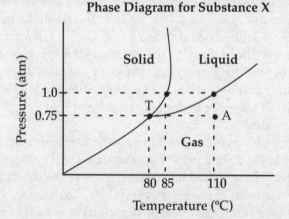

In this diagram, each region—solid, liquid, and gas—represents the phase that will exist for substance X at a given set of pressures and temperatures. For example, at a pressure of 0.75 atm and 110°C (point A), substance X is a gas. The normal freezing point (freezing point at 1 atm) for substance X is 85°C, and the normal boiling point (at 1 atm) is 110°C. Any point that lies on a line on the phase diagram represents a temperature and pressure at which the substance can exist in both phases. For instance, substance X can be a solid or a liquid at 1 atm and 85°C. Point T is a special combination of pressure and temperature called the **triple point**. At this particular pressure and temperature, the substance can exist as a solid, liquid, or a gas. For substance X, the triple point is at 0.75 atm and 80°C.

In general, when a substance is at relatively low pressure and high temperature it exists as a gas. When it is at relatively high pressure and low temperature, it is a solid. The liquid phase dominates at moderate pressures and temperatures. Keeping these relationships in mind can help you to predict how a change in pressure or temperature will affect the phase of a substance. For instance, if substance X, at 0.75 atm and 110°C (point A) is put under increasing pressure but its temperature is maintained, what phase change will eventually occur? Look at the phase diagram for substance X. Follow the dotted line up from point A (in the direction of increasing pressure). You'll see that beyond 1 atm (at 110° C), substance X will become a liquid. So an increase in pressure at constant temperature will cause substance X to condense.

VAPOR PRESSURE

Even if a solid is well below its melting point, a small number of its molecules will always have enough kinetic energy to enter the liquid phase. So when you have a block of ice stored in a freezer a little bit of it is always melting to form liquid. The molecules of that liquid immediately lose kinetic energy and form a solid again, but right away, a few other molecules gain enough kinetic energy to become liquid. They, too, become solid again after a few seconds. But a few other molecules take their place, becoming liquid, and then solid again. In other words, every solid is always melting—on the molecular level—and the molecules that melt are always refreezing.

The same goes for liquids. Even if it's well below the boiling point, a few molecules of a particular liquid always have enough kinetic energy to escape into the gaseous phase. This is called **evaporation**. If they're in a closed system (such as a pot with a lid on it), they quickly lose some kinetic energy and fall back into the liquid phase, only to be replaced continuously by a couple of other molecules that manage to escape. They, too, fall back into the liquid phase to be replaced by other molecules that manage to escape for a few seconds. So a sample of liquid below its boiling point is always evaporating—a little bit—and then condensing again (if the liquid is contained). When liquids below their boiling points are evaporating, a **vapor pressure** is created. All liquids in a closed system, at all temperatures, exert some vapor pressure.

But what if the liquid is *not* in a closed system but is out in the open environment? Here's what happens. A little bit evaporates and is blown away. Then a little more evaporates and is blown or drifts away. Ultimately the whole sample evaporates. If you put a pot of water outside, even at a temperature of 10°C, it will eventually evaporate, although it will take some time.

If we put the water on the stove and bring it to its boiling point, all of the molecules would have enough kinetic energy to escape as gas, and the whole sample would quickly vaporize.

Different liquids differ in their volatility; for instance, if you leave a bucket of gasoline and a bucket of water outside on a cold day—at a temperature well below the boiling point of either substance—both will eventually evaporate. But the gasoline will evaporate much more quickly than the water. This is because the intermolecular forces that attract gasoline molecules to each other are weaker than the hydrogen bonds that attract water molecules. Gasoline molecules need less kinetic energy than do water molecules to overcome the intermolecular forces that hold them in the liquid state. Because gasoline evaporates more readily than water, we can say that its *vapor pressure is higher*, and *it is more volatile* than water.

Learn to associate:

Vapor pressure with:	molecules of liquid escaping into gas phase although temperature of the liquid is below boiling point
More **volatile with:**	liquid that has higher vapor pressure; evaporates *more* readily when temperature is below boiling point (compared to a less volatile liquid)
Less **volatile with:**	liquid that has lower vapor pressure; evaporates *less* readily when temperature is below boiling point

ENERGY AND PHASE CHANGES

As we saw from the phase change diagram, a substance must absorb heat to change from a solid to a liquid to a gas. It must lose heat to turn from gas to liquid to solid. Heat, as you remember, is a form of energy. So, when you think of phases and energy, remember that among the three phases, solid is lowest in potential energy and gas is highest in potential energy.

One more thing: When ice melts, there is an increase in entropy, and when liquids vaporize, entropy increases even more. Under certain conditions, the increase in entropy (which the universe likes) is enough to overcome the increase in energy (which it dislikes) and make a phase change spontaneous. What are these conditions? Well, in the case of melting, if the substance is at a temperature above the melting point, the phase change will be spontaneous. In order for boiling to be spontaneous, the substance must be at a temperature above the boiling point.

> Solid ⟶ Liquid ⟶ Gas
> Low Potential Energy ⟶ High Potential Energy
> Low Entropy ⟶ High Entropy

Learn to associate:

Melting point/freezing point with:	solid to liquid/liquid to solid; heat of fusion
Boiling point with:	liquid to gas/gas to liquid; heat of vaporization/heat of condensation
Solid to liquid to gas with:	addition of heat; lower potential energy to higher potential energy; lower entropy to higher entropy
Gas to liquid to solid with:	removal of heat; higher potential energy to lower potential energy; higher entropy to lower entropy

Review what we've discussed since the last set of questions, and then try the following set.

QUESTION TYPE A

(A) $N_2O_4(g) + heat \rightarrow 2NO_2(g)$
(B) $I_2(s) \rightarrow I_2(g)$
(C) $CHCl_3(l) \rightarrow CHCl_3(g)$
(D) $Br_2(s) \rightarrow Br_2(l)$
(E) $O_2(g) \rightarrow O_2(l)$

12. At constant pressure, requires a decrease in heat to occur

13. Is an example of sublimation

14. Produces a decrease in system entropy

15. Enthalpy change for the process can equal heat of fusion for the process

QUESTION TYPE B

<u>Directions:</u> Each question below consists of two statements, I in the left-hand column and II in the right-hand column. For each question, determine whether statement I is true or false <u>and</u> whether statement II is true or false and fill in the corresponding T or F ovals on your answer sheet. <u>Fill in oval CE only if statement II is a correct explanation of statement I.</u>

I		II

111. A network solid has a high melting point   BECAUSE   hydrogen bonds are more difficult to break than covalent bonds.

	I		II	CE
111	T	F	T	F	⬭

112. A pot of water will boil above 100°C at high elevations   BECAUSE   the average kinetic energy of molecules must increase as the pressure on them increases.

	I		II	CE
112	T	F	T	F	⬭

QUESTION TYPE C

52. A 10-gram sample of which substance is held together by hydrogen bonding?

(A) H_2
(B) NH_3
(C) C_3H_8
(D) CaH_2
(E) HBr

60. A substance possessing a characteristically low
vapor pressure can be expected to have

(A) extremely weak intermolecular forces
(B) a relatively small heat of vaporization
(C) a relatively high boiling point
(D) a relatively high rate of evaporation
(E) a significantly high percentage of molecules
that have high kinetic energy

LET'S LOOK AT THE ANSWERS

Question 12: (E) Think back to the first phase change diagram. As heat was removed from the system, the substance moved from gas phase to liquid phase to solid phase. Which process is clearly doing that here? In choice E, a gas is condensing into a liquid, so E is the correct answer.

Question 13: (B) Remember that sublimation is the direct conversion of a solid into a gas, so B is correct.

Question 14: (E) A decrease in entropy means an increase in order. There is an increase in order (and restriction in molecular motion) as a gas condenses to a liquid. Choice E is correct.

Question 15: (D) Heat of fusion is associated with the process of melting or freezing. Do any choices involve one of these? Yes; in choice D, solid bromine melts. If this change took place solely at the melting point, then the heat of fusion of bromine would equal the enthalpy change for the process. D is the correct answer.

Question 111: (T, F) You know what to do with this question-type by now. Is statement I true or false? It's true. What about statement II? It's false. Hydrogen bonds are stronger than most intermolecular forces but far weaker than covalent or ionic bonds.

Question 112: (F, F) As you go up into higher elevations, the atmosphere exerts less pressure. As the pressure over a substance decreases, the boiling point of the substance will also decrease. Since water boils at 100° C at sea-level (1 atm), it will boil below 100° C at higher elevations. So statement I is false. Statement II is also false. Average kinetic energy is a measure of temperature, not pressure. So even if the pressure on a sample increases, if its temperature remains constant, so will its average kinetic energy.

Question 52: (B) Molecules that exhibit hydrogen bonding contain one or more hydrogen atoms (H) bonded to either N, O, or F. The partial positive end of one molecule (the H end) will become attracted to the partial negative end of a nearby molecule (in this case, the N end), creating a hydrogen bond. B is correct.

Question 60: (C) A substance with a low vapor pressure doesn't evaporate readily because it possesses relatively strong intermolecular attractions, so eliminate A and D. What would be the result of strong intermolecular forces? Recall that these must be overcome for a substance to boil. If they are strong, boiling will occur only at relatively high temperatures. C is correct.

Solutions

When you pour a teaspoon of table salt (NaCl) in a glass of water to create a solution, the water is considered the solvent, while the salt is considered the solute. The **solvent** is the component of the solution present in larger amounts, while the **solute** is the component present in lesser amounts. Salt water is an **aqueous** solution, meaning that the solution is water-based. A solute need not be solid. And solvents do not have to be liquids. In fact solutes and solvents can be solids, liquids, or gases. But since our focus is on what the SAT Chemistry Subject Test covers, and since it concentrates on solids (and occasionally gases) dissolved in water, this is what we'll focus on.

MEASURING CONCENTRATIONS

The most commonly used unit for concentration is **molarity**. Its symbol is M. Molarity is a measure of the number of moles of solute dissolved per liter of solution (volume).

$$\text{molarity } (M) = \frac{\text{number of moles solute}}{\text{number of liters solution}}$$

Molality, another fairly common unit for concentration, is a measure of the number of moles of solute dissolved per kilogram of solvent (mass). Its symbol is m.

$$\text{molality } (m) = \frac{\text{number of moles solute}}{\text{number of kilograms solvent}}$$

Learn to associate:

Molarity with:	moles of dissolved solute per *liter* of *solution*
Molality with:	moles of dissolved solute per *kilogram* of *solvent*

SOLUBILITY AND SATURATION

Suppose you take a glass of water and add table salt to it. The table salt dissolves. Suppose you keep adding table salt to it. After a while, the table salt doesn't dissolve, it just sits at the bottom of the glass. At that point the water is **saturated** with table salt. Another way to describe this is to say that the table salt has reached the limit of its **solubility** in water.

The temperature of the solvent affects solubility. Generally, a solid solute is *more* soluble in a liquid solvent at *higher* temperatures and *less* soluble at *lower* temperatures. If we took the glass of water and heated it, some of the table salt that hadn't dissolved, would dissolve. The increased temperature increases the table salt's water solubility.

Learn to associate:

Higher temperature with:	increased solubility of solutes in water
Lower temperature with:	decreased solubility of solutes in water

Substances that are held together by ionic bonds (such as table salt, NaCl) are generally soluble in water.

Other solutes are completely insoluble. For instance, if you place a pat of butter in a glass of water, it won't dissolve, ever, even if you heat it. This illustrates an important general principle; polar solutes such as NaCl dissolve in polar solvents such as water, and nonpolar solutes dissolve in nonpolar solvents. Butter, which is a fat, is nonpolar. Just remember, "like dissolves like."

The solubility of gases in water is quite different from that of solids. Think about a bottle of soda; its carbonation is the result of dissolved carbon dioxide gas. Once the bottle has been opened, should you store it where it's warm or cold to prevent it from going flat? You should store it where it's cold, of course. The CO_2 gas is more soluble in water at lower temperatures, and flat soda is simply soda after its CO_2 has diffused out into the air. This is typical of the solubility of gases in water. One more thing about the solubility of gases in water: the higher the pressure, the more soluble the gas. Again consider soda, bottled under pressure. Once you open the bottle, the pressure over the soda decreases, and CO_2 starts to come out of solution.

Learn to associate:

High temperature and low pressure with: decreased solubility of gases in water

Low temperature and high pressure with: increased solubility of gases in water

DISSOCIATION AND ELECTROLYTES

When an ionic substance ($NaCl$, KCl, $CaBr_2$, or $CuSO_4$) dissolves in water, its bonds break, and ions are released into solution. For instance, when KCl dissolves in water, K^+ ions and Cl^- ions dissociate into solution.

The dissociation of ionic compounds always creates an equal number of positive and negative charges in solution. One mole of $NaCl$ will dissociate into 1 mole of Na^+ ions and 1 mole of Cl^- ions, and 1 mole of $CaBr_2$ will dissociate into 2 moles of Br^- ions and 1 mole of Ca^{2+} ions. Both of these solutions have equal amounts of positive and negative charges and both are therefore neutral.

Although these solutions are neutral, the presence of charged particles—ions—enables the solution to conduct electricity. This is why ionic solutions are also called **electrolytic solutions**, and we call the ions **electrolytes**.

Learn to associate:

Ions in solution with: electrolytes;
electrolytic solutions;
electrical conduction

BOILING POINT ELEVATION AND FREEZING POINT DEPRESSION

When a solute is dissolved in a liquid solvent, the solvent's boiling point is raised, its freezing point is lowered, and its vapor pressure is lowered. By how much? The change in boiling point (ΔT_b) or freezing point (ΔT_f) is always equal to a constant (k) times the number of moles of *dissolved particles* of solute per kilogram of solvent.

$$\Delta T = km$$

The value of the constant k is different for different solvents; however, for all liquid solvents, *the extent of boiling point elevation or freezing point depression is directly proportional to the molality of the solution*. It's also directly proportional to the number of dissolved particles produced by each unit of solute. Suppose, therefore, that we dissolve 1 mole of sucrose (table sugar) in 1 kg of water. Sucrose does dissolve in water, but it isn't an ionic substance, so it doesn't dissociate into ions/electrolytes. The molality of the solution, therefore, is 1. There will be some elevation of boiling point and depression of freezing point.

Now, suppose we take the same amount of water and add 1 mole of KCl. KCl is an ionic substance; it dissociates in solution. Each unit of KCl produces two dissolved particles: 1 K^+ ion and 1 Cl^- ion. *The boiling point elevation and freezing point depression will be twice as great as they would be in the case of the dissolution of sucrose.*

Again, why is this? Boiling point elevation and freezing point depression are directly proportional to the number of particles dissolved in a solution, but independent of the *type* of particle (i.e., sucrose and KCl equally affect melting point and freezing point at the same molality). Sucrose doesn't ionize and KCl does. When 1 mole of sucrose is dissolved in water, it yields 1 mole of dissolved particles. When 1 mole of KCl is dissolved in water, it yields 2 moles of dissolved particles. If the sucrose elevated the water's boiling point by 0.5°C, the KCl would raise it by 1°C. If the sucrose depressed the water's freezing point by 2°C, the KCl would depress it by 4°C. Remember the relationship of proportionality we've just described.

There are many practical applications of boiling point elevation and freezing point depression. For example, spreading calcium chloride onto roadways during snow storms makes it harder for ice to form on them (since the freezing point of water is made lower).

Learn to associate:

**Boiling point elevation and
freezing point depression with:**   proportional to number of particles dissolved
                                      in solution

PRECIPITATION REACTIONS

Okay, so now you know that when ionic solids are dissolved in water, they dissociate. But what happens when soluble ions in separate solutions are mixed together, and they form an insoluble compound? Well, the product of this type of reaction will result in a solid substance that settles out of solution, called a **precipitate**. One example of this is the reaction between lead nitrate and potassium iodide.

$$2KI(aq) + Pb(NO_3)_2(aq) \rightarrow 2KNO_3(aq) + PbI(s)$$

Each of the reactants in this reaction is an ionic compound that's colorless in solution, but when they're combined, they react to form a product, lead iodide, which precipitates out of solution as a yellow solid. In this reaction, the anions and cations of the reactants are exchanged in a **double replacement reaction**, which typically results in the formation of a precipitate. But how do you know when a precipitation reaction will proceed? The **solubility rules** tell you which ionic compounds are soluble in water and which are not and enable you to make predictions about whether certain ions will react with one another to form a precipitate.

THE SOLUBILITY RULES

- Most silver, lead, and mercury salts are INSOLUBLE except their nitrates and perchlorates.

- Most hydroxides (OH^-) are INSOLUBLE except those of alkali metals and barium.

- All nitrates (NO_3^-) and perchlorates (ClO_4^-) are SOLUBLE.

- All alkali metal and ammonium (NH_4^+) compounds are SOLUBLE.

Enough said! Now review what we've said about solutions, and try the following set of questions.

QUESTION TYPE A

(A) Nitrogen dioxide, $NO_2(g)$
(B) Iodine, $I_2(s)$
(C) Glucose, $C_6H_{12}O_6(s)$
(D) Naphthalene, $C_{10}H_8(s)$
(E) Calcium oxide, $CaO(s)$

9. Yields an electrolytic solution upon dissolution in water

10. Solubility in water increases as temperature is decreased

11. Produces the greatest boiling point elevation per mole dissolved into 1 L of water

QUESTION TYPE B

Directions: Each question below consists of two statements, I in the left-hand column and II in the right-hand column. For each question, determine whether statement I is true or false and whether statement II is true or false and fill in the corresponding T or F ovals on your answer sheet. Fill in oval CE only if statement II is a correct explanation of statement I.

I		II

106. Aqueous solutions with ionic solutes conduct electricity   BECAUSE   a liquid solvent becomes saturated when the solute reaches the limit of its solubility.

107. Freezing point depression caused by a 2-molal aqueous solution of nonionic solute is equal to one half the freezing point depression caused by a 2-molal aqueous solution of NaCl   BECAUSE   the constant associated with freezing point depression does not vary with the nature of the solvent.

	I	II	CE
107	T F	T F	

QUESTION TYPE C

27. Which of the following will most likely increase the solubility of NaCl in water?

(A) Reducing the temperature of the water
(B) Raising the temperature of the water
(C) Reducing the molality of the solution
(D) Raising the molality of the solution
(E) Raising the molarity of the solution

34. Which of the following would most likely give a sample of water the capacity to conduct electricity?

(A) Reducing the temperature of the water
(B) Raising the temperature of the water
(C) Removing all electrolytes from the water
(D) Dissolving a nonionic substance in the water
(E) Dissolving $CaCl_2$ in the water

45. Aqueous solutions of barium chloride and sodium sulfate react to form -------, an insoluble white solid.

(A) $BaSO_4(s)$
(B) $Na_2SO_4(s)$
(C) $BaCl_2(s)$
(D) $NaCl(s)$
(E) $BaNa_2SO_4(s)$

LET'S LOOK AT THE ANSWERS

Question 9: (E) When ionic solutes dissolve in water, an electrolytic solution is produced. Are there any ionic solutes among the choices? Look for the combination of a metal and a nonmetal. Calcium oxide is ionic, and E is the correct answer.

Question 10: (A) When you are told that solubility increases as temperature decreases, think of dissolving a gas in aqueous solution. Are there any gases in the answer choices? Yes: NO_2. The correct answer is A.

Question 11: (E) Remember that the degree of boiling point elevation is proportional to the moles of dissolved particles. Choices A through D are substances composed solely of nonmetals. They are molecular compounds. In general, molecular compounds don't dissociate (acids, which we'll look at later, are an important exception), so 1 mole of the substances in A through D gives 1 mole of dissolved particles. Calcium oxide is different. As it dissolves, CaO dissociates into Ca^{2+} and O^{2-} ions, so 1 mole of CaO yields 2 moles of dissolved particles. CaO is the solute that will most raise water's boiling point; the correct answer is E.

Question 106: (T, T) Divide and conquer. Look at the first statement by itself. Is it true? Yes; you should associate "ions dissolved in solution" with the idea of conducting electricity.

The second statement is true. When a solvent can't dissolve any more solute, it's saturated—the solute has reached the limit of its solubility. Let's see whether the whole sentence makes sense. "Aqueous solutions with ionic solutes conduct electricity because a liquid solvent becomes saturated when the solute reaches the limit of its solubility." The sentence is nonsense—do not fill in the CE oval.

Question 107: (T, F) Again, divide and conquer. Is the first statement true or false? It's tricky but true. For each mole of original solute, a nonionic solute produces only 1 mole of particles in solution. One mole of NaCl, however, dissociates into 2 moles of particles. So the number of particles floating around in the NaCl solution will be twice the number of moles in the nonionic solution. The freezing point depression for the nonionic solution will be one half what it is for the NaCl solution.

What about the second statement? It's false. The freezing point depression constant does vary with the solvent.

Question 27: (B) You've learned to associate increased temperature with increased solubility of solids in water. This question is simple, and B is correct.

Question 34: (E) The question is about solutions that are capable of conducting electricity. Think of electrolytes, and remember that you should associate them with "ions in solution." Which of the answer choices lists an ionic compound capable of dissociating in solution? E does. Ca is a metal and Cl is a nonmetal, which tells you that $CaCl_2$ is most likely an ionic substance. E is the correct answer.

Question 45: (A) This question asks you to look for the insoluble product of this precipitation reaction. Because precipitations occur through double replacement reactions, the two products formed will be $NaCl(aq)$ and $BaSO_4(s)$. If you look back at the solubility rules, you can see that sodium chloride will be soluble; this means that you can eliminate this answer choice, which leaves you with the correct answer, A.

Kinetics and Equilibrium

Kinetics is the study of the rates of reactions—how quickly reactants are converted into products. **Equilibrium** is defined as the point in a chemical reaction at which the concentration of all the reactants and products ceases to change. As we will show you, no matter how often you may see the terms used together, these are two fundamentally different concepts.

KINETICS

The rate at which reactants are converted into products in a reaction is called the **reaction rate**. Remember that chemical reactions involve breaking old bonds (in the reactants) and making new bonds (in products). In order for bond breaking and bond making to occur, reactant molecules (or atoms or ions) must collide with sufficient energy and proper orientation. Why are energy and orientation important? Well, the reactant molecules need to collide with enough kinetic energy to break their bonds, and they need to collide with the proper orientation for new bonds to form. Consider the gas phase reaction.

$$H_2(g) + I_2(g) \rightarrow 2HI(g)$$

Notice that if an H_2 and I_2 molecule collide with enough kinetic energy and in the orientation shown below, the atoms are in an ideal position to form new H–I bonds.

First: Reactant molecules H_2 and I_2 move toward each other with sufficient energy.

$$
\begin{array}{cc}
\text{H} & \text{I} \\
| \rightarrow \leftarrow | \\
\text{H} & \text{I}
\end{array}
$$

Next: The collision causes H–H and I–I bonds to begin to break. Since the reactant molecules were properly aligned, new H–I bonds also start to form.

$$
\begin{array}{ccc}
\text{H} & \cdots\cdots & \text{I} \\
\vdots & & \vdots \\
\text{H} & \cdots\cdots & \text{I}
\end{array}
$$

The above species is an extremely unstable, high-energy arrangement of atoms called an **activated complex** or **transition state**. Reactants must form an activated complex before products can be made.

Finally: H–H and I–I bonds are completely broken, and H–I bonds are formed. The chemical reaction has produced hydrogen iodide.

$$
\begin{array}{c}
\text{H–I} \\
\text{H–I}
\end{array}
$$

Although this was a somewhat simplified account of what actually happens during a chemical reaction, the actual process does involve molecular collisions, bond breaking and making, and the formation of an activated complex.

FACTORS THAT AFFECT REACTION RATE

The test writers will expect you to be familiar with several key factors that influence the rate of a reaction. All of these factors impact the reaction rate by affecting the rate of molecular collisions, the energy of the collisions, or both.

1. **Concentration of Reactants:** Reactant molecules must collide in order to form products. If the rate at which reactant molecules collide is increased, then the reaction rate will also increase. One way to increase the rate of reactant collisions is to increase the amount of reactant present, or in other words, to increase the concentration of reactants. For example, wood burns much faster in a pure (100 percent) oxygen environment than in air (which is only about 20 percent oxygen by mass). An increase in the concentration of the reactant oxygen causes an increase in the rate of combustion. However, this is true only of reactants that are gaseous or in solution, whose concentrations can be changed. For instance, a gas can be compressed into a smaller volume (increasing the concentration of gas molecules per volume). Since the molecules in a pure solid or liquid are relatively close together, they cannot be significantly compressed, so their concentration is essentially constant. To sum up: *If one or more reactants are gaseous or in solution, the reaction rate can be increased by increasing the concentration of those reactants.* Obviously, a decrease in reactant concentration will produce a decrease in reaction rate. If the reactants are in gaseous phase, then increasing their pressure will also increase their concentration, thereby accelerating the reaction rate.

2. **Surface Area of Reactants:** The greater the surface area of the reactants, the greater the number of collisions hence the faster reaction rate. For instance, a cube of sugar will dissolve less quickly in water than will the same amount of sugar in loose form. Only the surface areas of solids and liquids can be changed: We can increase the surface area of a solid by breaking it up or grinding it into a powder, and a liquid's surface area can be increased by spraying it out as a mist of fine droplets.

3. **Temperature:** The factor that has perhaps the most profound effect on reaction rate is temperature. This is because a temperature change affects both rate of reactant collisions and the energy involved in the collisions. Remember that temperature is a measure of the average kinetic energy of molecules. As the temperature of the reactants is increased, the molecules move around faster; this results in more frequent and energetic collisions and increases the likelihood that a given collision will have sufficient energy to break bonds. A good rule of thumb says that, for every 10°C increase in temperature, the reaction rate will double.

4. **Nature of Reactants:** Since bond breaking is part of the reaction process, it makes sense that reactant molecules composed of weaker bonds will react more quickly than will reactant molecules held together by stronger bonds. Reactions between dissolved ions tend to be rapid, since bond breaking has already occurred, with the dissolution of the ionic substance.

5. **Catalysts:** A **catalyst** increases the rate of a chemical reaction without being consumed by it. Enzymes are examples of catalysts. They are involved in many important biological reactions. How do catalysts accelerate reaction rates? Before we get to that, let's first consider the energy changes that occur in the course of a reaction.

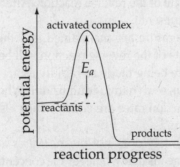

This figure is sometimes referred to as a potential energy diagram. The potential energy of the activated complex is greater than that of the reactants, and the energy difference between the two is called the activation energy (symbolized as E_a). The **activation energy** is the minimum energy that must be supplied for the activated complex to be formed. It is an energy barrier that must be overcome by reactant molecules; reactant molecules acquire the necessary activation energy by absorbing heat from the surroundings.

The size of the activation energy barrier indicates how difficult it is for the reaction to proceed. A relatively small barrier, indicating a low activation energy, means that collisions between reactant molecules need less energy to produce an activated complex. Thus, a greater percentage of reactant collisions are likely to lead to product formation, resulting in a relatively high rate of reaction.

Let's return to the question: *How do catalysts work?* Catalysts increase the reaction rate by enabling the reaction to proceed through a series of different steps, with a lower activation energy, than they ordinarily would. So a catalyst reduces the minimum energy requirement of the reaction. This leads to a greater percentage of product-forming collisions and thus an increased rate of reaction. Since a catalyst is not consumed by the process, a small amount of catalyst can be used to speed up a reaction with a fairly large reactant concentration.

Learn to associate:

Catalyst with: reduced activation energy;
                       not consumed during the reaction

CHEMICAL EQUILIBRIUM

We've been talking about chemical reactions as if they occur in only one direction—from reactants to products.

$$aA + bB \rightarrow cC + dD$$

However, many reactions are reversible; as products are formed, some of them go through the reverse reaction and re-form the reactants. Reversible reactions are written as follows:

$$aA + bB \rightleftharpoons cC + dD$$

What do the two arrows mean? They mean that the reaction is taking place in both directions. Reactants are forming products (the forward reaction), and products are forming reactants (the reverse reaction). Let's talk about how, exactly, this works. When a reaction first starts, the concentration of the reactants is high, and the concentration of the products is very low. At this point, the rate of the forward reaction is greater than the rate of the reverse reaction. After a while, as more of the products are formed, less of the reactants are present.

Ultimately, if pressure and temperature are maintained and the system is closed (meaning no species are allowed to escape), the rate of the reverse reaction will be equal to the rate of the forward reaction. In other words, reactants are being made as rapidly as are products. When this occurs, we say that the reaction is in **equilibrium**, or dynamic equilibrium. When a reaction is in **dynamic equilibrium**, the forward and reverse reaction rates are equal, which also means that the concentrations of products and reactants are constant.

But here's what equilibrium definitely does not mean: *It does not mean that the concentrations of products and reactants are equal.* It just means that whatever the concentrations of products and reactants may be, they aren't changing once the reaction reaches equilibrium.

If we want to know about the relative concentrations of products and reactants of a reaction at equilibrium, we must know two things: (1) the reaction's equilibrium constant, or K_{eq}, and (2) the reaction's equilibrium expression.

For the reaction $aA + bB \rightleftharpoons cC + dD$, the equilibrium expression is written as follows:

$$K_{eq} = \frac{[C]^c[D]^d}{[A]^a[B]^b}$$

(The symbol [ ] means "concentration of," so [A] means "the concentration of A.")

Keep in mind that the concentrations referred to in an equilibrium expression are those of the species at equilibrium; the coefficients in the balanced equation become exponents in the equilibrium expression; and only those species whose concentrations can be varied are included. So, only species that are gaseous or in solution (and not solids) belong in an equilibrium expression.

Thus, given the reaction

$$BF_3(g) + 3H_2O(l) \rightleftharpoons 3HF(aq) + H_3BO_3(aq)$$

(The notation (aq) indicates that a species is dissolved in water.) we get the equilibrium expression

$$K_{eq} = \frac{[HF]^3[H_3BO_3]}{[BF_3]}$$

Take a close look at the above equilibrium expression. Notice that the equilibrium constant K_{eq} is proportional to product concentrations over reactant concentrations, or $\frac{[products]}{[reactants]}$.

What's the significance of that ratio? Suppose that in a particular reaction, almost all of the reactants are converted into products and that products do not re-form reactants to any great extent. How would the K_{eq} of the reaction reflect such behavior? Well, product concentrations would be much greater than reactant concentrations at equilibrium. As a result K_{eq}, which is roughly a ratio of product concentrations to reactant concentrations, will be a relatively large number (greater than 100).

If, instead, we have a reaction in which reactants form relatively little product, then K_{eq} will be relatively small (smaller than $\frac{1}{100}$, or 1×10^{-2}). If product and reactant concentrations at equilibrium are somewhat close, then K_{eq} will be close to 1 (not particularly large or small). So the value of the equilibrium constant K_{eq} of the reaction can give us a good idea about the extent to which reactants form products.

Learn to associate:

**Equilibrium/
dynamic equilibrium with:**   constant but not equal concentrations of products and reactants

Equilibrium constant with: equilibrium concentration of products (multiplied together) over equilibrium concentration of reactants

**Equilibrium constant
> 1 with:**   *forward* reaction is favored (equilibrium concentration of products exceeds equilibrium concentration of reactants)

**Equilibrium constant
< 1 with:**   *reverse* reaction is favored (equilibrium concentration of reactants exceeds equilibrium concentration of products)

Phase Change Equilibrium

The principle of equilibrium does not only apply to chemical reactions but also to any system in which one thing(s) is (are) transforming, reversibly, into another—such as a phase change, for instance. Remember vapor pressure? Suppose water is in a sealed container, at a temperature below water's boiling point; some molecules will still gather enough kinetic energy to escape from the liquid and become gas. Then they will lose their kinetic energy—they will cool down and fall back into the container as water. Other liquid molecules gain enough kinetic energy to escape into the gas phase, and the process continues. Some liquid is converted to gas, and some gas is converted to liquid. The process is in equilibrium.

Le Chatelier's Principle

The Effects of Substrate Concentration on Equilibrium

Look at this equilibrium.

$$A + B \rightleftharpoons C + D$$

On the left side of the equilibrium equation, we find A and B. On the right side, we find C and D. A and B act together to produce C and D; meanwhile, C and D act together to produce A and B.

If we add more A to the reaction system, the reaction will shift to the right, to produce *more* C and D at equilibrium.

$$A \searrow \quad A + B \rightleftharpoons \uparrow C + \uparrow D$$

If we add more B to the reaction, the reaction will shift to the right, to produce more C and D at equilibrium.

$$B \searrow \quad A + B \rightleftharpoons \uparrow C + \uparrow D$$

Adding more A *and* B, of course, will also increase the production of C and D.

$$A \searrow \atop B \searrow \quad A + B \rightleftharpoons \uparrow\uparrow C + \uparrow\uparrow D$$

Adding more C or more D to the system has an analogous but opposite effect.

$$\uparrow\uparrow A + \uparrow\uparrow B \rightleftharpoons C + D \quad {C \swarrow \atop D \swarrow}$$

Think about it this way. When you add more A to the system, you're increasing the amount of reactant available to react and form products. Similarly, if you add more C or D to the system, you're increasing the amount of product available to react and form reactants. The system will adjust by moving to the left to reestablish equilibrium.

When we increase the concentration of one species on the left side of an equation, what happens to the concentration of the *other* species on the left side of the equation? Say we add more A to the system: There will be more collisions between A particles and B particles. Since we did not add any B to the system, the increased collisions among A and B particles, along with the increased production of C and D, will tend to reduce the concentration of B at equilibrium. After equilibrium has shifted, there will be more A particles than there were before we added any more A. There will be fewer B particles than there were before we began, and there will, of course, be more C and D particles.

To give you an idea of what we mean by "driving or shifting equilibrium to the right," consider this example.

Suppose for the reaction, $2A(g) + B(g) \leftrightarrows C(g)$, equilibrium concentrations at a particular temperature are $[A] = 2\ M$, $[B] = 6\ M$, and $[C] = 8\ M$.

When we plug these into the equilibrium expression $K_{eq} = \dfrac{[C]}{[A]^2[B]}$ we get $K_{eq} = \dfrac{[8]}{[2]^2[6]} = \dfrac{1}{3}$.

Now, according to Le Chatelier's principle, if we add more A into the system at equilibrium, equilibrium will shift to the right. So once equilibrium is reestablished, the concentration of C will be greater than $8\ M$, and the concentration of B will be less than $6\ M$. Of course the concentration of A will also be greater than before. But as long as we maintain the original temperature, K_{eq} will stay the same. So when the new equilibrium concentrations are plugged back into the equilibrium expression, it will still equal $\dfrac{1}{3}$. For instance, the new equilibrium concentrations could be $[A] = 3\ M$, $[B] = 4\ M$, and $[C] = 12\ M$. The equilibrium concentrations have changed but the K_{eq} has not.

The Effects of Heat on Equilibrium

Consider this equilibrium equation.

$$H + I + Heat \leftrightarrows J + K$$

The reaction consumes heat in the forward direction, and it produces heat in the reverse direction. In a sense, you can think of heat as being one of the reactants in this equation. So what happens if we increase the temperature of this reaction? That is, what happens if we add heat to the system? According to Le Chatelier's principle, we drive the equilibrium to the right. What happens if we decrease the temperature of the system? We drive the equilibrium to the left.

There is one important thing to know about temperature changes: This is the only type of stress that causes an equilibrium shift *and* changes the value of K_{eq} for a given reaction. The others do *not* alter K_{eq}.

So to summarize, **Le Chatelier's principle** says that if some stress is placed on a reaction at equilibrium, then the equilibrium will shift in a direction that relieves the stress.

Learn to associate:	
Le Chatelier's principle with:	a shift in the reaction in the direction that relieves the stress placed on the system

The Effects of Pressure Changes on Equilibrium

If one or more of the species in the reaction are gaseous, then changing the system's pressure can affect equilibrium. Consider the important ammonia-producing reaction that is at the heart of what is known as the **Haber process**.

$$N_2(g) + 3H_2(g) \rightleftharpoons 2NH_3(g)$$

If the above reaction at equilibrium is stressed by a reduction of its volume (which would increase the pressure of the system), then the reaction will relieve this stress by shifting equilibrium in the direction that produces fewer moles of gas. Therefore, in the above reaction, equilibrium would shift to the right. If the reaction system was stressed by an increase in its volume (which would decrease the pressure of the system) then equilibrium would shift to the left. The equilibrium of a reaction that involved equal moles of gaseous reactants and products would not be affected by either a change in volume or a change in pressure.

The Effects of Catalysts on Equilibrium

So how does the presence of a catalyst affect equilibrium? The answer is simple: It doesn't. Catalysts change reaction rates, but they do not affect equilibrium. A catalyst can aid the reaction in achieving equilibrium more quickly, but it won't affect the concentration of product at equilibrium. This emphasizes what we said at the start of this chapter: Kinetics and equilibrium address quite different aspects of a chemical reaction.

EQUILIBRIUM IN PRECIPITATION REACTIONS

As you learned in the last chapter, some combinations of cation and anion form ionic solids with very low water solubilities or precipitates. However, even the most insoluble ionic precipitate dissolves into ions in water to a certain degree. If pressure and temperature are maintained for a precipitate in water, equilibrium exists between the precipitate and its dissolved ions. For instance, consider the equilibrium between the precipitate lead chloride ($PbCl_2$) and its dissolved ions.

$$PbCl_2(s) \rightleftharpoons Pb^{2+}(aq) + 2Cl^-(aq)$$

The equilibrium expression for the above equilibrium is

$$K_{sys} = [Pb^{2+}][Cl^-]^2$$

Remember that solids are not included in equilibrium expressions! When we consider equilibrium between a so-called insoluble ionic solid and its dissolved ions, we call the equilibrium constant a **solubility product constant** and symbolize it as K_{sp}. As you might expect, since the forward reaction is so insignificant for these precipitates, K_{sp} values are typically very small. For $PbCl_2$ at 25°C, $K_{sp} = 1.6 \times 10^{-5}$ (or 0.000016). The smaller K_{sp} is for a given ionic solid, the more insoluble it is.

Review everything we've said about kinetics, reversible reactions, and equilibrium, then answer the following questions.

QUESTION TYPE A

(A) $Ca^{2+}(aq) + CO_3^{2-}(aq) \rightleftharpoons CaCO_3(s)$

(B) $N_2(g) + 2O_2(g) \rightleftharpoons 2NO_2(g)$

(C) $4NH_3(g) + 5O_2(g) \rightleftharpoons 4NO(g) + 6H_2O(g)$

(D) $H_2(g) + I_2(g) \rightleftharpoons 2HI(g)$

(E) $Na_2O_2(s) + H_2O(l) \rightleftharpoons NaOH(aq) + H_2O_2(aq)$

18. Reaction rate can be increased by increasing the surface area of reactants

19. Increasing system pressure by decreasing reaction volume shifts equilibrium to the right

20. Impossible to increase rate of reverse reaction by increasing the concentration of reactant(s)

QUESTION TYPE B

Directions: Each question below consists of two statements, I in the left-hand column and II in the right-hand column. For each question, determine whether statement I is true or false and whether statement II is true or false and fill in the corresponding T or F ovals on your answer sheet. Fill in oval CE only if statement II is a correct explanation of statement I.

I		**II**
109. For any chemical reaction in dynamic equilibrium, increasing the concentration of one product will decrease the concentration of all reactants	BECAUSE	a dynamic equilibrium will shift in a direction that tends to relieve a stress imposed on it.

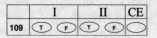

| 110. When a reversible chemical reaction reaches equilibrium, concentrations of products and reactants are always equal | BECAUSE | on the right side of any equilibrium expression, numerator and denominator are always equal. |

| 111. Increasing the concentration of a gaseous reactant typically increases the reaction rate | BECAUSE | the reaction rate is increased as the energy per molecular collision increases. |

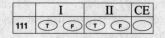

(1) $N_2(g) + 3H_2(g) \rightleftharpoons 2NH_3(g)$, K_{eq} (472°C) = 0.105

(2) $H_2(g) + I_2(g) \rightleftharpoons 2HI(g)$, K_{eq} (448°C) = 50

53. In comparing the two reactions above, performed at the indicated temperatures, which of the following is true?

   (A) Reaction 1 is favored in the forward direction, and reaction 2 is favored in the reverse direction.
   (B) Reaction 1 is favored in the reverse direction, and reaction 2 is favored in the forward direction.
   (C) Both reactions 1 and 2 are favored in the forward direction.
   (D) Both reactions 1 and 2 are favored in the reverse direction.
   (E) Neither reaction favors either the forward or reverse direction.

$$2SO_3(g) \rightleftharpoons 2SO_2(g) + O_2(g)$$

56. If the reaction given above is at equilibrium, the result of a sudden increase in the concentration of O_2 will result in

   (A) increased concentration of SO_2 and decreased concentration of SO_3
   (B) increased concentration of SO_2 and increased concentration of SO_3
   (C) decreased concentration of SO_2 and increased concentration of SO_3
   (D) decreased concentration of SO_2 and decreased concentration of SO_3
   (E) no change in concentration of any product or reactant

58. All of the following are true regarding the activated complex EXCEPT:

   (A) It represents the highest energy state achieved during the course of a reaction.
   (B) It is not consumed during the course of a reaction.
   (C) It is very unstable.
   (D) It is formed before reactant bonds are completely broken.
   (E) It is formed before product bonds are completely formed.

LET'S LOOK AT THE ANSWERS

Question 18: (E) While the surface area of solids and liquids can be increased (through crushing a solid or spraying a liquid), the surface area of gases cannot. Which answer choice has solid or liquid reactants? E does, and it's the correct answer.

Question 19: (B) When the volume of a system is decreased, equilibrium will shift in the direction that produces fewer moles of gas. Eliminate A and E—neither reaction involves a gaseous species, so pressure changes will not affect their equilibrium. Now, look at the other three choices: Which reaction involves fewer moles of gas on the right than on the left? B does (3 moles on the left, and 2 on the right). So the correct answer is B.

Question 20: (A) We're asked about reverse reactions, so read choices A to E from right to left. Recall that only gaseous and aqueous species can have their concentration increased. Choices B, C, D, and E have either a gaseous or aqueous species on the right side (this is a bit tricky—these would be the reactants of the *reverse* reaction). That leaves A, which has a single solid reactant for its reverse reaction. The concentration of pure solids cannot be changed, so A is correct.

Question 109: (F, T) Divide and conquer! Assess the first statement by itself. Is it true or false? If you increase the concentration of a product, equilibrium shifts in the direction that creates more reactant, so in this case, to the left. This means that we will see an increase, not a decrease, in the concentration of reactants. The statement is false.

What about the second statement? It is a statement of Le Chatelier's principle, so it's true. The first statement is false, and the second is true.

Question 110: (F, F) Divide and conquer. Is the first statement true or false? Don't be tricked! At equilibrium, the rates of forward and reverse reactions are equal, but the concentrations of products and reactants are usually not. This statement is false.

Let's look at the second statement. What do they mean by the "right side of any equilibrium expression?" Equilibrium expressions, remember, look like this

$$K_{eq} = \frac{[\text{products}]}{[\text{reactants}]}$$

What's on the right side? The fraction showing product concentrations and reactant concentrations. As we know, those are not usually equal at equilibrium, so both statements are false.

Question 111: (T, T) As concentrations of reactants increase, so do molecular collisions, and this produces a higher reaction rate. Statement I is true.

What about statement II? It's also true. As collisions become more energetic, they are more likely to lead to product formation.

Now put the sentences together. Does it make sense? It sounds good, but don't fall into the temptation trap: Only a temperature change, not a concentration change, can change the *energy* of molecular collisions. Don't fill in the CE oval.

Question 53: (B) Remember what we said about the size of K_{eq}.

> **Learn to associate:**
>
> **An equilibrium
> constant > 1 with:**   a reaction that favors the forward direction
>
> **An equilibrium
> constant < 1 with:**   a reaction that favors the reverse direction

The K_{eq} is less than 1 for the first reaction and greater than 1 for the second, which means that the reverse direction is favored in the first reaction, and the forward direction is favored in the second reaction. B is correct.

Question 56: (C) Think of Le Chatelier's principle, and look at what's happening here. Someone increases the concentration of the product O_2 in a reaction at equilibrium. This means that the concentration of the other product, SO_2, will decrease, and the concentration of the reactant(s) will increase. C is the correct answer.

Question 58: (B) Don't fall into the temptation trap. You've probably heard the phrase "not consumed by the reaction" in connection with catalysts, in kinetics. But here they're asking about an activated complex. An activated complex is quickly broken down to form the products of a reaction. B is the correct answer.

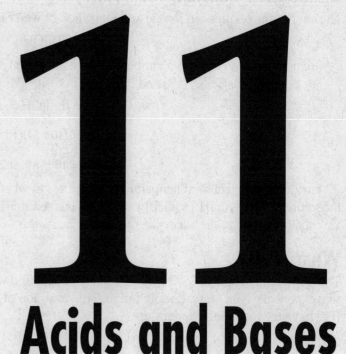

11
Acids and Bases

In order to do well on the SAT Chemistry Subject Test, you'll need to know a few things about acids and bases, including what they are, how they behave in water, and how they react with each other. Let's get started.

THE AUTOIONIZATION OF H_2O

This might surprise you, but a glass of water is not entirely composed of molecules of H_2O. Small amounts of $H^+(aq)$ and $OH^-(aq)$ are also present; these are formed during the spontaneous dissociation of water, a process called *autoionization*.

$$H_2O\ (aq) \rightleftharpoons H^+(aq) + OH^-(aq)$$

Autoionization is reversible, and an equilibrium exists in which $[H^+]$, $[OH^-]$, and $[H_2O]$ are stable.

This equilibrium can be upset by the addition of compounds that alter $[H^+]$ or $[OH^-]$, as predicted by Le Chatelier's principle. In fact, you'll see that aqueous acid-base chemistry is nothing new; it is simply the study of how other compounds introduced into solution can disturb the autoionization equilibrium of water.

Dissociation Constant for Water, K_w

The equilibrium expression for the autoionization of water is

$$K_w = [H^+][OH^-]$$

(Remember that H_2O doesn't appear in the equilibrium expression because it is the solvent.)
For pure water at 25°C, $[H^+]$ and $[OH^-]$ are both 10^{-7} M. Therefore, in pure water

$$K_w = [H^+][OH^-]$$

$$= (10^{-7} \, M)(10^{-7} \, M)$$

$$= 10^{-14} \, M^2 \text{ at } 25°C$$

Furthermore, at constant temperature, regardless of whether more $[H^+]$ or more $[OH^-]$ is added to the solution, the K_w, or $[H^+] \times [OH^-]$, of any aqueous solution is equal to 10^{-14} M^2 at 25°C. That's because *the only way to change the value of an equilibrium constant is to change the temperature of the solution.*

What Is pH?

The $[H^+]$ of pure water at 25°C is 10^{-7} M. Many people find working with exponents, especially negative exponents, a bit scary. Luckily for you, the tradition of pH was conceived and created; pH and $[H^+]$ have the following relationship:

$$\text{If } [H^+] = 10^{-7} \, M$$
$$\text{then pH} = -\log(10^{-7}) = 7$$

Note that "p" is the abbreviation for the numerical operation of $-\log$; the $-\log$ is taken from whatever number follows the p. For example, given that

$$K_w = [H^+][OH^-] = 10^{-14} \, M^2$$

taking the p of every term gives

$$pK_w = p[H^+] + p[OH^-] = 14$$

Notice that we don't include units here, so after taking the $-\log$, the resulting number has no units.

Doing Log_{10} in Your Head

For some people, having to figure out a base ten logarithm ($\log_{10}$) is just as daunting as working with exponents. If you are one of these people, try the following trick:

Look at the number, and ask the question: *What's this number's exponent when it is written as a base ten number (in other words, 10 to some power)?*

For example

$$\log 10^4 = ?$$

Ask yourself, "What's the exponent of 10^4 when it's written as 10? Well, it's already written as 10, so the answer is 4.

Answer: 4

Try these.

$$\log 10^{-8} =$$

$$\log 1{,}000 =$$

$$\log 0.01 =$$

$$\log 1 =$$

The answers are –8, 3, –2, and 0, respectively.

But taking a logarithm of a number that isn't an even factor of 10 can seem tough. For example

$$\log 58 = ?$$

Well, for this test, you can just make a good guess: 58 is between 10 and 100. Since log 10 = 1 and log 100 = 2, log 58 must be between 1 and 2.

And that's good enough for the SAT Chemistry Subject Test.

ACIDS AND BASES

Over the years, several different definitions for acids and bases have been introduced. For example

Arrhenius:	Acids produce H^+ in aqueous solution; Bases produce OH^- in aqueous solution.
Lewis:	Acids are electron acceptors in solution; Bases are electron donors in solution.
Bronsted-Lowry:	Acids are proton donors; Bases are proton acceptors.

The Bronsted-Lowry definition is the one that's most widely used today, although it is commonplace for chemists to flip between the Bronsted-Lowry and Arrhenius definitions.

Bronsted-Lowry Acids and Bases

The most important thing to remember about the Bronsted-Lowry definition of acids and bases is that *acids are proton donors and bases are proton acceptors*. The term *proton* is used to mean $H^+(aq)$, and $H^+(aq)$ reacts with water to form the **hydrodium ion**, $H_3O^+(aq)$.

The dissociation of an
acid looks like this:

$$HA(aq) \rightarrow H^+(aq) + A^-(aq)$$

Which can also be written as

$$HA(aq) + H_2O(l) \rightarrow H_3O^+(aq) + A^-(aq)$$

The reaction of a
base looks like this:

$$A^-(aq) + H^+(aq) \rightarrow HA(aq)$$

Which can also be written as

$$A^-(aq) + H_2O(l) \rightarrow HA(aq) + OH^-(aq)$$

Most compounds behave either just as acids or just as bases no matter what other chemical species are in solution. However, a handful of molecules/ions can act as either acids or bases. They elect to either donate or accept $H^+(aq)$ in response to whatever else is in solution; these are called **amphoteric** molecules/ions. One example of an amphoteric ion is the bicarbonate ion, $HCO_3^-(aq)$.

In acidic solutions, the following reaction occurs:

$$HCO_3^-(aq) + H^+(aq) \rightarrow H_2CO_3(aq)$$

While in basic solutions, the following reaction takes place:

$$HCO_3^-(aq) + OH^-(aq) \rightarrow CO_3^{2-}(aq) + H_2O(l)$$

Strong Acids and Bases

Acids and bases that dissociate completely and stay dissociated are referred to as strong acids and bases. The term *strong* is NOT used as a common adjective in acid-base chemistry; it has a very specific meaning. It means completely dissociating. For example, HCl is a strong acid and NaOH is a strong base.

$$HCl(aq) \rightarrow H^+(aq) + Cl^-(aq)$$

$$NaOH(aq) \rightarrow Na^+(aq) + OH^-(aq)$$

In the case of strong acids and bases, dissociation is considered 100 percent and irreversible, so a one-way reaction arrow is used in reactions of strong acids and bases. (Keep this in mind when you're asked to calculate the pH of strong acid-base solutions; it makes the math simpler.)

For the test, you MUST memorize the following list of strong acids and bases:

Strong Acids

HCl	hydrochloric acid
HBr	hydrobromic acid
HI	hydroiodic acid
HNO_3	nitric acid
H_2SO_4	sulfuric acid (only the first H is strong)
$HClO_4$	perchloric acid

Strong Bases

Group 1 hydroxides such as LiOH, NaOH, KOH, etc.

Calculating pH for Strong Acid or Base Solutions

We've said that strong acids and bases completely dissociate. This means that, for strong acids, $[H^+]$ equals the [STRONG ACID], and for strong bases, $[OH^-]$ equals the [STRONG BASE].

Example:　　　What is the pH of 1.0 M $HNO_3(aq)$?

Solution:　　　First, write the balanced chemical equation.

$$HNO_3(aq) \rightarrow H^+ (aq) \ + \ NO_3^-(aq)$$

Second, realize that there is really no $HNO_3(aq)$ in solution; it has all dissociated. Therefore, what we really have is

$$HNO_3(aq) \rightarrow H^+(aq) \ + \ NO_3^-(aq)$$
$$\cancel{1.0\,M}1.0\,M \quad 1.0\,M$$

Third, since pH is the $-log[H^+]$, we get

$$pH = -log[H^+]$$

$$= -log(1.0 \ M) = -log(10^0 \ M)$$

$$= 0$$

It's a good idea to remember that for a 1.0 M solution of any strong acid, pH = 0 because these solutions are commonly used in the SAT Chemistry laboratory questions. Don't make the mistake of thinking that $-log(1) = 1$!

Example: What is the pH of 1.0 M KOH(aq)?

Solution: First, write the balanced chemical equation.

$$KOH(aq) \rightarrow K^+(aq) \ + \ OH^-(aq)$$

Second, realize that there is really no KOH(aq) in solution. It's all dissociated. Therefore, what we really have is

$$KOH(aq) \rightarrow K^+(aq) \ + \ OH^-(aq)$$

~~1.0 M~~   1.0 M 1.0 M

Third, take the pOH since that's what we have.

$$pOH = -log[OH^-]$$

$$= -log(1.0 \ M) = \quad -log(10^0 \ M)$$

$$= 0$$

Fourth, recall that pH + pOH = 14 (at 25°C), and solve for pH.

$$pH = 14 - pOH$$

$$= 14 - 0 = 14$$

It is also a good idea to remember that for 1.0 M strong base, pH = 14 because these solutions are also commonly used in the SAT Chemistry laboratory questions.

WEAK ACIDS AND BASES

Acids and bases that partially, reversibly dissociate are referred to as weak acids or bases. Again, the term *weak* is NOT used as a common adjective in acid-base chemistry. It has a very specific meaning; it means *partial* or *reversible dissociation*. For example, HF is a weak acid, and NH_3 is a weak base.

$$HF(aq) \rightleftharpoons H^+(aq) + F^-(aq)$$

$$NH_3(aq) + H_2O(l) \rightleftharpoons NH_4^+(aq) + OH^-(aq)$$

The reversible double-reaction arrow is used in weak acid-base dissociation reactions.

Being able to identify weak acids and bases will really help you on test day. No one memorizes the list of weak acids and weak bases because there are tens of thousands of them. The way to identify a weak acid or weak base is first to recognize whether a compound is acidic or basic, then know that if it isn't one of the strong acids or strong bases, it must be weak.

Weak Acids

an acid that isn't one of the six strong acids

Weak Bases

a base that isn't one of the strong bases

Calculating pH for Weak Acids or Base Solutions

Weak acids and bases partially, reversibly dissociate. For this reaction, a dissociation constant, K_a for acids and K_b for bases, must be used to calculate the pH of a solution of weak acid or base.

Example: Given that $K_{aHF} = 7 \times 10^{-4}$, what is the pH of 1.5 M HF(aq)?

Solution: First, write the balanced chemical equation.

$$HF(aq) \rightleftharpoons H^+(aq) + F^-(aq)$$

Second, write the equilibrium expression, so we can use K_{aHF}.

$$K_{aHF} = \frac{[H^+][F^-]}{[HF]}$$

Third, write the algebraic expression (plug in numbers where you have them, and plug in letters where you don't).

$$(7 \times 10^{-4}) = (x)(x) \ / \ (1.5\ M - x)$$

A couple of things about this last step: First of all, the reaction indicates that for every 1 HF molecule that dissociates, 1 H^+ and 1 F^- are produced. That's why we used just x's in the algebraic expression instead of using three unrelated variables. Second of all, the equation above is actually a quadratic equation and can therefore be solved using the quadratic equation. However, in cases where [HA] is *at least* 3 orders of magnitude (10^3) larger than K_a, the fraction of HA lost due to dissociation is tiny and is completely ignored by chemists (this same rule applies for weak bases). So, for this problem, we can now write

$$(7 \times 10^{-4}) = \frac{(x)(x)}{(1.5\ M)}$$

Fourth, solve the algebraic expression.

$$(7 \times 10^{-4}) = \frac{(x)(x)}{(1.5\ M)}$$

$$x^2 = (7 \times 10^{-4}) \times (1.5\ M) = 1 \times 10^{-3}$$

$$x = 1 \times 10^{-1.5}$$

Fifth, don't worry about the fractional exponent because it will disappear when you calculate pH.

$$pH = -log[H^+]$$

$$= -log(1 \times 10^{-1.5}\ M)$$

$$= 1.5$$

Try another example to make sure you've got it.

Example: Given that $K_{bNH3} = 1.8 \times 10^{-5}$, what is the pH of 0.5 M NH$_3$(aq)?

Solution: First, write the balanced chemical equation.

$$\text{NH}_3(aq) + \text{H}_2\text{O}(l) \rightleftharpoons \text{NH}_4^+(aq) + \text{OH}^-(aq)$$

Second, write the equilibrium expression (use K_{bNH3}).

$$K_{bNH3} = \frac{[\text{NH}_4^+][\text{OH}^-]}{[\text{NH}_3]}$$

Third, write the algebraic expression (plug in numbers where you have them, and plug in letters where you don't).

$$(1.8 \times 10^{-5}) = \frac{(x)(x)}{(0.5\ M - x)}$$

Since [NH$_3$] is AT LEAST 3 orders of magnitude larger than K_{bNH3}, we can now write

$$(1.8 \times 10^{-5}) = \frac{(x)(x)}{(0.5\ M)}$$

Fourth, solve the algebraic expression.

$$(1.8 \times 10^{-5}) = \frac{(x)(x)}{(0.5\ M)}$$

$$x^2 = (1.8 \times 10^{-5}) \times (0.5\ M) \cong 1 \times 10^{-5}$$

$$x = 1 \times 10^{-2.5}$$

Fifth, don't worry about the fractional exponent because it will disappear when you calculate pOH.

$$\text{pOH} = -log[\text{OH}^-]$$

$$= -log(1 \times 10^{-2.5}\ M)$$

$$= 2.5$$

Sixth, remember that pH + pOH = 14 (at 25°C), and solve for pH.

$$\text{pH} = 14 - \text{pOH}$$

$$= 14 - 2.5$$

$$= 11.5$$

CONJUGATE ACID-BASE PAIRS

A **conjugate pair** of molecules refers to two molecules that have identical molecular formulas except that one of them has an additional H^+.

Some examples of conjugate pairs are

$$HCl \text{ and } Cl^-$$

$$H_2O \text{ and } OH^-$$

$$H_2PO_4^- \text{ and } HPO_4^{2-}$$

$$Na^+ \text{ and } NaOH^*$$

* Note that $Na^+(aq)$ can also be thought of as $Na(H_2O)^+$, or simply remember that aqueous metal ions are the conjugates of their metal hydroxides.

Some molecules/ions that are often *mistaken* for conjugate pairs are

$$H_3O^+/OH^-, \ H_2SO_4/SO_4^{2-}, \ H_2CO_3/CO_3^{2-}$$

Since all of these differ by more than 1 H^+, they do NOT qualify as conjugate pairs.

Now, the member of a conjugate pair that has an extra H^+ is called the **conjugate acid**, and the member that has one fewer H^+ is the **conjugate base**.

A word of caution: *Just because a molecule is called conjugate acid or base does not mean it's actually acidic or basic in solution.*

For example, given the conjugate pair

$$OH^-/O^{2-}$$

we see that by definition, hydroxide is the conjugate acid of the pair, but of course, OH^- is actually a base in solution.

Calculating Equilibrium Constants (*K*) for Weak Conjugate Acid/Base Pairs

Keep in mind that weak acids and bases do not completely ionize in aqueous solution. There is a measurable equilibrium, called the **ionic equilibrium**, between the weak acid and its conjugate base (or between the weak base and its conjugate acid). Here's a derivation that is pretty important to look through before test day. If you take any conjugate pair of a weak acid and weak base, such as NH_4^+ and NH_3, writing out the balanced dissociation reactions in water for each gives the following:

For $NH_4^+(aq)$: $NH_4^+(aq) \rightleftharpoons H^+(aq) + NH_3(aq)$

For $NH_3(aq)$: $NH_3(aq) + H_2O(l) \rightleftharpoons NH_4^+(aq) + OH^-(aq)$

Then, writing out the equilibrium expressions for each gives

For $NH_4^+(aq)$: $K_{aNH4+} = [NH_3][H^+] / [NH_4^+]$

For $NH_3(aq)$: $K_{bNH3} = [NH_4^+][OH^-] / [NH_3]$

Rearranging each so that $[NH_4^+]$ is by itself on the left yields

For $NH_4^+(aq)$: $[NH_4^+] = [NH_3][H^+] / K_{aNH4+}$

For $NH_3(aq)$: $[NH_4^+] = K_{bNH3} [NH_3] / [OH^-]$

Now these can be set equal to one another as follows:

$$[NH_3][H^+] / K_{aNH4+} = K_{bNH3} [NH_3] / [OH^-]$$

The $[NH_3]$'s cancel out, and then grouping the *K*'s and concentration, respectively, leaves

$$(K_{aNH4+})(K_{bNH3}) = [OH^-][H^+]$$

Since we've already seen that $[OH^-] \times [H^+] = K_w = 10^{-14}\ M^2$ at 25°C for any aqueous solution, then

$$(K_{aNH4+})(K_{bNH3}) = [OH^-][H^+] = K_w = 10^{-14}\ M^2, \text{ or}$$

$$pK_{aNH4+} + pK_{bNH3} = 14$$

In other words, the *sum of the pK$_a$ and pK$_b$ of a conjugate pair of a weak acid and weak base must always be equal to 14 at 25°C.*

If the acid-base properties of one member of a conjugate pair are already known, then the acid-base properties of the other can be inferred using the conjugate rules. There are four conjugate rules that cover all of the possible combinations of strong/weak acids/bases.

1. The conjugate acid of a strong base is neutral.
   Example: Na^+ (the conjugate acid of NaOH) is neutral.

2. The conjugate base of a strong acid is neutral.
   Example: Cl^- (the conjugate base of HCl) is neutral.

3. The conjugate acid of a weak base is an acid.
   Example: NH_4^+ (the conjugate acid of NH_3) is acidic.

4. The conjugate base of a weak acid is a base.
   Example: F^- (the conjugate base of HF) is basic.

Memorize these conjugate rules. You'll need to know them in order to make sense of acid-base titration experiments.

BUFFERS

Buffers are solutions used to minimize (not prevent) a change in pH when an additional acid or base is introduced into solution. Buffers are made out of conjugate weak acids and bases—the acid/base pair must be conjugates because if they weren't they would immediately react, neutralize one another, and fail to establish a reversible reaction. Therefore, a **buffer** consists of a conjugate pair of a weak acid and weak base.

Calculating the pH of Buffers

Thanks to the algebraic skills of Henderson and Hasselbalch, calculating the pH of a buffer solution has been reduced to a relatively simple exercise in plug and chug. The most common version of the Henderson-Hasselbalch equation is

$$pH = pK_a + \log \frac{[\text{conjugate acid}]}{[\text{conjugate base}]}$$

or

$$pH = pK_a + \log \frac{[A^-]}{[HA]}$$

Unfortunately, people often remember this equation incorrectly, either because they're used to taking –logs in acid-base chemistry or because they're confused about whether $[A^-]$ or $[HA]$ is in the numerator. So here is a test to check to make sure that the Henderson-Hasselbalch equation you jot down on test day is correct.

The addition of a base to any solution, whether it's buffered or not, will cause the pH of the solution to increase—that's a fact. The only difference between a buffered and normal solution is the magnitude of the pH change. So look at any version of the Henderson-Hasselbalch equation, and see what happens as $[A^-]$ increases. If the pH doesn't increase, then something's amiss. So, given

$$pH = pK_a + \log\left(\frac{[\text{conjugate acid}]}{[\text{conjugate base}]}\right)$$

Increasing $[A^-]$ makes the numerator of the fraction $\left(\frac{[A^-]}{[HA]}\right)$ bigger, which

makes $\left(\frac{[A^-]}{[HA]}\right)$ bigger. Now, the logarithm of a bigger number is also

bigger (100 is bigger than 10; log 100 = 2 and log 10 = 1). Therefore, if the

$+\log\left(\frac{[A^-]}{[HA]}\right)$ is bigger, then adding it to pK_a gives a bigger pH. So this

equation is correct.

Of course, the Henderson-Hasselbalch equation can be worked out for pOH, as illustrated below.

$$pOH = pK_b + \log\left(\frac{[HA]}{[A^-]}\right)$$

This passes the above test because increasing the amount of acid [HA] should always increase the pOH of any solution.

Example: Given the $K_{a(\text{Acetic acid})} = 1.8 \times 10^{-5}$, what is the pH of a solution of 0.1 M acetic acid and 0.01 M sodium acetate?

Solution: First, write the balanced chemical equation that establishes the equilibrium.

$$HC_2H_3O_2(aq) \rightleftharpoons H^+(aq) + C_2H_3O_2^-(aq)$$

Of course, Na^+ is ignored because the conjugate rules tell us that it doesn't affect pH in any way.

Second, write the relevant version of the Henderson-Hasselbalch equation.

$$pH = pK_{a(\text{Acetic acid})} + \log\left(\frac{[C_2H_3O_2^-]}{[HC_2H_3O_2]}\right)$$

Third, covert the K_a to pK_a, and write the algebraic expression.

$$pH = 4.7 + \log\left(\frac{[0.01\ M]}{[0.1\ M]}\right)$$

Fourth, solve it.

$$pH = 4.7 + \log\left(\frac{[0.01\ M]}{[0.1\ M]}\right)$$

$$= 4.7 + \log 10^{-1}$$

$$= 4.7 + (-1)$$

$$= 3.7$$

Some Final Facts About Buffers

Here's another look at the Henderson-Hasselbalch equation, but this time the concentration terms, M, are expanded into the equivalent (moles/V).

$$pH = pK_a + \log\left(\frac{\dfrac{moles}{V}_{(A^-)}}{\dfrac{moles}{V}_{(HA)}}\right)$$

Since HA(aq) and A$^-$(aq) are in the same solution, the volumes of both $V_{(HA)}$ and $V_{(A-)}$ must be equal. Therefore, volume cancels out, leaving

$$pH = pK_a + \log\left(\frac{moles_{(A^-)}}{moles_{(HA)}}\right)$$

Examining this version of the Henderson-Hasselbalch equation reveals some additional properties of buffers.

1. If you're given the number of moles of HA and A$^-$ in the test question, don't waste time converting to molarity just to plug into the Henderson-Hasselbalch equation, just use moles.

2. If the number of moles of HA and A$^-$ are equal, then the Henderson-Hasselbalch equation can be simplified to $pH = pK_a$ (or $pOH = pK_b$).

3. The pH of a buffer solution doesn't change with changing volume, since volume does not appear in the equation. Therefore, diluting or concentrating (through evaporation or osmosis) a buffer will not change its pH.

The third point is arguably the most important chemical property of a buffer, so memorize it.

Diluting or concentrating a buffered solution DOES NOT change its pH.

ACID-BASE TITRATIONS

An acid-base titration is an experimental technique used to acquire information about a solution containing an acid or base. Specifically, an acid-base titration can be used to figure out the following:

1. concentration of an acid or base

2. whether an unknown acid or base is strong or weak

3. pK_a of an unknown acid or pK_b of unknown base

Titration experiments are all carried out in the same way. The procedure consists of adding a strong acid or base of known identity and concentration, called the **titrant**, to the unknown acid or base solution. The titrant is carefully added step-wise, and changes in pH are monitored and recorded. With each small sample of titrant, a fraction of the unknown base or acid molecules is neutralized and converted into their conjugates.

This procedure continues until either the pH of the solution starts to level off or a color change is observed using a pH indicator.

Analyzing a **titration curve**—a curve obtained by plotting pH as a function of the volume of added titrant—provides information about the unknown solution's concentration.

THE EQUIVALENCE POINT

The most important feature of any titration curve is the **equivalence point** (also called the **inflection** and the **end point**). This is the point during the titration where just enough titrant (in moles) has been added to completely neutralize the subject acid or base. At the equivalence point, no unreacted titrant or unknown base/acid remain in solution. Keep in mind that conjugate acids and bases need not be neutral (recall the conjugate rules). Therefore, do not make the mistake of automatically associating the equivalence point with pH 7.

You can locate the equivalence point by eyeballing the titration curve: It is the point at which the curve is the steepest.

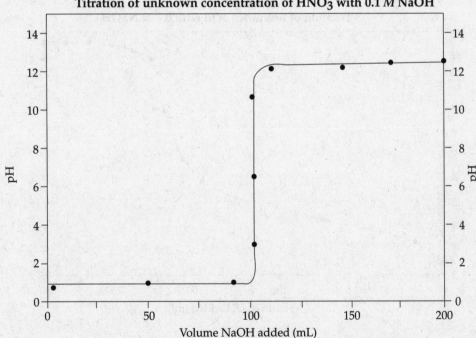

Titration of unknown concentration of HNO$_3$ with 0.1 M NaOH

DETERMINING CONCENTRATION

As we said earlier, the equivalence point is that point in the titration where just enough titrant has been added to completely neutralize the unknown acid or base. Therefore, since the number of moles must be equal at the equivalence point, if we know the concentration of the titrant, and the amount of the titrant we've added, we can calculate the concentration of the unknown solution, using an adaptation of the dilution equation, $M_iV_i = M_fV_f$.

$$\text{Molarity}_{(subject)} \times \text{Volume}_{(subject)} = \text{Molarity}_{(titrant)} \times \text{Volume}_{(titrant)}$$

Rearranging this to solve for Molarity $_{(subject)}$ gives

$$\text{Molarity}_{(subject)} = (\text{Molarity}_{(titrant)} \times \text{Volume}_{(titrant)}) / \text{Volume}_{(subject)}$$

Therefore, for the titration curve we just saw

$$\text{Molarity}_{(HNO_3)} = (0.1 \ M \times 100 \ \text{mL}) / 100 \ \text{mL}$$

$$= 0.1 \ M$$

The concentration of HNO_3 was 0.1 M.

In a titration, the pH at the equivalence point indicates whether the unknown acid or base is strong or weak. If the pH at the equivalence point is exactly 7, then the unknown acid or base is strong. If the pH at the equivalence point is greater or less than 7, the unknown acid or base is weak.

This is true because all of the acid/base and added titrant have been neutralized into their conjugates at the equivalence point. Remember the conjugate rules: *The conjugates of strong acids and bases are neutral, while the conjugates of weak acids and bases are in fact basic and acidic, respectively.*

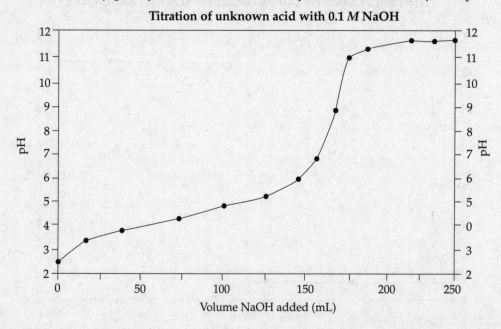

Titration of unknown acid with 0.1 M NaOH

Since the equivalence point for this titration curve lies above pH = 7 (around pH = 9), and the titration was done using an NaOH solution as the titrant, the original solution contained a weak acid.

Determining pK_a (pK_b)

First, a warning: NEVER try to figure out the pK_a or pK_b of a strong acid or base—remember, they react completely.

Now, figuring out the pK_a of a weak unknown acid (or pK_b for a weak unknown base) requires finding a second location on the titration curve: the **half-equivalence point**. The half-equivalence point, as its name suggests, is the point at which enough titrant has been added to neutralize exactly one-half of the original unknown acid or base. You can identify this point by locating the equivalence point and then backtracking halfway to zero along the x-axis.

The half-equivalence point is an important location on the titration curve because at this point, equal amounts of the unknown acid or base and its conjugates exist in the solution. That means the solution is a buffer, so the Henderson-Hasselbalch equation applies.

For titration of weak acid with strong base: $\quad \text{pH} = \text{p}K_a + \log\left(\dfrac{[\text{A}^-]}{[\text{HA}]}\right)$

For titration of weak base with strong acid: $\quad \text{pOH} = \text{p}K_b + \log\left(\dfrac{[\text{HA}]}{[\text{A}^-]}\right)$

Furthermore, since $[\text{A}^-] = [\text{HA}]$ at the half-equivalence point, the Henderson-Hasselbalch equation simplifies to the following:

For titration of weak acid with strong base: $\quad \text{pH}_{\text{(at the half-eq point)}} = \text{p}K_a$

For titration of weak base with strong acid: $\quad \text{pOH}_{\text{(at the half-eq point)}} = \text{p}K_b$

Therefore, the solution's pH at the half-equivalence point is actually the pK_a of the unknown weak acid. For a weak base, the pK_b can be quickly calculated as follows:

$$\text{p}K_b = \text{pOH}_{\text{(at the half-eq point)}} = 14 - \text{pH}_{\text{(at the half-eq point)}}$$

For the titration curve we just showed, the unknown weak acid has a p$K_a = 4.5$.

Acid-Base Indicators

An indicator is just the conjugate pair of a weak acid or base, where each conjugate is a different color. For example

$$\text{H-Indicator}(aq) \rightleftharpoons \text{H}^+(aq) + \text{Indicator}^-(aq)$$
$$\qquad (red) \qquad\qquad\qquad\qquad (yellow)$$

Since only a trace amount of an indicator is used in a titration, the acid-base dissociation doesn't impact the solution's overall pH. Instead, the indicator's dissociation equilibrium is shifted one way or another depending upon the solution's pH, according to Le Chatelier's principle. If the indicator above were used in a titration, then in acidic solutions the indicator would be driven to the conjugate acid form (*red*) and in basic solutions it would be driven to the conjugate base form (*yellow*).

All you really need to know for this test is that a chemical acid-base indicator is a substance that changes color in a pH range ±1 of its pK_a.

For example, thymol blue, which has a p$K_a = 2$, undergoes a red-to-blue color change in the pH range 1 to 3. Also, litmus paper changes color at about pH 7. At pH's lower than 7, the paper is red, while at pH's greater than 7, the paper is blue. Keep these things in mind when selecting an appropriate chemical indicator.

Incidentally, the test writers will want you to know how we add acid to base or base to acid, and the answer is: use a buret. A **buret** is a little measuring device that allows us to drop small, known amounts of liquid into a container.

Review this section on acids and bases, and then try the following questions.

QUESTION TYPE A

(A) HBr (aq)
(B) NH_3 (aq)
(C) H_2O (l)
(D) HF (aq)
(E) H_2CO_3 (aq)

17. A strip of litmus paper will appear blue in it

18. At 25°C, it has a pH > 7

19. Is essentially a nonelectrolyte

20. Its aqueous ionization goes virtually to completion

QUESTION TYPE B

Directions: Each question below consists of two statements, I in the left-hand column and II in the right-hand column. For each question, determine whether statement I is true or false and whether statement II is true or false and fill in the corresponding T or F ovals on your answer sheet. Fill in oval CE only if statement II is a correct explanation of statement I.

	I		II
110.	If an acid is added to water with an original pH of 7, the concentration of hydroxide ions will increase	BECAUSE	the product of hydroxide ions and protons is equal to 1.0×10^{-14} in all aqueous solutions at 25°C.

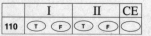

	I		II
111.	An aqueous solution of HI is considered to be a Bronsted-Lowry base	BECAUSE	HI (aq) can accept an H+ ion from another species.

QUESTION TYPE C

50. HNO_3 (aq) + OH^- $(aq) \rightleftharpoons H_2O$ (l) + NO_3^- (aq)

In the reaction above, which species is the conjugate acid?

(A) HNO_3 (aq)
(B) OH^- (aq)
(C) H_2O (l)
(D) NO_3^- (aq)
(E) There is no conjugate acid in the above reaction.

53. A titration experiment is conducted in which 15 milliliters of a 0.015 M Ba(OH)$_2$ solution is added to 30 milliliters of an HCl solution of unknown concentration and titration is complete. What is the approximate concentration of the HCl solution?

(A) 0.015 M
(B) 0.03 M
(C) 1.5 M
(D) 2.5 M
(E) 3.0 M

55. Which is true regarding an aqueous solution of H$_3$PO$_4$ at 25 °C?

(A) It has a very large acid ionization constant.
(B) It has a bitter taste.
(C) The concentration of [OH$^-$] > 1.0×10^{-7} M.
(D) It is a weak electrolyte.
(E) It can be formed by the reaction of a metal oxide and water.

LET'S LOOK AT THE ANSWERS

Question 17: (B) Litmus is an indicator that is blue in basic solutions. Since NH$_3$ is the most obvious base among the choices, the answer is B.

Question 18: (B) At 25°C, a pH greater than 7 indicates a basic solution. B is correct.

Question 19: (C) A nonelectrolyte does not dissociate into ions in water. Soluble ionic compounds, strong acids, and strong bases are all strong electrolytes, so eliminate A (a strong acid). Weak acids and bases ionize to a slight extent, and, therefore, are weak electrolytes. So eliminate B (weak base) and D and E (both weak acids). What's left? Water. But doesn't water ionize to a slight extent? Yes, but check out how slight: K_w (equilibrium constant for the ionization of water) at 25°C is 1.0×10^{-14}. That's so small that we can consider water to be a nonelectrolyte. C is correct.

Question 20: (A) The same species that makes strong electrolytes (soluble ionic compounds, strong acids, and strong bases) has an ionization reaction that essentially goes to completion. Are any of these answer choices strong acids or bases? Yes. HBr is a strong acid. It completely ionizes into H+ and Br$^-$ ions in water, so A is correct.

Question 110: (F, T) Divide and conquer! Look at statement I by itself, and decide if it's true or false. It's false. If you add an acid to neutral water you *increase* the hydrogen ion concentration and *decrease* the hydroxide ion concentration.

Is the second statement true or false? This is a true statement about water's ion product. So, statement I is false, and statement II is true.

Question 111: (F, F) Remember the six common strong acids? HI is one of them, so statement I is false.

What about the second statement? Because HI is a strong acid it will donate, not accept, H$^+$ ions. Both statements are false.

Question 50: (C) Conjugate acids and bases appear on the right side of the equation, so eliminate A and B. A conjugate acid donates an H^+ ion. Does either H_2O or NO_3^- do that? Yes: H_2O donates an H^+ ion to NO_3^- to re-form the reactants HNO_3 and OH^-. So H_2O is the conjugate acid, and the answer is C.

Question 53: (A) We know that if we fully titrate an acid we need equal amounts of H^+ and OH^- ions. There are 2 moles of OH^- ion for each mole of $Ba(OH)_2$, and we're dealing with 0.015 L of a 0.015 M solution, so

$$(2)(0.015)(0.015) = 0.00045 \text{ moles } OH^-$$

We need 0.00045 moles of H^+ ion, too. We have 0.03 L of the HCl solution, and there's just 1 mole of H^+ ion per mole of HCl, so

$$(1)(0.03)(x) = 0.00045 \text{ moles } OH^-$$

$$x = 0.015 \ M$$

A is the correct answer.

Question 55: (D) H_3PO_4 looks like the formula of an acid, and it is—phosphoric acid. Choices B, C, and E are properties of bases, so eliminate them. Is H_3PO_4 on our list of strong acids? No; so it must be a weak acid. Would a weak acid have a large K_a? No; so eliminate A. A weak acid is a weak electrolyte. D is the correct answer.

Redox and Electrochemistry

Another important type of reaction you'll need to know about for this test is the oxidation-reduction or "redox" reaction. **Electrochemistry** involves using redox reactions to generate electricity.

OXIDATION AND REDUCTION

When an atom becomes involved in a bond, the atom is either oxidized or reduced. But what do these terms mean? Well, any chemistry teacher will tell you: An atom that loses electrons is **oxidized**; an atom that gains electrons is **reduced**. They'll tell you to recite "LEO says GER," which means Lose Electrons Oxidized and Gain Electrons Reduced. You should definitely remember that sentence for this exam.

The only kind of reaction in which an atom truly loses an electron and another truly gains one is one that results in an ionic bond. But, as a way of keeping track of electrons, chemists assign each term in a compound a positive or a negative charge based upon the relative electronegativities of the atoms. For example, take HF. H-F has a covalent bond; F has a higher electronegativity value than does H. Although this isn't an ionic bond, chemists will assign the H a +1 charge and the F a –1 charge. These charges are called oxidation numbers and are always whole numbers.

The following are some important points to remember about oxidation states:

- The atoms in any compound can be assigned oxidation states. The charges given to the atoms are formal charges that reflect their electronegativities.

- For any compound, the total number of electrons given up by atoms is the same as the number gained. Thus the oxidation states of all of the atoms in a neutral compound always add up to zero.

OXIDATION STATES AND OXIDATION NUMBERS

Each atom in a compound can also be assigned what's called an oxidation state. The **oxidation state** is positive if the atom is likely to lose electrons and negative if the atom is likely to gain electrons.

If, for instance, we imagine that some atom has gained two electrons, its oxidation state is –2, and if it has lost one electron, its oxidation state would be +1. Since total reduction has to equal total oxidation for all compounds, the sum of all oxidation numbers of a compound is always zero. It is important to remember that we assign oxidation states to atoms only when they aren't in their elemental forms. For example, each atom of H_2, O_2, Cl_2, N_2, Na, or Fe has an oxidation state of zero. Atoms in all other compounds, such as those in H_2CO_3, CaO, or N_2O, can be assigned an oxidation number that is not zero.

On the SAT Chemistry, the writers might show you some compound or other and ask you to calculate the oxidation states of its atoms. If you remember a few simple rules, you'll always be able to answer these questions.

For some elements, oxidation state is almost always the same, no matter what compound they're sitting in, while for other elements, oxidation state varies depending on the compound. Here are the important points to remember.

1. When oxygen is in a compound, its oxidation state is usually –2 (it has been reduced). One important exception is oxygen in a peroxide such as hydrogen peroxide (H_2O_2). In a peroxide, oxygen has an oxidation state of –1.

2. When an alkali metal (Li, Na, etc.) is involved in a compound, its oxidation state is always +1 (it's been oxidized).

3. When an alkaline earth metal (Be, Mg, etc.) is involved in a compound, its oxidation state is +2.

4. When a halogen (F, Cl, etc.) is involved in a compound, its oxidation state is often –1. The oxidation state of fluorine in a compound is always –1.

5. When hydrogen is combined with a nonmetal its oxidation state is +1. When hydrogen is combined with a metal its oxidation state is –1.

6. In any compound, the sum of all oxidation states is zero.

Remember those six simple rules, and you'll be able to answer the questions about oxidation state on the exam.

What is the oxidation state for nitrogen, in the compound nitrogen monoxide (NO)?

- Oxygen's oxidation number is –2; there's 1 oxygen atom in the molecule, so oxygen contributes a total reduction of –2.

- Since the total reduction (gain of electrons) must equal the total oxidation (loss of electrons), nitrogen must have an oxidation state of +2 (which means it has been oxidized, having lost two electrons).

Try another one. What is the oxidation number of carbon in iron(III) carbonate, $Fe_2(CO_3)_3$?

If Fe's subscript is 2 and CO_3's is 3, that means the charge on Fe must be +3, and the charge on CO_3 must be –2. The oxidation state of an ion is equal to its charge. So the oxidation state of Fe is +3. The total oxidation state of CO_3 is –2. The oxidation state of oxygen is –2. Since there are 3 oxygen atoms in CO_3, the total contribution by oxygen is –6. This means that carbon's oxidation state must be +4 so that CO_3's total oxidation state is (+4) + 3(–2) = –2.

Now let's consider how these oxidation states add to give the total oxidation state of $Fe_2(CO_3)_3$.

- Oxygen contributes total reduction of (3)(3)(–2) = –18.

- Carbon contributes total oxidation of 3(+4) = +12.

- Iron contributes total oxidation of 2(+3) = +6.

So the oxidation state of $Fe_2(CO_3)_3$ is (–18) + (+12) + (+6) = 0. This is just what we would expect. Each iron atom has lost 3 electrons, each oxygen atom has gained 2 electrons, and each carbon atom has lost 4 electrons. The losses equal the gains; total oxidation equals total reduction.

REDOX REACTIONS

In **oxidation reduction** or **redox reactions,** as reactants form products, one or more atoms are reduced while one or more other atoms are oxidized. If reduction occurs in a reaction, then oxidation must also take place. If one species gains electrons, another must have lost them. If we want to represent just the reduction or just the oxidation in a redox reaction, we write something called a **half-reaction.**

Look at this reaction.

$$Fe + 2HCl \rightarrow FeCl_2 + H_2$$

On the left side of the equation, iron's oxidation state is 0 and hydrogen's is +1. On the right side of the equation, iron's oxidation state is +2 and hydrogen's is 0. So iron has been oxidized (each atom has gone from an oxidation state of 0 to +2, so each has lost two electrons), and hydrogen has been reduced (each atom has gone from an oxidation state of +1 to 0, so each has gained one electron). We can write two half-reactions, one showing the oxidation of iron and the other showing the reduction of hydrogen. Here they are.

- **Oxidation:** $Fe \rightarrow Fe^{+2} + 2e^-$
  1 iron atom loses 2 electrons and takes on an oxidation state of +2.

- **Reduction:** $2H^+ + 2e^- \rightarrow H_2$
  2 hydrogen atoms each gain 1 electron to yield 2 hydrogen atoms with an oxidation state of 0.

Notice that if we take the two half-reactions together, oxidation equals reduction: In the oxidation half-reaction, iron loses 2 electrons. In the reduction half-reaction, 2 hydrogen atoms each gain 1 electron; the total electron gain is 2.

That's how these redox half-reactions work. Let's try writing the half-reactions for the following:

$$4NH_3 + 5O_2 \rightarrow 4NO + 6H_2O$$

- Hydrogen's oxidation state doesn't change (it's +1 on both sides).

- Oxygen's oxidation state changes from 0 to –2. This means that nitrogen's oxidation state must change to balance the reduction of oxygen.

- What is the change in nitrogen's oxidation state? On the left side of the equation, its oxidation state is –3 (to balance the total +3 oxidation state of the 3 hydrogen atoms to which each is bonded). On the right side of the equation, its oxidation state is +2 (to balance the –2 oxidation of the oxygen atom to which each is bonded). So its oxidation state changes from –3 to +2; nitrogen is oxidized.

Here's the half-reaction that tells us what's happening to it.

- **Oxidation:** $4N^{-3} \rightarrow 4N^{+2} + 20e^-$
  1 nitrogen atom loses 5 electrons.

You now know that reduction has to balance oxidation. The nitrogen atoms lost a total of 20 electrons; some other atoms must gain a total of 20 electrons. What gains electrons and is reduced? Oxygen does. Its oxidation state goes from 0 on the left to –2 on the right, and here's that half-reaction.

- **Reduction:** $5O_2 + 20e^- \rightarrow 10 \, O^{-2}$

Of the 10 oxygen atoms that have a –2 oxidation state on the right side, 4 are in NO and 6 are in H_2O. The nitrogen atoms lose a total of 20 electrons, and the oxygen atoms gain a total of 20 electrons.

Many important reactions are redox reactions. In a **combustion reaction,** a compound containing carbon and hydrogen reacts with molecular oxygen, O_2, to produce CO_2 and H_2O. Look closely at the combustion of acetylene (C_2H_2), and you'll see it's a redox reaction.

$$2C_2^{-1}H_2^{+1} + 5O_2^{0} \rightarrow 4 \, C^{+4}O_2^{-2} + 2 \, H_2^{+1}O^{-2}$$

Carbon is oxidized and oxygen is reduced in this reaction. The rusting of iron is also a redox reaction. Here's a simplified expression of this process.

$$4Fe^0 + 3O_2^{0} \rightarrow 2 \, Fe_2^{+3} O_3^{-2}$$

As you can see, iron is oxidized, and oxygen is reduced. The result is that iron is converted into the reddish-brown iron(II) oxide, commonly called rust.

OXIDIZING AND REDUCING AGENTS

There are two other terms that you should be familiar with: oxidizing agent (or oxidant) and reducing agent (or reductant). An **oxidizing agent** causes another species to be oxidized by undergoing reduction. A **reducing agent**—by itself being oxidized—causes another substance to be reduced. Consider the two redox reactions we examined earlier.

- $Fe + 2HCl \rightarrow FeCl_2 + H_2$

- $4NH_3 + 5O_2 \rightarrow 4NO + 6 H_2O$

In the first reaction, Fe (which is oxidized) is the reducing agent, and HCl (which contains the species being reduced, H) is the oxidizing agent.

In the second reaction, NH_3 (which contains the species being oxidized, N) is the reducing agent and O_2 (which is reduced) is the oxidizing agent. Note that oxygen (O_2) is an excellent oxidizing agent, and fluorine (F_2) is also a powerful oxidizing agent. The active metals make strong reducing agents.

ELECTROCHEMISTRY

Electrochemistry is the study of the relationship between chemical reactions and electricity.

ELECTROCHEMICAL CELLS

An **electrochemical cell** (sometimes called a **voltaic** or **galvanic cell**) is a device used to produce an electric current from a spontaneous redox reaction. How do we know that a redox reaction is spontaneous? We must consider something called the **standard electrode potential** for both the oxidation and reduction half-reactions. ("Standard" means the solutions are 1 M, and the gases are at 1 atm.) The standard electrode potential (symbolized by E^0) measures, in volts, the electric potential difference (which is like potential energy) of a given half-reaction relative to the following half-reaction:

$$2H^+(aq) + 2e^- \rightarrow H_2(g)$$

If we're measuring E^0_{ox} (oxidation potential), it's relative to the above reduction. If we're measuring E^0_{red} (reduction potential), it's relative to the *reverse* of the above reaction. To determine if a redox reaction is spontaneous, simply add E^0_{ox} for the oxidation half-reaction and E^0_{red} for the reduction half-reaction. The sum of E^0_{ox} and E^0_{red} is E^0_{cell}, which is the electric potential difference for the overall redox reaction. If E^0_{cell} is greater than 0, then the redox reaction is spontaneous. One other thing about E^0_{ox} and E^0_{red} values: Even if a half-reaction is multiplied by some coefficient, never, ever multiply E^0_{ox} by that coefficient. *Never multiply E^0 values by anything!* The test writers will supply you with all the E^0 values you'll need. Now consider the following redox reaction:

$$Cu^{2+}(aq) + Zn(s) \rightarrow Cu(s) + Zn^{2+}(aq)$$

Here are the half-reactions and E^0 values.

- **Oxidation:** $Zn(s) \rightarrow Zn^{2+}(aq) + 2e^-$; $E^0_{ox} = 0.76$ V

- **Reduction:** $Cu^{2+}(aq) + 2e^- \rightarrow Cu(s)$; $E^0_{red} = 0.34$ V

For the above reaction, E^0_{cell} is 0.76 V + 0.34 V = 1.10 V. Since $E^0_{cell} > 0$, this redox reaction is spontaneous, which means that we can turn the energy that this reaction releases into electrical energy. But how?

If we simply drop some zinc metal into an aqueous solution of Cu^{2+} ion (say, a water solution of $Cu(NO_3)_2$), this spontaneous redox reaction will happen. Electrons will leave the zinc metal as it is oxidized and be captured by the Cu^{2+} ions, which will be reduced. All of this will happen, yet we will get no electrical energy out of the reaction. Why not? Because the electrons will immediately travel from the zinc atoms to the Cu^{2+} ions. Electrical energy involves the flow of electrons, so if we want to derive electrical energy from this reaction, we must force the electrons that leave zinc to flow through a wire in order to reach Cu^{2+}. This is precisely what the electrochemical cell does. In an electrochemical cell, the oxidation and reduction half-reactions occur in separate vessels. Each vessel contains an aqueous solution containing the ions participating (as reactants or products) in the reaction. For example, we can use $Zn(NO_3)_2(aq)$ and $Cu(NO_3)_2(aq)$ for the redox reaction shown on the previous page. A strip of metal called an **electrode** is placed in each solution; each electrode is made out of a metal that also participates in the reaction. The electrode in the vessel in which **oxidation** occurs is called the **anode**. The **cathode** is the electrode in the vessel in which **reduction** takes place. Each electrode is made out of a metal that also participates in the reaction. In our electrochemical cell, the anode is a strip of zinc metal, and the cathode is a strip of copper metal.

Just remember: **AN OX** and **RED CAT**

Oxidation occurs at the cathode;

Reduction occurs at the anode.

As we mentioned, the anode and cathode are connected by an electricity-conducting wire. As electrons are freed by the oxidation process at the anode, they travel through the wire to the cathode, where they participate in reduction. This flow of electrons creates electrical energy, and it has been generated by the spontaneous redox reaction. Here's what an electrochemical cell will look like for the reaction between Zn and Cu^{2+}.

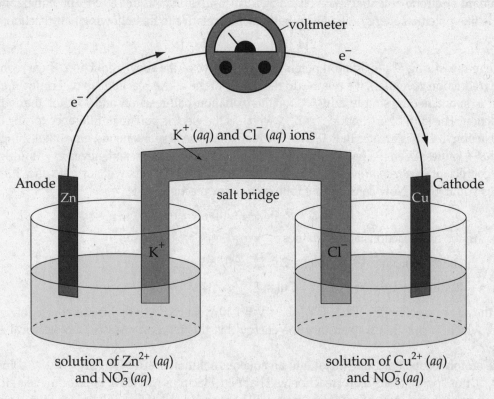

As electrons leave the vessel in which oxidation is occurring, a net positive charge accumulates in the vessel. A net negative charge grows in the reduction vessel, where the electrons are ending up. If these charge buildups were not neutralized, then the redox reaction would be short-lived, since electrons will not readily flow from a region of positive charge to a region of negative charge. So, what neutralizes any excess charge buildup? The **salt bridge** does. The salt bridge contains a cation and an anion that don't participate in the redox reaction. As positive charge accumulates in the oxidation vessel, anions flow into it from the salt bridge. Cations leave the salt bridge to flow into the reduction vessel and neutralize the negative charge buildup. In our electrochemical cell, we would fill the salt bridge with an aqueous solution of potassium chloride (KCl). K^+ ions flow into the reduction vessel, and Cl^- ions flow into the oxidation vessel.

We can connect a **voltmeter** to the wire to measure the voltage (electric potential) of the electrochemical cell. The actual electric potential is theoretically equal to E^0_{cell}; however, electrical resistance in the wire always causes the actual electric potential to be less than E^0_{cell}. As an electrochemical cell runs, its voltage decreases. When the voltage becomes 0, the spontaneous redox reaction has attained equilibrium, and the electrochemical cell is "dead."

ELECTROLYSIS

Electrolysis is the process by which electrical energy is put into a nonspontaneous redox reaction to force it to occur. This means that, during electrolysis, electrical energy is converted into chemical energy. Electrolysis is a useful way to separate ionic compounds into their constituent elements. For example, running electricity through a sample of molten NaCl can produce sodium metal (Na) and chlorine gas (Cl^2).

Electroplating is a type of electrolysis in which one metal is deposited on another. For instance, a coating of silver can be electroplated onto a cheaper metal to make quality silverware.

Review what we've said about oxidation-reduction and electrochemistry, and try the following questions.

QUESTION TYPE A

(A) Anode
(B) Cathode
(C) Salt bridge
(D) Voltmeter
(E) Electrical wire

11. Serves to maintain charge neutrality in both half-reaction vessels

12. Location of oxidation in an electrochemical cell

13. Necessary to connect two electrodes

14. Increases in mass during the operation of an electrochemical cell

QUESTION TYPE B

Directions: Each question below consists of two statements, I in the left-hand column and II in the right-hand column. For each question, determine whether statement I is true or false <u>and</u> whether statement II is true or false and fill in the corresponding T or F ovals on your answer sheet. <u>Fill in oval CE only if statement II is a correct explanation of statement I.</u>

	I		II
104.	Any reaction in which one atom is oxidized requires that another atom be reduced	BECAUSE	if one species donates electrons another must acquire them.

	I		II	CE
104	T F	T F	

105.	Electrolysis requires the input of electrical energy	BECAUSE	a redox reaction that has a positive overall E^0 is nonspontaneous.

	I		II	CE
105	T F	T F	

QUESTION TYPE C

32. $2Na + \ldots Cl_2 \rightarrow \ldots 2NaCl$

    Which of the following is true of the reaction given by the equation above?

    (A) Chlorine is oxidized.
    (B) Sodium is oxidized.
    (C) Sodium is the oxidizing agent.
    (D) Both sodium and chlorine are oxidized.
    (E) Neither sodium nor chlorine are oxidized nor reduced.

35. The oxidation state of manganese (Mn) in the compound potassium permanganate ($KMnO_4$) is

    (A) +7
    (B) +4
    (C) 0
    (D) −4
    (E) −7

54. $2Al + 6HCl \rightarrow 2AlCl_3 + 3H_2$

If 2 moles of Al and 6 moles of HCl react according to the above equation, then how many moles of electrons are transferred during the redox reaction?

(A) 1
(B) 2
(C) 3
(D) 5
(E) 6

LET'S LOOK AT THE ANSWERS

Question 11: (C) Remember the parts of an electrochemical cell and what they do. A salt bridge neutralizes charge buildup in the half-reaction vessels. C is the answer.

Question 12: (A) Did you remember AN OX and RED CAT? If so, then you know that *oxidation* occurs at the *an*ode. The correct answer is A.

Question 13: (E) You might have been tempted to pick C. However, a salt bridge doesn't physically connect the anode to the cathode. An electrical wire (whether or not a voltmeter is also attached) connects the electrodes, so E is correct.

Question 14: (B) Think about what happens during the operation of an electrochemical cell. The anode is oxidized into an aqueous cation. That causes the anode to decrease in mass as the redox reaction progresses. The opposite happens at the cathode. An aqueous ion acquires electrons to form more of the metal that composes the cathode, so the cathode gets more massive as the reaction happens. The answer is B.

Question 104: (T, T, CE) Divide and conquer. Look at the first statement, and evaluate it on its own. Is it true? Yes. Wherever there's oxidation there must be reduction.

Look at the second statement by itself. Is it true? Yes. If one species gives up electrons, something else must accept them. Now see whether the whole sentence makes sense: *Any reaction in which one atom is oxidized requires that another atom be reduced because if one species donates electrons another must acquire them.* Does it? Absolutely. Oxidation means losing electrons, and reduction means gaining electrons. Oxidation must accompany reduction because if electrons are lost from one place, they must be gained by another. The second statement explains the first, so fill in oval CE.

Question 105: (T, F) Evaluate the first statement on its own: Does electrolysis require the input of electricity? It sure does, so statement I is true.

What about the second statement? A spontaneous redox reaction has *positive* overall E^0_{cell}, so statement II is false.

Question 32: (B) Do some simple oxidation/reduction arithmetic. Sodium starts with an oxidation state of 0 because it isn't in a compound. When Cl is in a compound, its oxidation state is usually –1. In NaCl, Cl has an oxidation state of –1, and Na has an oxidation state of +1. The oxidation state of Na was 0 and is now +1; Na has lost electrons—it has been oxidized. B is the correct answer.

Question 35: (A) Again, some simple oxidation/reduction arithmetic is necessary. Oxygen's oxidation state here is –2. Since there are 4 oxygen atoms in the formula, oxygen contributes total oxidation of $(-2)(4) = -8$. Potassium's oxidation state is +1. The oxidation state of the overall compound is 0. So $1 + (-8) + x = 0$. $x = +7$. That's why A is correct.

Let's begin by applying the rules for assigning oxidation states to the given reaction.

$$2Al^0 + 6H^{+1}Cl^{-1} \rightarrow 2\,Al^{+3}Cl_3^{-1} + 3H_2^0$$

Notice that each mole of Al that's oxidized to Al^{+3} loses 3 moles of electrons, so 2 moles of Al lose 6 moles of electrons during oxidation. The 6 moles of electrons that are given up by Al are acquired by H^+ ions to form H_2. E is the correct answer.

13

Organic Chemistry and Environmental Chemistry

There are two other fields of chemistry that you should have some knowledge about for the SAT Chemistry Subject Test. One is **organic chemistry**, which is the study of carbon compounds, and the other is **environmental chemistry**, which is the study of chemicals (their interaction with each other, and our interactions with them, in the environment). Let's start by talking about organic chemistry.

ORGANIC CHEMISTRY

Carbon compounds are especially important because all living things on Earth are made up of carbon (in addition to a few other elements). Each carbon atom can form up to four bonds with other atoms; this enables carbon to form long chains with itself and certain other atoms, which is what makes it such an important biomolecule. Organic molecules almost always contain nonpolar covalent bonds.

Here are some other properties of organic compounds that you should know.

- Organic compounds are much more soluble in nonpolar solvents than in polar solvents. Remember, like dissolves like, so since carbon compounds are generally nonpolar, they will be soluble in nonpolar solvents. That means that organic substances are not very soluble in water, which is a highly polar solvent.

- Organic compounds don't dissociate in solution; since organic compounds do not contain ionic bonds, they will not dissociate into ions. That means that organic solutions are poor conductors of electricity, and organic compounds do not behave as electrolytes in solution.

There is an infinite variety of organic molecules. Sometimes two organic molecules may have the same chemical makeup with identical constituent elements, but these elements are arranged in a different geometrical arrangement. In these cases, the two compounds have completely different chemical properties and are said to be **isomers**.

HYDROCARBONS

The simplest organic compounds are hydrocarbons, compounds that contain only carbon and hydrogen. Hydrocarbons can be grouped into three categories: **alkanes**, which contain only single carbon-carbon bonds; **alkenes**, which contain carbon-carbon double bonds; and **alkynes**, which contain carbon-carbon triple bonds.

Alkanes

Alkanes are hydrocarbons that contain only single bonds. They are also known as **saturated hydrocarbons** because each carbon atom is bonded to as many other atoms as possible.

Alkane (C_nH_{2n+2}) Formula

Methane CH_4

Ethane C_2H_6

Propane C_3H_8

Butane C_4H_{10}

Pentane C_5H_{12}

The prefixes (*meth-*, *eth-*, *prop-*, *etc.*) indicate the number of carbons in the hydrocarbon chain.

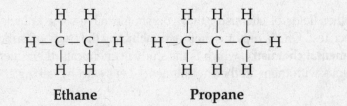

Ethane   **Propane**

Alkenes

Alkenes are hydrocarbons that contain at least one double bond. They are said to be unsaturated hydrocarbons because each carbon atom is not bonded to as many atoms as possible—the two or more carbons double bonded to one another could theoretically instead bond to other H atoms, for example.

Alkene (C$_n$H$_{2n}$) Formula

Ethylene C$_2$H$_4$

Propene C$_3$H$_6$

Butene C$_4$H$_8$

Pentene C$_5$H$_{10}$

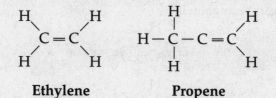

Ethylene   **Propene**

Alkynes

Alkynes are hydrocarbons that contain triple bonds; they are also unsaturated hydrocarbons.

Alkyne (C$_n$H$_{2n-2}$) Formula

Ethyne C$_2$H$_2$

Propyne C$_3$H$_4$

Butyne C$_4$H$_6$

Pentyne C$_5$H$_8$

$$H-C\equiv C-H \qquad H-C\equiv C-\underset{\underset{\textstyle H}{|}}{\overset{\overset{\textstyle H}{|}}{C}}-H$$

Ethyne   **Propyne**

Hydrocarbon Rings

Many hydrocarbons form rings instead of chains. One of the most important classes of these compounds is the **aromatic hydrocarbons**, the simplest of which is benzene, C$_6$H$_6$.

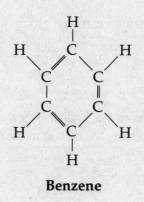

Benzene

FUNCTIONAL GROUPS

The presence of certain groups of atoms, called functional groups, in organic compounds can give the compounds specific chemical properties.

Alcohols—Alcohols are organic compounds in which a hydrogen has been replaced with a hydroxyl group (OH). The hydroxyl group makes the alcohol polar, which means that alcohols are more soluble in water than most other organic compounds.

$$H-\underset{\displaystyle \underset{H}{|}}{\overset{\displaystyle \overset{H}{|}}{C}}-O-H$$

Methanol

Halides—Halides are organic compounds in which one or more hydrogens have been replaced with a halide (F, Cl, Br, I).

$$H-\underset{\displaystyle \underset{H}{|}}{\overset{\displaystyle \overset{H}{|}}{C}}-Cl$$

Organic Acids—Organic acids are organic compounds in which a hydrogen has been replaced with a carboxyl group (COOH).

The "R" in the diagram stands for the rest of the hydrocarbon chain.

Amines—In an amine, a hydrogen atom has been replaced by an amino group (NH$_2$).

$$R-NH_2$$

Aldehydes—An aldehyde contains a carbonyl group $C=O$ connected to at least one hydrogen atom.

$$R-\underset{\displaystyle \underset{H}{|}}{C}=O$$

Ketones—A ketone is similar to an aldehyde in that it also contains a carbonyl group $C=O$; but in a ketone, the carbon in the carbonyl is not connected to any hydrogen atoms.

Ethers—In an ether, an oxygen atom serves as a link in the hydrocarbon chain.

$$R_1 - O - R_2$$

Esters—In an ester, an ester group (COO) serves as a link in the hydrocarbon chain.

$$R_1 - \overset{\displaystyle O}{\overset{\|}{C}} - O - R_2$$

ORGANIC REACTIONS

You should be familiar with a handful of organic reactions, so study the reactions below carefully.

Addition—In an addition reaction, a carbon-carbon double bond is converted into a single bond, freeing each of the two carbons to bond with another element. Also in an addition reaction, a triple bond can be converted into a double bond.

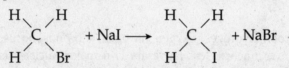

Substitution—In a substitution reaction, one atom or group in a compound is replaced with another atom or group. Chemically, this very rarely happens (i.e., direct replacement of H).

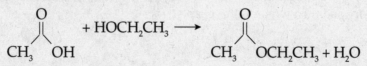

Polymerization—In polymerization, two smaller compounds, called *monomers*, are joined to form a larger third compound. In condensation polymerization, two monomers are joined in a reaction that produces water.

Cracking—In cracking, a larger compound is broken down into smaller compounds.

Oxidation—An organic compound can react with oxygen at high temperatures to form carbon dioxide and water. This reaction should be familiar to you as **combustion** or burning.

$$CH_4 + 2O_2 \rightarrow CO_2 + 2H_2O$$

Esterification—In esterification, an organic acid reacts with an alcohol to produce an ester and water.

$$\underset{CH_3 \quad\quad OH}{\overset{\displaystyle O}{\overset{\|}{C}}} + HOCH_2CH_3 \longrightarrow \underset{CH_3 \quad\quad OCH_2CH_3}{\overset{\displaystyle O}{\overset{\|}{C}}} + H_2O$$

Fermentation—In fermentation, an organic compound reacts in the *absence* of oxygen to produce an alcohol and carbon dioxide.

THE FOUR MAJOR GROUPS OF BIOMOLECULES

Four important types of organic molecules that you'll hear a lot about if you go into the fields of biochemistry (for instance, if you're planning on being premed in college) or biology are lipids, carbohydrates, nucleic acids, and proteins. All of these biomolecules are carbon compounds, and each of them is characterized by different functional groups, which gives them different functions in the human body.

Lipids

Lipids are made up of carbon, hydrogen, and oxygen atoms, connected in long branching chains. The most common examples of lipids are fats and oils. One group of lipids commonly talked about in biology is the **triglycerides**. Triglycerides are made up of three long fatty acid chains (long hydrocarbon chains) attached to a head group that consists of a molecule of glycerol. (No need to know the structure of glycerol for the test.) The molecules that make up cell walls are a type of lipid, specifically known as phospholipids. And one final note about lipids: lipids are not water-soluble and tend to aggregate to form droplets when placed in water.

Carbohydrates

Carbohydrates are also known as sugars; they are organic compounds that contain carbon, hydrogen, and oxygen, usually in a ratio of 1:2:1. They are polymers made up of sugar monomers. Some simple types of carbohydrates are glucose and fructose, for example. Both of these are examples of monosaccharides, carbohydrates made up of just one unit of sugar. Larger sugars, called polysaccharides, are the energy storage units in both plants and animals—the storage carbohydrate of animals is glycogen, and the storage carbohydrate of plants is cellulose. Carbohydrates can be straight chains of these sugar monomers, or they can be extensively branched.

Nucleic Acids

Nucleic acids contain carbon, hydrogen, oxygen, nitrogen, and phosphorus. They are polymers made up of monomers known as nucleotides. There are two major nucleic acids: DNA (which you've probably heard of, stands for deoxyribonucleic acid) and RNA (you might have heard of this type of nucleic acid too—ribonucleic acid). **DNA** is the genetic material of all living things; it contains the blueprints for all life.

Proteins

Proteins are polymers that are made up of amino acid monomers. Amino acids all have two functional groups in common—an amino group (remember, $-NH_2$) and a carboxyl group ($-COOH$). This means that they are amphoteric and can act as either an acid or a base. All of the 20 different amino acid monomers that make up proteins differ in their side chain or R group. Chains of linked amino acids are known as **polypeptides**, and proteins are formed by the folding of the polypeptide chains (and oftentimes the association of one or more polypeptide chains). Recall our discussion of catalysts: **Enzymes**, which are biological catalysts that speed up the rate of nearly all cellular reactions, are all proteins.

Okay, that's it for organic chemistry—let's briefly review what you'll need to know about environmental chemistry and then wrap up this chapter!

ENVIRONMENTAL CHEMISTRY

Here we'll cover three main topics that fall under the broad category of environmental chemistry: the earth's atmosphere, the Greenhouse Effect, and the causes and effects of acid rain.

THE CHEMISTRY OF EARTH'S ATMOSPHERE

For this test, you should remember that the earth's atmosphere is about 78 percent nitrogen, 2 percent oxygen, less than 1 percent argon, and then contains a trace amount of the following other elements; carbon dioxide, neon, helium, methane, krypton, hydrogen, nitrous oxide, and xenon. While the test won't ask you about the trace elements of the atmosphere, it could ask you about its major components. The atmosphere is divided into four regions: the **troposphere**, which is the layer of the atmosphere that's closest to the earth; the **stratosphere**, which is the layer above the troposphere; the **mesosphere**, which is further out; and then the **thermosphere**, which is the furthest out of all.

One molecular component of the atmosphere that you should be aware of is **ozone**, O_3, which you've probably heard about before in conjunction with global warming. Ozone is the result of the collision of elemental oxygen, O, and diatomic oxygen, O_2. But how come oxygen can exist in the atmosphere in elemental form, if it's supposed to be one of those diatomic molecules? Well, O is produced in the atmosphere in the following reaction:

$$O_2(g) + h\gamma = 2O(g)$$

This type of reaction is called photodissociation—in **photodissociation**, a bond is broken as a molecule absorbs a photon of light energy.

In the next step in the production of ozone, elemental oxygen and diatomic oxygen collide.

$$O(g) + O_2(g) \rightarrow O_3(g)$$

Atmospheric ozone absorbs solar radiation and decomposes back to elemental and diatomic oxygen. If ozone didn't absorb this high-energy radiation, the damaging rays would reach the planet and destroy much of its plant and animal life. As you have probably read about or seen in the news, certain chemicals produced by humans are thought to be responsible for the gradual degradation of the ozone layer. The primary culprits in ozone layer destruction are **chlorofluorocarbons**, which have been created for use as propellants in spray cans and car air conditioners. Chloroflourocarbons react with light energy to form, among other compounds, free chlorine. This chlorine reacts with ozone to form chlorine monoxide, ClO and oxygen. The fact that ozone is a reactant in this chemical reaction means that it is slowly being consumed; the earth's atmosphere is slowly being robbed of its protective ozone layer.

THE GREENHOUSE EFFECT

Another environmental topic that's hotly debated in the news is the Greenhouse Effect. In short, the **Greenhouse Effect** refers to the buildup of carbon dioxide, CO_2, and other greenhouse gases in the atmosphere. Greenhouse gases are the result of the combustion of fossil fuels such as coal and oil; they absorb infrared radiation that reflects off the earth from the sun, effectively trapping it in the atmosphere and creating an effect much like that in a greenhouse (hence the name).

ACID RAIN

The SAT Chemistry might also expect you to know a little something about what acid rain is and how it's formed. By definition, **acid rain** is rain that has an abnormally low pH, due to the presence of certain oxides, which are pollutants produced by human activities. One of the most prevalent classes of oxide pollutants is the sulfur oxides, in the form SO_2. SO_2 is produced when coal and oil are combusted and can react with either ozone or diatomic oxygen to form SO_3. In turn, SO_3 reacts with rainwater to produce sulfuric acid, in the following reaction:

$$SO_3(g) + H_2O(l) \rightarrow H_2SO_4(aq)$$

Other oxides that also contribute to the production of acid rain are the nitrogen oxides, which combine with water to form nitric acid.

Acid rain is harmful to buildings and other structures because it reacts with metals and is corrosive. It's also harmful for organisms that live in ponds and lakes; most natural ponds and lakes have a pH of about 7, which is neutral, and a drop in pH has many negative effects on the inhabitants of these bodies of water. In fact, the fall of acid rain has significantly reduced the number of fish and other aquatic organisms in many polluted areas of the world.

The last air pollutant that you'll need to know about for this test is carbon monoxide, CO. Carbon monoxide is found in car exhaust and cigarette smoke and can be dangerous for humans because it binds irreversibly to hemoglobin, the biomolecule that is responsible for transporting oxygen around the body through the bloodstream.

Okay, we're done with environmental chemistry—now read through the laboratory chapter, and you'll be all set to take the three practice exams at the back of the book.

14
Laboratory

SAFETY RULES

Always wear safety goggles in the laboratory.

Always work with good ventilation; many common chemicals are toxic.

Take extra care when working with an open flame.

When diluting an acid, always add the acid to the water to avoid spattering the acid solution.

When heating substances, do it slowly. When you heat things too quickly, they can spatter, burn, or explode.

ACCURACY

- When titrating, rinse the buret not with water but with the solution to be used in the titration. If you rinse the buret with water, you might dilute the solution, which will cause the volume added from the buret to be too large.

- Allow hot objects to return to room temperature before weighing them. Hot objects on a scale create convection currents that may make the object seem lighter than it is.

- Don't weigh reagents directly on a scale. Use a glass or porcelain container to prevent corrosion of the balance pan.

- Don't contaminate your chemicals. Never insert another piece of equipment into a bottle containing a chemical. Instead you should always pour the chemical into another clean container. Also, don't let the inside of the stopper for a bottle containing a chemical touch another surface.

- When mixing chemicals, stir slowly to ensure even distribution.

- Be conscious of significant figures when you record your results. The number of significant figures that you use should indicate the accuracy of your results.

SIGNIFICANT FIGURES

When you do calculations based on measurements that you take in the lab, your answers can only be as precise as the measurements that you took. The way to make sure all your calculations reflect the precision of your measurements is to be aware of significant figures (or significant digits). The more significant figures in the numbers you use, the more precise your answer will be. The number of significant figures you use will be determined by the precision of your measuring device.

The rules for recognizing and calculating with significant figures are given below.

- Nonzero digits and zeros between nonzero digits are significant.

    | 362 | 3 significant figures |
    | 4.609 | 4 significant figures |
    | 103.06 | 5 significant figures |

- Zeros to the left of the first nonzero digit in a number are not significant.

    | 0.004 | 1 significant figure |
    | 0.0802 | 3 significant figures |

- Zeros at the end of a number to the right of the decimal point are significant.

    | 67.000 | 5 significant figures |
    | 0.030 | 2 significant figures |
    | 2.0 | 2 significant figures |

- Zeros at the end of a number greater than 1 are not significant, unless their significance is indicated by the presence of a decimal point.

2,600	2 significant figures
2,600.	4 significant figures
50	1 significant figure
50.	2 significant figures

- The coefficients of a balanced equation and numbers obtained by counting objects are infinitely significant. So if a balanced equation calls for 3 moles of carbon, we can think of it as 3.00 moles of carbon.

When multiplying and dividing, the result should have the same number of significant figures as the number in the calculation that has the smallest number of significant figures.

$$0.352 \times 0.90876 = 0.320$$

$$864 \times 12 = 1.0 \times 10^4$$

$$7.0 \times 0.567 = 12$$

When adding and subtracting, the result should have the same number of decimal places as the number in the calculation that has the smallest number of decimal places.

$$26 + 45.88 + 0.09534 = 72.$$

$$780 + 35 + 4 = 820$$

Remember: *The result of a calculation cannot be more accurate than the least accurate number in the calculation.*

And one more thing to remember for test day. Accurate and precise do NOT mean the same thing! **Accuracy** is a measure of how correct a measurement is, compared to some standard, while **precision** is a measure of how exact a measurement is, compared to the real value of the measurement.

LAB PROCEDURES

METHODS OF SEPARATION

Filtration—In filtration, solids are separated from liquids as the mixture is passed through a filter. Typically, porous paper is used as the filter. To find the amount of solid that is filtered out of a mixture, the filter paper containing the solid is allowed to dry and is then weighed. The initial weight of the clean dry filter is then subtracted from the weight of the dried filter paper and solid.

Distillation—In distillation, the differences in the boiling points of liquids can be used to separate them. The temperature of the mixture is raised to a temperature that is greater than the boiling point of the more volatile substance and lower than the boiling point of the less volatile substance. The more volatile substance will vaporize, leaving the less volatile substance as a liquid.

Chromatography—In chromatography, substances are separated by the differences in the degree to which they are adsorbed onto a surface. The substances are passed over the adsorbing surface, and the ones that stick to the surface with greater attraction will move more slowly than the substances that are less attracted to the surface. This difference in speeds is what separates the substances.

TITRATION

Titration is one of the most important laboratory procedures. In titration, an acid-base neutralization reaction is used to find the concentration of an unknown acid or base. It takes exactly 1 mole of hydroxide ions (base) to neutralize 1 mole of hydrogen ions (acid), so the concentration of an unknown acid solution can be found by finding out how much of a known basic solution is required to neutralize a sample of given volume. The most important formula in titration experiments is derived from the definition of molarity.

Molarity = moles/Liters

moles = (Molarity)(Liters)

The moment when exactly enough base has been added to the sample to neutralize the acid present is called the equivalence point. In the lab, an indicator is used to tell when the equivalence point has been reached. An indicator is a substance that is one color in acid solution and a different color in basic solution. Two popular indicators are **phenolphthalein**, which is clear in acidic solution and pink in basic solution; and **litmus**, which is pink in acidic solution and blue in basic solution.

IDENTIFYING CHEMICALS

Precipitation—Unknown ions in solution can be identified by precipitation. If you know which salts are soluble and which are insoluble, you can use process of elimination to identify unknown ions in solution. For instance, nearly all salts containing chlorine are soluble, but silver chloride is not; if you put chloride ions into a solution and a precipitate is formed, silver ions were probably present in the solution.

Conduction—You can tell whether a solution contains ions or not by checking to see if the solution conducts electricity. Ionic solutes conduct electricity in solution, nonionic solutes do not.

Flame Tests—Certain chemicals burn with distinctly colored flames. This is especially true of the alkali metals and the alkaline earth metals.

Colored Solutions—The color of a solution will sometimes indicate which chemicals are present. For instance, the colors of solutions containing transition metals will vary depending on the element present.

LABORATORY EQUIPMENT

The pictures below show some standard chemistry lab equipment.

Beaker

Buret

Burner

Dropper pipette

Rubber policeman

Safety goggles

Ring clamp

Evaporating dish

Erlenmeyer flask

Forceps

Funnel

Platform balance (triple beam)

Mortar and pestle

Metal spatula

Pipette bulb

Graduated cylinder

Thermometer

Crucible tongs

Graduated pipette

Volumetric pipette

Florence flask

Test tube

YOU'RE READY!

If you've gone through this whole book, answered our questions, and read our explanations along the way, you're going to do well on the SAT Chemistry. Take our practice tests. If you like, you can also take the SAT Chemistry Subject Tests the College Board has released.

Will there be some questions you can't answer? Of course—but that's okay. Use our elimination strategies and guess from among the choices that remain, and there will be so many questions that you can answer, you won't be bothered by the few that you have to guess at. We've taught you all the chemistry you need, so go to it, and good luck!

PART ◆ III

The Princeton Review Practice SAT Chemistry Subject Tests and Answers and Explanations

Practice SAT Chemistry
Subject Test 1

15

Practice SAT Chemistry
Subject Test 1

PRACTICE SAT CHEMISTRY
SUBJECT TEST 1

You are about to take the first of three practice SAT Chemistry Subject Tests. After answering questions 1–23, which constitute Part A, you'll be directed to answer questions 101–116, which constitute Part B. Then you will begin again at question 24. Questions 24–69 constitute Part C.

When you're ready to score yourself, refer to the scoring instructions and answer key on pages 180 and 181. Full explanations regarding the correct answers to all questions start on page 183.

Material in the following table may be useful in answering the questions in this examination.

(handwritten annotations): strong acid — NO_3, SO_4, ClO_4 → all strong acids —

PERIODIC TABLE OF THE ELEMENTS

1 H 1.0																		2 He 4.0
3 Li 6.9	4 Be 9.0											5 B 10.8	6 C 12.0	7 N 14.0	8 O 16.0	9 F 19.0	10 Ne 20.2
11 Na 23.0	12 Mg 24.3											13 Al 27.0	14 Si 28.1	15 P 31.0	16 S 32.1	17 Cl 35.5	18 Ar 39.9
19 K 39.1	20 Ca 40.1	21 Sc 45.0	22 Ti 47.9	23 V 50.9	24 Cr 52.0	25 Mn 54.9	26 Fe 55.8	27 Co 58.9	28 Ni 58.7	29 Cu 63.5	30 Zn 65.4	31 Ga 69.7	32 Ge 72.6	33 As 74.9	34 Se 79.0	35 Br 79.9	36 Kr 83.8
37 Rb 85.5	38 Sr 87.6	39 Y 88.9	40 Zr 91.2	41 Nb 92.9	42 Mo 95.9	43 Tc (98)	44 Ru 101.1	45 Rh 102.9	46 Pd 106.4	47 Ag 107.9	48 Cd 112.4	49 In 114.8	50 Sn 118.7	51 Sb 121.8	52 Te 127.6	53 I 126.9	54 Xe 131.3
55 Cs 132.9	56 Ba 137.3	57 *La 138.9	72 Hf 178.5	73 Ta 180.9	74 W 183.9	75 Re 186.2	76 Os 190.2	77 Ir 192.2	78 Pt 195.1	79 Au 197.0	80 Hg 200.6	81 Tl 204.4	82 Pb 207.2	83 Bi 209.0	84 Po (209)	85 At (210)	86 Rn (222)
87 Fr (223)	88 Ra 226.0	89 †Ac 227.0															

(handwritten annotation under Li/Na/K/Cs column): strong bases

*Lanthanum Series	58 Ce 140.1	59 Pr 140.9	60 Nd 144.2	61 Pm (145)	62 Sm 150.4	63 Eu 152.0	64 Gd 157.3	65 Tb 158.9	66 Dy 162.5	67 Ho 164.9	68 Er 167.3	69 Tm 168.9	70 Yb 173.0	71 Lu 175.0
†Actinium Series	90 Th 232.0	91 Pa 231.0	92 U 238.0	93 Np 237.0	94 Pu (244)	95 Am (243)	96 Cm (247)	97 Bk (247)	98 Cf (251)	99 Es (252)	100 Fm (258)	101 Md (258)	102 No (259)	103 Lr (260)

DO NOT DETACH FROM BOOK.

CHEMISTRY SUBJECT TEST 1

Note: For all questions involving solutions and/or chemical equations, assume that the system is in pure water unless otherwise stated.

Part A

Directions: Each set of lettered choices below refers to the numbered statements or questions immediately following it. Select the one lettered choice that best fits each statement or answers each question, and then fill in the corresponding oval on the answer sheet. A choice may be used once, more than once, or not at all in each set.

Questions 1–4

    (A)   Thermometer
    (B)   Conductivity tester
    (C)   Salt bridge
    (D)   Buret
    (E)   Graduated cylinder

1. May be used in combination with a calorimeter to compare the specific heats of two substances

2. Is used to measure the volume of a solid by water displacement

3. Useful for adding small quantities of acid into a base

4. Completes the circuit of an electrochemical cell

Questions 5–9

    (A)   Nucleic acids
    (B)   Proteins
    (C)   Carbohydrates
    (D)   Lipids
    (E)   Electrolytes

5. Always amphoteric in nature

6. Found as both straight-chained and branched polymers

7. Deoxyribose in DNA nucleotides belongs to this family of biologically important molecules

8. Always ionic in nature

9. Tend not to be water soluble, and aggregate into droplets or molecular bilayers

GO ON TO THE NEXT PAGE

Questions 10–13

(A) $Ag^+ + Br^- \rightarrow AgBr$

(B) $^{14}_{6}C \rightarrow ^{14}_{7}N + ^{0}_{-1}e$

(C) $^{234}_{92}U \rightarrow ^{230}_{90}Th + ^{4}_{2}He$

(D) $^{30}_{15}P \rightarrow ^{30}_{14}Si + ^{0}_{1}e$

(E) $2HgO \rightarrow 2Hg + O_2$

3+8
=11+5
=16+10
=26

10. Represents the decomposition of a compound into its constituent elements

E

11. Represents alpha decay

C

12. Represents an oxidation-reduction reaction

A

13. Causes the neutron-to-proton ratio in a nucleus to be lowered

B

Questions 14–16

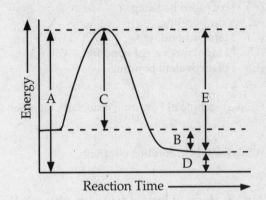

14. Is the activation energy of the reverse reaction

E

15. Is the enthalpy change of the forward reaction

B

16. Represents energy of the activated complex

A

GO ON TO THE NEXT PAGE

CHEMISTRY SUBJECT TEST 1—*Continued*

Questions 17–20

(A) Hydrogen bonding
(B) Ionic bonding
(C) Metallic bonding
(D) Nonpolar covalent bonding
(E) Polar covalent bonding

17. Holds a sample of barium iodide, BaI_2, together

18. Allows solids to conduct electricity

19. Attracts atoms of hydrogen to each other in a H_2 molecule

20. Responsible for relatively low vapor pressure of water

Questions 21–23

(A) Iron(III) chloride, $FeCl_3(s)$
(B) Iodine, $I_2(s)$
(C) Sodium hydroxide, $NaOH(s)$
(D) Sucrose, $C_{12}H_{22}O_{11}(s)$
(E) Graphite, $C(s)$

21. Gives off a purplish vapor as it sublimes

22. Can conduct electricity in the solid state

23. Its dissolution in water is highly exothermic

GO ON TO THE NEXT PAGE

CHEMISTRY SUBJECT TEST 1—*Continued*

PLEASE GO TO THE SPECIAL SECTION AT THE LOWER RIGHT-HAND CORNER OF PAGE 2 OF YOUR ANSWER SHEET LABELED CHEMISTRY AND ANSWER QUESTIONS 101–116 ACCORDING TO THE FOLLOWING DIRECTIONS.

Part B

<u>Directions:</u> Each question below consists of two statements, I in the left-hand column and II in the right-hand column. For each question, determine whether statement I is true or false <u>and</u> whether statement II is true or false and fill in the corresponding T or F ovals on your answer sheet. <u>Fill in oval CE only if statement II is a correct explanation of statement I.</u>

EXAMPLES:

	I		II
EX 1.	H_2SO_4 is a strong acid	BECAUSE	H_2SO_4 contains sulfur.
EX 2.	An atom of oxygen is electrically neutral	BECAUSE	an oxygen atom contains an equal number of protons and electrons.

SAMPLE ANSWERS

	I	II	CE
EX 1	● F	● F	○
EX 2	● F	● F	●

	I		II
101.	Carbon is a nonmetal	BECAUSE	carbon atoms can bond with each other.
102.	Two isotopes of the same element have the same mass number	BECAUSE	isotopes have the same number of protons.
103.	The density of a sample of water is doubled by doubling its mass	BECAUSE	compared to a gas, the molecules in a liquid are relatively far apart.
104.	Sodium and cesium exhibit similar chemical properties	BECAUSE	their atoms have the same number of valence electrons.
105.	An endothermic reaction can be spontaneous	BECAUSE	both enthalpy and entropy changes affect the value of a reaction's Gibbs free energy change.
106.	The 4s orbital fills before the 3d orbitals	BECAUSE	subshells fill in the order from lower to higher energy.
107.	Calcium acts as a reducing agent when it reacts with bromine	BECAUSE	mass is conserved in a chemical reaction.
108.	If an acid is added to pure water, it increases the water's pH	BECAUSE	adding an acid to water raises the hydrogen ion concentration in the water.

GO ON TO THE NEXT PAGE

	I		**II**
109.	Covalent bonds must be broken for a liquid to boil	BECAUSE	heat must be released for a liquid to change into a gas.
110.	Alpha particles can be detected using a Geiger counter	BECAUSE	all radioactive elements are highly chemically reactive.
111.	As ice absorbs heat and begins to melt, its temperature remains constant	BECAUSE	the absorbed heat is consumed by the breaking of intermolecular interactions.
112.	When a solute is added to pure water, the vapor pressure of the water will decrease	BECAUSE	all solutes dissociate into positive and negative ions.
113.	The rate of a reaction is accelerated by increasing temperature	BECAUSE	a large equilibrium constant favors the formation of product.
114.	Hydrofluoric acid, HF(*aq*), is a weaker electrolyte than hydrochloric acid, HCl(*aq*)	BECAUSE	fluorine has a lower electronegativity than chlorine.
115.	A nonpolar molecule can have polar bonds	BECAUSE	polar bonds can be symmetrically arranged in a molecule so that there are no net poles.
116.	The electrolysis of potassium iodide, KI, produces electrical energy	BECAUSE	electrons flow from the anode to the cathode.

RETURN TO THE SECTION OF YOUR ANSWER SHEET YOU STARTED FOR CHEMISTRY AND ANSWER QUESTIONS 24–69.

GO ON TO THE NEXT PAGE →

Part C

Directions: Each of the questions or incomplete statements below is followed by five suggested answers or completions. Select the one that is best in each case and then fill in the corresponding oval on the answer sheet.

24. What is the number of protons and neutrons in an atom with mass number 89 and atomic number 39?

    (A) 50 protons and 50 neutrons
    (B) 50 protons and 39 neutrons
    (C) 39 protons and 89 neutrons
    (D) 39 protons and 50 neutrons
    (E) 39 protons and 39 neutrons

25. $2 \cdot C_4H_{10}(g) + 13 O_2(g) \rightarrow 8 \cdot CO_2(g) + 10 H_2O(l)$

    When the above equation is balanced using the lowest whole-number terms, the coefficient of CO_2 is

    (A) 2
    (B) 4
    (C) 8
    (D) 10
    (E) 13

26. Which of the following is closest in mass to a proton?

    (A) Alpha particle
    (B) Positron
    (C) Neutron
    (D) Electron
    (E) Hydrogen molecule

27. What is the approximate percentage composition by mass of the element oxygen in the compound $HClO_4$?

    (A) 16%
    (B) 32%
    (C) 50%
    (D) 64%
    (E) 75%

28. If two atoms that differ in electronegativity combine by chemical reaction and share electrons, the bond that joins them will be

    (A) metallic
    (B) ionic
    (C) a hydrogen bond
    (D) nonpolar covalent
    (E) polar covalent

29. When the temperature of a 20-gram sample of water is increased from 10°C to 30°C, the heat transferred to the water is

    (A) 600 calories
    (B) 400 calories
    (C) 200 calories
    (D) 30 calories
    (E) 20 calories

30. What is the oxidation state of chromium, Cr, in the compound potassium dichromate, $K_2Cr_2O_7$?

    (A) +1
    (B) +2
    (C) +3
    (D) +6
    (E) +12

31. An aqueous solution with pH 5 at 25°C has a hydroxide ion (OH⁻) concentration of

    (A) 1×10^{-11} molar
    (B) 1×10^{-9} molar
    (C) 1×10^{-7} molar
    (D) 1×10^{-5} molar
    (E) 1×10^{-3} molar

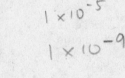

GO ON TO THE NEXT PAGE

CHEMISTRY SUBJECT TEST 1—*Continued*

32. $2H_2O(g) \rightarrow 2H_2(g) + O_2(g)$

    The volume of water vapor required to produce 44.8 liters of oxygen by the above reaction is

    (A) 11.2 liters
    (B) 22.4 liters
    (C) 44.8 liters
    (D) 89.6 liters
    (E) 100.0 liters

33. When 190 grams of $MgCl_2$ are dissolved in water and the resulting solution is 500 milliliters in volume, what is the molar concentration of $MgCl_2$ in the solution?

    (A) 2.0 M
    (B) 4.0 M
    (C) 8.0 M
    (D) 12.0 M
    (E) 16.0 M

34. When a fixed amount of gas has its Kelvin temperature doubled and its pressure doubled, the new volume of the gas is

    (A) four times greater than its original volume
    (B) twice its original volume
    (C) unchanged
    (D) one-half its original volume
    (E) one-fourth its original volume

    $\frac{2P}{2V} = \frac{P}{V}$

35. In 12.4 hours, a 100 gram sample of an element decays so that its mass is 25 grams. What is the approximate half-life of this radioactive substance?

    (A) 1.6 hours
    (B) 3.1 hours
    (C) 6.2 hours
    (D) 24.8 hours
    (E) 49.6 hours

    12.4 hours
    100 g
    6.2 = 50
    3.1

36. In the equation $Q \rightarrow {}^{4}_{2}He + {}^{216}_{85}At$, the species represented by Q is

    (A) ${}^{220}_{87}Fr$

    (B) ${}^{212}_{83}Bi$

    (C) ${}^{220}_{87}At$

    (D) ${}^{212}_{83}Fr$

    (E) ${}^{216}_{85}Bi$

37. A compound with a molecular weight of 56 amu has an empirical formula of CH_2. What is its molecular formula?

    56 AMU

    (A) C_2H_2
    (B) C_2H_4
    (C) C_4H_8
    (D) C_4H_{10}
    (E) C_6H_{12}

38. The change in heat energy for a reaction is best expressed as a change in

    (A) enthalpy
    (B) absolute temperature
    (C) specific heat
    (D) entropy
    (E) kinetic energy

39. $...NF_3(g) + ...H_2O(g) \rightarrow ...HF(g) + ...NO(g) + ...NO_2(g)$

    When the equation for the reaction above is balanced, how many moles of NF_3 would be required to react completely with 6 moles of H_2O ?

    (A) 0.5 mole
    (B) 1 mole
    (C) 2 moles
    (D) 3 moles
    (E) 4 moles

40. Which characteristic is associated with bases?

    (A) React with metal to produce hydrogen gas
    (B) Donate an unshared electron pair
    (C) Always contain the hydroxide ion in their structure
    (D) Taste sour
    (E) Formed by the reaction of a nonmetal oxide and water

GO ON TO THE NEXT PAGE

41. An element has the following properties: shiny, brittle, poor electrical conductivity, and high melting point. This element can be best classified as a(n)

    (A) alkali metal
    (B) halogen
    (C) metalloid
    (D) transition metal
    (E) noble gas

42. Which of the following forward processes produces a decrease in entropy?

    I. $H_2O(g) \rightarrow H_2O(l)$
    II. $Fe^{2+}(aq) + S^{2-}(aq) \rightarrow FeS(s)$
    III. $2SO_3(g) \rightleftharpoons 2SO_2(g) + O_2(g)$

    (A) I only
    (B) III only
    (C) I and II only
    (D) II and III only
    (E) I, II, and III

43. Which of the following will raise the boiling point of a sample of water?

    (A) Heat the water
    (B) Mix gasoline into the water
    (C) Bring the water sample to a higher altitude
    (D) Place the water sample on a magnetic stirrer
    (E) Dissolve table sugar into the water

44. Elements H and J lie in the same period. If the atoms of H are smaller than the atoms of J, then compared to atoms of J, atoms of H are most likely to

    (A) exist in a greater number of isotopes
    (B) exist in a lesser number of isotopes
    (C) exist in a greater number of oxidation states
    (D) have a greater positive charge in their nuclei
    (E) have a lesser positive charge in their nuclei

45. $\underline{\quad} Al(s) + \underline{\quad} O_2(g) \rightarrow \underline{\quad} Al_2O_3(s)$

    When the equation representing the reaction shown above is completed and balanced and all coefficients are reduced to lowest whole-number terms, the coefficient of $O_2(g)$ is

    (A) 1
    (B) 2
    (C) 3
    (D) 4
    (E) 6

46. Which of the following solids has a brilliant blue color?

    (A) $Ca(OH)_2$
    (B) KCl
    (C) NaBr
    (D) Fe_2O_3
    (E) $CuSO_4$

47. Twenty-five percent of element X exists as ^{210}X and 75 percent of it exists as ^{214}X. What is the atomic weight of element X in amu?

    (A) 85
    (B) 211
    (C) 212
    (D) 213
    (E) 214

48. A 600-milliliters container holds 2 moles of $O_2(g)$, 3 moles of $H_2(g)$, and 1 mole of He(g). Total pressure within the container is 760 torr. What is the partial pressure of O_2?

    (A) 127 torr
    (B) 253 torr
    (C) 380 torr
    (D) 507 torr
    (E) 760 torr

GO ON TO THE NEXT PAGE

49. $Fe(OH)_3(s) \rightleftharpoons Fe^{3+}(aq) + 3OH^-(aq)$

The ionic solid $Fe(OH)_3$ is added to water and dissociates into its component ions, as shown above. The solubility product expression for the saturated solution is

(A) $K_{sp} = [Fe^{3+}][OH^-]$
(B) $K_{sp} = [Fe^{3+}][3OH^-]$
(C) $K_{sp} = [Fe^{3+}][3OH^-]^3$
(D) $K_{sp} = [Fe^{3+}][OH^-]^3$
(E) $K_{sp} = \dfrac{[Fe^{3+}][OH^-]^3}{[Fe(OH)_3]}$

50. Which of the following electron configurations represent an atom of magnesium in an excited state?

(A) $1s^22s^22p^6$
(B) $1s^22s^22p^63s^2$
(C) $1s^22s^22p^53s^23p^2$
(D) $1s^22s^22p^63s^13p^1$
(E) $1s^22s^22p^63s^13p^2$

51. All of the following when added to water will produce an electrolytic solution EXCEPT

(A) $N_2(g)$
(B) $HCl(g)$
(C) $KOH(s)$
(D) $NaI(s)$
(E) $CaCl_2(s)$

52. $NH_3(aq) + H_2CO_3(aq) \rightleftharpoons NH_4^+(aq) + HCO_3^-(aq)$

In the reaction represented above, NH_4^+ acts as a(n)

(A) indicator
(B) hydrate
(C) acid
(D) base
(E) salt

53. Which species has the ground state electron configuration $1s^22s^22p^63s^23p^6$?

(A) Sulfide ion, S^{2-}
(B) Bromide ion, Br^-
(C) Neon atom, Ne
(D) Chromium ion, Cr^{3+}
(E) Potassium atom, K

54. Which of the following species is amphoteric?

(A) Na_3PO_4
(B) HSO_4^-
(C) KOH
(D) HNO_3
(E) $C_2O_4^{2-}$

55. An ideal gas has a volume of 10 liters at 20°C and a pressure of 750 mmHg. Which of the following expressions is needed to determine the volume of the same amount of gas at STP?

(A) $10 \times \dfrac{750}{760} \times \dfrac{0}{20}$ L
(B) $10 \times \dfrac{750}{760} \times \dfrac{293}{273}$ L
(C) $10 \times \dfrac{760}{750} \times \dfrac{0}{20}$ L
(D) $10 \times \dfrac{760}{750} \times \dfrac{273}{293}$ L
(E) $10 \times \dfrac{750}{760} \times \dfrac{273}{293}$ L

GO ON TO THE NEXT PAGE

Questions 56–57 pertain to the phase diagram for substance Z below:

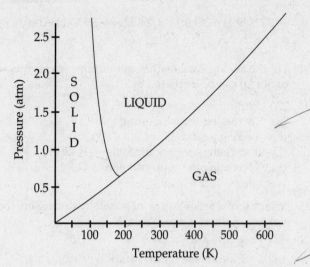

56. Substance Z is at 0.5 atm and 200 K. If the pressure on substance Z is steadily increased and its temperature is kept constant, what phase change will eventually occur?

(A) Condensation
(B) Freezing
(C) Melting
(D) Sublimation
(E) Vaporization

57. The normal boiling point of substance Z is closest to

(A) 100 K
(B) 200 K
(C) 300 K
(D) 400 K
(E) 500 K

58. The shape of a PCl_3 molecule is described as

(A) bent
(B) trigonal pyramidal
(C) linear
(D) trigonal planar
(E) tetrahedral

59. What volume of 0.4 M $Ba(OH)_2$ (aq) is needed to exactly neutralize 100 milliliters of 0.2 M HBr(aq)?

(A) 25 ml
(B) 50 ml
(C) 100 ml
(D) 200 ml
(E) 400 ml

60. Which of the following is true regarding the aqueous dissociation of HCN, $K_a = 4.9 \times 10^{-10}$ at 25°C ?

I. At equilibrium, $[H^+] = [CN^-]$
II. At equilibrium, $[H^+] > [HCN]$
III. HCN(aq) is a strong acid.

(A) I only
(B) II only
(C) I and II only
(D) II and III only
(E) I, II, and III

61. Which of the following atoms has the largest second ionization energy?

(A) Silicon, Si
(B) Calcium, Ca
(C) Chlorine, Cl
(D) Iron, Fe
(E) Sodium, Na

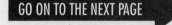GO ON TO THE NEXT PAGE

Question 62 refers to the overall reaction and half-reactions with standard reduction potentials below.

$$2Fe^{2+} + Cl_2 \rightarrow 2Fe^{3+} + 2Cl^-$$

$$Fe^{3+} + e^- \rightarrow Fe^{2+}; E^\circ_{red} = 0.77 \text{ volts}$$

$$Cl_2 + 2e^- \rightarrow 2Cl^-; E^\circ_{red} = 1.36 \text{ volts}$$

62. The standard potential difference of an electrochemical cell using the overall reaction above is

(A) 0.18 volts
(B) 0.59 volts
(C) 1.05 volts
(D) 2.13 volts
(E) 2.90 volts

63. The reaction of zinc metal, Zn, and hydrochloric acid, HCl, produces which of the following?

I. $H_2(g)$
II. $Cl_2(g)$
III. $Zn^{2+}(aq)$

(A) II only
(B) III only
(C) I and II only
(D) I and III only
(E) I, II, and III

Questions 64–65 refer to the following reaction:

$$2H_2S(g) + 3O_2(g) \rightleftharpoons 2SO_2(g) + 2H_2O(g) + \text{heat}$$

64. For the above reaction, the equilibrium concentration of $SO_2(g)$ can be increased by

(A) adding neon gas
(B) increasing the temperature
(C) adding a catalyst
(D) increasing the concentration of $H_2O(g)$
(E) increasing the concentration of $O_2(g)$

65. Which of the following is increased by decreasing the volume of the reaction system?

I. Rate of reaction
II. Equilibrium concentration of reactants
III. Value of K_{eq}

(A) I only
(B) III only
(C) I and II only
(D) II and III only
(E) I, II, and III

GO ON TO THE NEXT PAGE

66. $Fe_2O_3(s) + 3CO(g) \rightarrow 2Fe(s) + 3CO_2(g)$

When 3 moles of Fe_2O_3 are allowed to completely react with 56 grams of CO according to the above equation, approximately how many moles of iron, Fe, are produced?

(A) 0.7
(B) 1.3
(C) 2.0
(D) 2.7
(E) 6.0

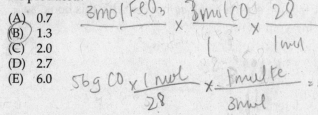

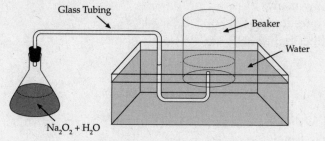

Glass Tubing

Beaker

Water

$Na_2O_2 + H_2O$

$2Na_2O_2(s) + 2H_2O(l) \rightarrow 4NaOH(aq) + O_2(g)$

67. Sodium peroxide, Na_2O_2, and water react in the flask at 25°C according to the equation and in the diagram above. If water levels are equal inside and outside the beaker, then the gas pressure inside the beaker is equal to the

(A) pressure of oxygen gas collected
(B) vapor pressure of water at 25°C
(C) sum of pressure of oxygen gas collected and atmospheric pressure
(D) sum of vapor pressure of water at 25°C and atmospheric pressure
(E) sum of pressure of oxygen gas collected and vapor pressure of water at 25°C

$NaO_2 + H_2O$ @25°

68. Which of the following molecules has the strongest carbon-to-carbon bond?

(A) C_2H_2
(B) C_2H_4
(C) C_2H_6
(D) C_3H_8
(E) C_4H_{10}

69. $N_2O_4(g) \rightleftharpoons 2NO_2(g)$

The following concentration data were gathered for the above reaction at 5 minute intervals from the start of an experiment:

Time After Start of Experiment	$[N_2O_4]$	$[NO_2]$
0 min (start)	0.00 M	0.50 M
5 min	0.10 M	0.33 M
10 min	0.20 M	0.20 M
15 min	0.25 M	0.15 M
20 min	0.28 M	0.13 M
25 min	0.28 M	0.13 M

If the experiment was carried out in a closed system at constant temperature, then during which time interval (from the start of the experiment) did the reaction most likely achieve equilibrium?

(A) 0 min (start) to 5 min
(B) 5 min to 10 min
(C) 10 min to 15 min
(D) 15 min to 20 min
(E) 20 min to 25 min

STOP

IF YOU FINISH BEFORE TIME IS CALLED, YOU MAY CHECK YOUR WORK ON THIS TEST ONLY.
DO NOT TURN TO ANY OTHER TEST IN THIS BOOK.

HOW TO SCORE THE PRINCETON REVIEW PRACTICE SAT CHEMISTRY SUBJECT TEST

When you take the real exam, the proctors will collect your test booklet and bubble sheet and send your answer sheet to New Jersey where a computer looks at the pattern of filled-in ovals on your answer sheet and gives you a score. We couldn't include even a small computer with this book, so we are providing this more primitive way of scoring your exam.

DETERMINING YOUR SCORE

STEP 1   Using the answer key on the next page, determine how many questions you got right and how many you got wrong on the test. Remember, questions that you do not answer don't count as either right or wrong answers.

STEP 2   List the number of right answers here.

(A) _____

STEP 3   List the number of wrong answers here. Now divide that number by 4. (Use a calculator if you're feeling particularly lazy.)

(B) _____ ÷ 4 = (C) _____

STEP 4   Subtract the number of wrong answers divided by 4 from the number of correct answers. Round this score to the nearest whole number. This is your raw score.

(A) _____ – (C) _____ = _____

STEP 5   To determine your real score, take the number from Step 4 above, and look it up in the left column of the Score Conversion Table on page 182; the corresponding score on the right is your score on the exam.

ANSWERS TO THE PRINCETON REVIEW
PRACTICE SAT CHEMISTRY SUBJECT TEST 1

Question Number	Correct Answer	Right	Wrong	Question Number	Correct Answer	Right	Wrong
1.	A	___	___	46.	E	___	___
2.	E	___	___	47.	D	___	___
3.	D	___	___	48.	B	___	___
4.	C	___	___	49.	D	___	___
5.	B	___	___	50.	D	___	___
6.	C	___	___	51.	A	___	___
7.	C	___	___	52.	C	___	___
8.	E	___	___	53.	A	___	___
9.	D	___	___	54.	B	___	___
10.	E	___	___	55.	E	___	___
11.	C	___	___	56.	A	___	___
12.	E	___	___	57.	C	___	___
13.	B	___	___	58.	B	___	___
14.	E	___	___	59.	A	___	___
15.	B	___	___	60.	A	___	___
16.	A	___	___	61.	E	___	___
17.	B	___	___	62.	B	___	___
18.	C	___	___	63.	D	___	___
19.	D	___	___	64.	E	___	___
20.	A	___	___	65.	A	___	___
21.	B	___	___	66.	B	___	___
22.	E	___	___	67.	E	___	___
23.	C	___	___	68.	A	___	___
24.	D	___	___	69.	D	___	___
25.	C	___	___				
26.	C	___	___				
27.	D	___	___	101.	T, T		
28.	E	___	___	102.	F, T		
29.	B	___	___	103.	F, F		
30.	D	___	___	104.	T, T, CE		
31.	B	___	___	105.	T, T, CE		
32.	D	___	___	106.	T, T, CE		
33.	B	___	___	107.	T, T		
34.	C	___	___	108.	F, T		
35.	C	___	___	109.	F, F		
36.	A	___	___	110.	T, F		
37.	C	___	___	111.	T, T, CE		
38.	A	___	___	112.	T, F		
39.	E	___	___	113.	T, T		
40.	B	___	___	114.	T, F		
41.	C	___	___	115.	T, T, CE		
42.	C	___	___	116.	F, T		
43.	E	___	___				
44.	D	___	___				
45.	C	___	___				

THE PRINCETON REVIEW PRACTICE SAT CHEMISTRY SUBJECT TEST SCORE CONVERSION TABLE

Raw Score	Scaled Score	Raw Score	Scaled Score	Raw Score	Scaled Score
85	800	45	620	5	390
84	800	44	620	4	390
83	800	43	610	3	380
82	800	42	610	2	380
81	800	41	600	1	370
80	800	40	590	0	370
79	800	39	590	−1	370
78	790	38	580	−2	360
77	780	37	580	−3	360
76	780	36	570	−4	350
75	780	35	560	−5	340
74	780	34	560	−6	340
73	780	33	550	−7	330
72	770	32	550	−8	330
71	770	31	540	−9	320
70	750	30	530	−10	310
69	750	29	530	−11	310
68	740	28	520	−12	300
67	740	27	520	−13	300
66	740	26	520	−14	290
65	730	25	510	−15	280
64	730	24	510	−16	280
63	710	23	500	−17	270
62	710	22	500	−18	270
61	710	21	490	−19	260
60	700	20	480	−20	250
59	700	19	480	−21	250
58	690	18	470		
57	690	17	470		
56	680	16	460		
55	680	15	450		
54	680	14	450		
53	670	13	440		
52	670	12	440		
51	660	11	430		
50	650	10	420		
49	650	9	420		
48	630	8	410		
47	630	7	410		
46	630	6	400		

Practice SAT Chemistry Subject Test 1: Answers and Explanations

PART A

QUESTIONS 1–4

(A) Thermometer
(B) Conductivity tester
(C) Salt bridge
(D) Buret
(E) Graduated cylinder

1. May be used in combination with a calorimeter
   to compare the specific heats of two substances

A is correct. When we talk about specific heat, we're talking about the amount of heat necessary to produce a change in temperature. The calorimeter can be used to measure heat input or output, and the thermometer, choice A, would be used in combination with it to ascertain the associated change in temperature.

2. Is used to measure the volume of a solid by
   water displacement

E is correct. A graduated cylinder can be used to help find the volume of an irregularly-shaped solid. How? Fill the graduated cylinder with water, and read the water's volume. Next add the solid. The difference between the volume of both the water and solid and the volume of the water alone is the volume of the solid.

3. Useful for adding small quantities of acid
   into a base

D is correct. When an acid and base are combined, think *titration*, and when you consider titration remember that a buret is typically used to deliver small amounts of acid into a base and vice versa.

4. Completes the circuit of an electrochemical
   cell

C is correct. Electrons travel from the anode to the cathode in an electrochemical cell. But what allows the redox reaction to go on by maintaining charge neutrality in each vessel? That's the function of a salt bridge. The salt bridge completes the circuit of the electrochemical cell.

QUESTIONS 5–9

(A) Nucleic acids
(B) Proteins
(C) Carbohydrates
(D) Lipids
(E) Electrolytes

5. Always amphoteric in nature

B is correct. An amphoteric molecule can act either as an acid or a base. Proteins are polypeptides made from amino acids, and all amino acids have both an acid group (carboxylic acid group) and a base group (amino group). Therefore, proteins are always amphoteric.

6. Found as both straight-chained and branched
   polymers

C is correct. Proteins and carbohydrates are both polymers; however, only carbohydrates commonly form branched polymers. Glycogen and cellulose are both carbohydrate polymers made up of glucose monomers; glycogen is a highly branched polymer while cellulose is primarily straight-chained.

7. Deoxyribose in DNA nucleotides belongs to this
   family of biologically important molecules

C is correct. Deoxyribose is a ribose sugar molecule missing an oxygen atom. As with all molecules with the suffix *-ose*, ribose is a carbohydrate. In general, proteins tend to have the suffix *-in* (or *-ase* if they are an enzyme) and nucleic acids have the suffix *-ine* (except for uracil).

8. Always ionic in nature

E is correct. Electrolytes are substances that increase the electrical conductivity of water by dissolving in solution to form ions. Therefore, all ionic compounds, or salts, are electrolytes.

9. Tend not to be water soluble, and aggregate into
   droplets or molecular bilayers

D is correct. Most lipids are insoluble in water. For example, fat-based oils (such as corn oil), a subfamily of lipids, form droplets in water. Several other fat derivatives form double-layered sheets in water; this type of lipids serves as the principle structural element in cell membranes.

QUESTIONS 10–13

(A) $Ag^+ + Br^- \rightarrow AgBr$

(B) $^{14}_{6}C \rightarrow ^{14}_{7}N + ^{0}_{-1}e$

(C) $^{234}_{92}U \rightarrow ^{230}_{90}Th + ^{4}_{2}He$

(D) $^{30}_{15}P \rightarrow ^{30}_{14}Si + ^{0}_{1}e$

(E) $2HgO \rightarrow 2Hg + O_2$

10. Represents the decomposition of a compound into
    its constituent elements

E is correct. Don't let phrases such as "constituent elements" throw you off course. The question asks you to identify a situation in which a compound is broken down into its elements. Mercury(II) oxide, HgO, is decomposed into the elements mercury, Hg, and oxygen, O_2, in choice E.

11. Represents alpha decay

C is correct. When a radioactive atom undergoes alpha decay, it loses 2 protons and 2 neutrons. That means that its atomic number decreases by 2, and its mass number decreases by 4. That's exactly what has happened here. Uranium (atomic number = 92, mass number = 234) has been converted to thorium (atomic number = 90, mass number = 230).

12. Represents an oxidation-reduction reaction

E is correct. The phrase "oxidation-reduction reaction" describes a reaction in which one atom loses electron(s) to another. The atom that loses electrons is oxidized, and the one that gains electrons is reduced. In HgO, the oxidation state of Hg is +2 and that of oxygen is –2. HgO is decomposed into the free elements Hg and O_2, each of which has an oxidation state of 0. So the oxidation state of Hg goes from +2 to 0; it has been reduced. Oxygen has been oxidized; its oxidation state has changed from –2 to 0. This is clearly a redox reaction.

13. Causes the neutron-to-proton ratio in a nucleus to be lowered

B is correct. Look at choice B. In an atom of carbon-14 there are 8 neutrons and 6 protons, a ratio greater than 1. In nitrogen-14, the neutron-to-proton ratio is 7:7 or equivalent to 1. Choice B is an example of beta decay. As you can see, beta decay causes the neutron-to-proton ratio to decrease.

QUESTIONS 14–16

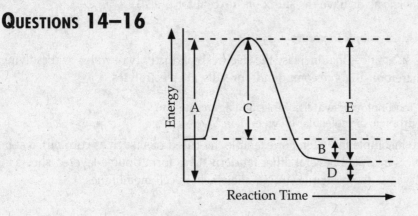

14. Is the activation energy of the reverse reaction

E is correct. The activation energy of forward and reverse reactions is always characterized by the "hump" that you see in pictures of this kind. It's the energy necessary to get the reaction going. The reactants of the reverse reaction have energy that is expressed by the flat portion of the curve to the right of the hump. For a reaction to occur, these reactants must gain an energy equal to that represented by the top of the hump. This energy that must be acquired is represented by E. Remember that catalysts reduce activation energy and the rate of the reaction.

15. Is the enthalpy change of the forward reaction

B is correct. The enthalpy change of a reaction is the amount of heat the reaction absorbs or gives off. In this case, the reactants begin at one energy level (represented by the flat portion of the curve to the left of the hump), and the products are associated with another (represented by the flat portion of the curve to the right of the hump). The difference represents the enthalpy change of the reaction (which, in this case, is negative—the reaction liberates heat; it's exothermic).

16. Represents energy of the activated complex

A is correct. Recall that the activated complex represents the highest energy state reactants achieve as they are transformed into new substances. So the energy of the activated complex is measured from the very bottom of the diagram to the top of the activation energy barrier. This distance is represented by A.

QUESTIONS 17–20

    (A) Hydrogen bonding
    (B) Ionic bonding
    (C) Metallic bonding
    (D) Nonpolar covalent bonding
    (E) Polar covalent bonding

17. Holds a sample of barium iodide, BaI_2, together

B is correct. BaI_2 is composed of a metal (Ba) and nonmetal (I) bonded together. This is an ionic compound which is held together by—surprise—ionic bonding.

18. Allows solids to conduct electricity

C is correct. You may be tempted to go with "ionic bonding" here, but resist that impulse. The ions in an ionic solid are too restricted in their movement to conduct a charge, so B is incorrect. Now think: What solids conduct electricity? Metals, of course. And why can copper wire be used to conduct electricity? Because the metallic bonds that hold a sample of copper together do so through the motion of many free electrons, which can conduct electricity as they move.

19. Attracts atoms of hydrogen to each other in a H_2 molecule

D is correct. Don't be fooled by A. Hydrogen bonds occur *between*, not *within* molecules. A hydrogen molecule consists of nonmetal hydrogen atoms in a bond. Nonmetals form covalent bonds, and identical nonmetal atoms form nonpolar covalent bonds.

20. Responsible for relatively low vapor pressure of water

A is correct. Water's vapor pressure (its tendency to evaporate) is low compared to other similarly-sized molecules. What keeps molecules together in the liquid state? Intermolecular forces do, and the intermolecular force most prevalent in water is hydrogen bonding. Since hydrogen bonds are a relatively strong intermolecular force, water molecules are significantly attracted to each other, and water does not evaporate readily.

QUESTIONS 21–23

    (A) Iron(III) chloride, $FeCl_3(s)$
    (B) Iodine, $I_2(s)$
    (C) Sodium hydroxide, $NaOH(s)$
    (D) Sucrose, $C_{12}H_{22}O_{11}(s)$
    (E) Graphite, $C(s)$

21. Gives off a purplish vapor as it sublimes

B is correct. You might be asking yourself: purplish vapor? How am I supposed to know that? Unfortunately there will be a few questions on the test that will test your familiarity with the properties of certain substances. We hope your experiences in chemistry lab will carry you through. If not, don't panic. You'll see only a few of these types of questions. Iodine is a grayish-purple solid that gives off a similarly colored vapor as it sublimes.

22. Can conduct electricity in the solid state

E is correct. If you don't know that graphite, a form of carbon, can conduct electricity, you can still get the answer by eliminating the other choices. A and C are ionic solids—they can conduct electricity in solution or in the molten state, but not as solids. Choices B and D (table sugar) are molecular solids. You wouldn't expect molecular solids to be particularly conductive. That leaves graphite, which is a network solid.

23. Its dissolution in water is highly exothermic

C is correct. If you've dissolved sodium hydroxide pellets in a beaker of water and felt the side of the beaker, you know that the process gives off heat.

PART B

101. Carbon is a nonmetal   BECAUSE   carbon atoms can bond with each other.

T, T Use the divide and conquer strategy. Carbon is a nonmetal, so statement I is true. Do carbon atoms bond with each other? They sure do. Otherwise we wouldn't have oils, waxes, fossil fuels, diamonds, and literally thousands of different substances. Now, does the sentence make sense? No. Metal atoms can also bond with each other, so this ability is not unique to nonmetals. Fill in both true ovals, but not the CE oval.

102. Two isotopes of the same   BECAUSE   isotopes have the same number of
      element have the same mass   protons.
      number

F, T Isotopes of the same element do not have the same mass number, but since they are the same element, their atomic numbers are identical. The first statement is false and the second is true.

103. The density of a sample of   BECAUSE   compared to a gas, the molecules
      water is doubled by doubling   in a liquid are relatively far apart.
      its mass

F, F Divide and conquer. At a given temperature, the density of water stays the same whether we have 10 grams or 20 grams, so statement I is false. Statement II is also false: Molecules in the liquid (and solid) state are much closer than they are in the gaseous state.

104. Sodium and cesium exhibit   BECAUSE   their atoms have the same number
      similar chemical properties   of valence electrons.

T, T, CE Sodium and cesium are both in the alkali metal family. As such, they have similar chemical properties, so statement I is true. Statement II is also true: Alkali metals such as sodium and cesium have 1 valence electron in their atoms. Do the two statements make sense when they are combined? Do sodium and cesium exhibit similar chemical properties because their atoms have the same number of valence electrons? Yes, so fill in oval CE.

105. An endothermic reaction   BECAUSE   both enthalpy and entropy changes
     can be spontaneous   affect the value of a reaction's
                                            Gibbs free energy change.

T, T, CE Divide and conquer. Can an endothermic reaction be spontaneous? Have you ever seen an ice cube melt at room temperature? That's a spontaneous endothermic process, so the first statement is true. What about the second statement? Remember that the change in Gibbs free energy, ΔG, depends on enthalpy change, ΔH, and entropy change, ΔS: $\Delta G = \Delta H - T \Delta S$. Statement II is also true. Does the second statement explain the first? Yes, it does. That ice cube melts at room temperature because the increase in entropy for the process overcomes the change to a higher energy state. Fill in the CE oval.

106. The 4s orbital fills before   BECAUSE   subshells fill in the order from lower
     the 3d orbitals   to higher energy.

T, T, CE The first statement is true. The 3d orbitals are of higher energy than the 4s orbital, so the 4s orbital fills first. Evaluate the second statement. It is true. Subshells *do* fill in order of lower to higher energy. Does the second statement explain the first? Yes, it does. The 4s orbital fills before the 3d orbitals because it is lower in energy. Fill in oval CE.

107. Calcium acts as a reducing   BECAUSE   mass is conserved in a chemical
     agent when it reacts with   reaction.
     bromine

T, T Divide and conquer. Here's what happens when calcium and bromine react: $Ca + Br_2 \rightarrow CaBr_2$. Bromine's oxidation state decreases from 0 to –1; it is reduced. Calcium (which is oxidized) is responsible for reducing bromine. In other words, calcium acts as a reducing agent. Statement I is true. Look at statement II. Is mass conserved in a chemical reaction? Yes. If it weren't, there would be no need to balance equations. Both statements are true. Does statement II explain why statement I is true? No, it doesn't. Do not fill in oval CE.

108. If an acid is added to pure   BECAUSE   adding an acid to water raises the
     water, it increases the   hydrogen ion concentration in
     water's pH   water.

F, T Adding an acid to water increases the hydrogen ion concentration in the water, which means that the water's pH is *reduced*. The first statement is false and the second is true.

109. Covalent bonds must be   BECAUSE   heat must be released for a liquid
     broken for a liquid to boil   to change into a gas.

F, F For a liquid to boil, the intermolecular forces in the liquid must be overcome, not the bonds within individual molecules. When water boils, its H_2O molecules are still intact. While we're considering boiling, take a look at statement II. You need to heat water to make it boil, so boiling absorbs, not releases, heat. Both statements are false.

110. Alpha particles can be   BECAUSE   all radioactive elements are highly
     detected using a Geiger   chemically reactive.
     counter

T, F Divide and conquer. A Geiger counter is used to detect radioactive particles, so statement I is true. Be careful with statement II. Radioactive elements have atoms with unstable nuclei. However, that has nothing to do with an atom's valence electrons. Radon (Rn) is a perfect example. The nuclei of radon atoms emit alpha particles. However, radon is a noble gas. Radon atoms have filled valence shells and are therefore unreactive chemically. Statement II is false.

111. As ice absorbs heat and   BECAUSE   the absorbed heat is consumed by
     begins to melt, its temperature   the breaking of intermolecular
     remains constant   interactions.

T, T, CE The first statement is true. If the temperature of a substance didn't remain constant during melting there would be no such thing as a melting point. Instead, at a given pressure, a substance would melt over a range of temperatures. Statement II is also true. The heat absorbed by the ice is being used to break intermolecular hydrogen bonds, so we don't see the temperature rise although heat is being added. Does the second statement explain the first? Yes, it does. Since the average kinetic energy of molecules stays constant during a phase change (such as melting), the temperature also remains constant. Fill in the CE oval.

112. When a solute is added to   BECAUSE   all solutes dissociate into positive
     pure water, the vapor pressure   and negative ions.
     of the water will decrease

T, F The first statement is true. Adding a solute to a solvent reduces its freezing point, raises its boiling point, and reduces its vapor pressure. The second statement is false. Some, but not all, solutes dissociate into positive and negative ions.

113. The rate of a reaction is   BECAUSE   a large equilibrium constant favors
     accelerated by increasing   the formation of product.
     temperature

T, T Divide and conquer. Statement I is true. A reaction will proceed more quickly if its temperature is raised. Look at the second statement. A large K_{eq} absolutely means that a reaction favors the forward reaction or, in other words, favors product formation. Both statements are true. Put them together. Does the second explain the first? No, it doesn't. The first deals with reaction rates (kinetics) and the second with equilibrium. These are different areas of chemistry, so don't fill in CE.

114. Hydrofluoric acid, HF(*aq*), is   BECAUSE   fluorine has a lower
     a weaker electrolyte than   electronegativity than chlorine.
     hydrochloric acid, HCl (*aq*)

T, F Hydrofluoric acid is not one of the six common strong acids; thus, it will partially ionize and is a weak electrolyte. Hydrochloric acid is a strong acid, and it ionizes completely. So HCl(*aq*) is a strong electrolyte. Statement I is true. The second statement is false. Remember that electronegativity values decrease down a given column. So from fluorine to chlorine, electronegativity decreases.

115. A nonpolar molecule can   BECAUSE   polar bonds can be symmetrically
     have polar bonds   arranged in a molecule so that
                                                      there are no net poles.

T, T, CE The first statement is true. An example of this is the carbon tetrachloride molecule, CCl_4. It consists of four polar bonds. However, the bonds are arranged such that the overall molecule is nonpolar. Therefore, the second statement is true. Since the second statement explains the first, fill in the CE oval.

116. The electrolysis of potassium   BECAUSE   electrons flow from the anode to
iodide, KI, produces electrical   the cathode.
energy

F, T Divide and conquer. Does electrolysis generate electricity? No, electrolysis involves the *use* of electrical energy to force a chemical reaction to occur, so statement I is false. What about statement II? It's true. Electrons flow from the anode to the cathode in both electrochemical and electrolytic cells.

PART C

24. What is the number of protons and neutrons in an atom with mass number 89 and atomic number 39?

    (A) 50 protons and 50 neutrons
    (B) 50 protons and 39 neutrons
    (C) 39 protons and 89 neutrons
    (D) 39 protons and 50 neutrons
    (E) 39 protons and 39 neutrons

D is correct. The atomic number is the number of protons in the nucleus, and the mass number is the sum: number of protons + number of neutrons. If the atomic number is 39 and the mass number is 89, then the number of neutrons in the nucleus must be (89) − (39) = 50.

25. $\ldots C_4H_{10}(g) + \ldots O_2(g) \rightarrow \ldots CO_2(g) + \ldots H_2O(l)$

When the above equation is balanced using the lowest whole-number terms, the coefficient of CO_2 is

    (A) 2
    (B) 4
    (C) 8
    (D) 10
    (E) 13

C is correct. Use the plug-in balancing strategy. Since there are at least 4 carbon atoms on the left, the coefficient of CO_2 cannot be 2, so eliminate A. If the coefficient of carbon is 4, we must place a 1 in front of C_4H_{10} to keep carbons in balance. This will give 10 hydrogens on the left. If we put a 5 in front of H_2O on the right, we then have 13 oxygens on the right. The only way we can get 13 oxygens on the left is to place $\frac{13}{2}$ in front of O_2 on the left. This puts all the elements in balance, but violates the rule of using only whole numbers, so B is wrong. However, if we multiply the coefficients we just determined by 2, we will maintain balance and have all whole numbers. So the balanced equation becomes: $2C_4H_{10}(g) + 13O_2(g) \rightarrow 8CO_2(g) + 10H_2O(l)$.

26. Which of the following is closest in mass to a proton?

    (A) Alpha particle
    (B) Positron
    (C) Neutron
    (D) Electron
    (E) Hydrogen molecule

C is correct. The mass of a proton is approximately 1 amu, and this is very nearly the mass of a neutron. A positron and an electron are both much lighter than 1 amu. A hydrogen molecule weighs roughly twice as much as a proton, and an alpha particle weighs about four times as much.

27. What is the approximate percentage composition by mass of the element oxygen in the compound $HClO_4$?

   (A) 16%
   (B) 32%
   (C) 50%
   (D) 64%
   (E) 75%

D is correct. Add up the mass of 1 mole of this substance. From the periodic table, we know that

- 1 mole of hydrogen atoms has a mass of about 1 g.

- 1 mole of chlorine atoms has a mass of about 35 g.

- 4 moles of oxygen atoms have a mass of about 64 g.

The total gram-molecular weight of this substance, then, is 100 g. Oxygen's contribution is 64 g, which means the compound is 64 percent oxygen by mass.

28. If two atoms that differ in electronegativity combine by chemical reaction and share electrons, the bond that joins them will be

   (A) metallic
   (B) ionic
   (C) a hydrogen bond
   (D) nonpolar covalent
   (E) polar covalent

E is correct. As soon as you hear the term *electron sharing*, you know you're dealing with a covalent bond, so eliminate A, B, and C. The fact that the two atoms differ in electronegativity tells you that one has more attraction for the shared electrons than the other. The result? A polar covalent bond—the molecule has a negative and a positive pole.

29. When the temperature of a 20-gram sample of water is increased from 10°C to 30°C, the heat transferred to the water is

   (A) 600 calories
   (B) 400 calories
   (C) 200 calories
   (D) 30 calories
   (E) 20 calories

B is correct. Use $q = mc\Delta T$ to compute the amount of heat transfer. For water, the specific heat, c, is about 1 calorie/g–°C, so a 20 g sample of water experiencing a 20°C increase in temperature has (20 g) (1 calorie/g–°C)(20° C), or 400 calories of heat, transferred to it.

30. What is the oxidation state of chromium, Cr, in the compound potassium dichromate, $K_2Cr_2O_7$?

(A) +1
(B) +2
(C) +3
(D) +6
(E) +12

D is correct. Remember the oxidation state rules. An oxygen atom usually has a –2 state. Potassium atoms are always given a +1 state. In $K_2Cr_2O_7$, we have 2 potassium atoms and 7 oxygen atoms. So potassium atoms contribute 2(+1) or a state of +2. Oxygen atoms contribute 2(–7) or –14. For $K_2Cr_2O_7$ to be neutral, each chromium atom must have a state of +6.

31. An aqueous solution with pH 5 at 25°C has a hydroxide ion (OH⁻) concentration of

(A) 1×10^{-11} molar
(B) 1×10^{-9} molar
(C) 1×10^{-7} molar
(D) 1×10^{-5} molar
(E) 1×10^{-3} molar

B is correct. If the pH is 5, then [H⁺] is 1×10^{-5} moles/L. Water's ion product is 1×10^{-14} at 25°C, meaning that the product [H⁺] × [OH⁻] is 1×10^{-14}. So [OH⁻] = $(1 \times 10^{-14})(1 \times 10^{-5}) = 1 \times 10^{-9}$ moles/L. B is correct.

32.
$$2H_2O(g) \rightarrow 2H_2(g) + O_2(g)$$

The volume of water vapor required to produce 44.8 liters of oxygen by the above reaction is

(A) 11.2 liters
(B) 22.4 liters
(C) 44.8 liters
(D) 89.6 liters
(E) 100.0 liters

D is correct. Based on the balanced equation, the ratio of water vapor consumed to oxygen produced is 2 moles H_2O to 1 mole O_2. The volume of gas will also be in this 2:1 ratio. So 89.6 liters of $H_2O(g)$ are required to produce 44.8 liters of $O_2(g)$.

33. When 190 grams of $MgCl_2$ are dissolved in water and the resulting solution is 500 milliters in volume, what is the molar concentration of $MgCl_2$ in the solution?

(A) 2.0 M
(B) 4.0 M
(C) 8.0 M
(D) 12.0 M
(E) 16.0 M

B is correct. Molarity refers to moles of solute per liter of solution. We know we have 500 milliliters of solution, but we don't know how many moles of solute we have. Let's first figure out the mass of 1 mole of $MgCl_2$. Looking at the periodic table, we find that 1 mole of Mg has a mass of 24.3 g. Two moles of Cl have a mass of about 71 g. One mole of $MgCl_2$, therefore, has a mass of 95.3 g.

Now, we're dealing with 190 g of $MgCl_2$, which is equal to $\dfrac{190}{95.3}$ = about 2 moles. But don't be duped into choosing A! You're looking for the solution's molarity. There are 2 moles of solute in 500 milliliters (0.5 liters) of solution, which means that the molarity is 4 moles/L. That's why B is correct.

34. When a fixed amount of gas has its Kelvin temperature doubled and its pressure doubled, the new volume of the gas is

    (A) four times greater than its original volume
    (B) twice its original volume
    (C) unchanged
    (D) one-half its original volume
    (E) one-fourth its original volume

C is correct. Think of the ideal gas equation: $PV = nRT$. What does this equation tell us? It means that volume is directly related to Kelvin temperature and inversely related to pressure. Doubling a gas's Kelvin temperature will double its volume if other variables are held constant. Doubling a gas's pressure will halve its volume if other variables are held constant. So the effect on volume of doubling pressure cancels out the effect of doubling Kelvin temperature, and the net result is that the gas's volume will stay the same.

35. In 12.4 hours, a 100 gram sample of an element decays so that its mass is 25 grams. What is the approximate half-life of this radioactive substance?

    (A)   1.6 hours
    (B)   3.1 hours
    (C)   6.2 hours
    (D)   24.8 hours
    (E)   49.6 hours

C is correct. After 1 half-life, a 100 g sample will have a mass of 50 g. After 2 half-lives it will have a mass of 25 g, so we're talking about the expiration of 2 half-lives. If 2 half-lives = 12.4 hours, then 1 half-life = 6.2 hours.

36. In the equation $Q \rightarrow {}^{4}_{2}He + {}^{216}_{85}At$, the species represented by Q is

    (A) ${}^{220}_{87}Fr$

    (B) ${}^{212}_{83}Bi$

    (C) ${}^{220}_{87}At$

    (D) ${}^{212}_{83}Fr$

    (E) ${}^{216}_{85}Bi$

A is correct. This is alpha decay, in which a radioactive atom loses 2 protons and 2 neutrons. The loss of 2 protons means the atomic number decreases by 2, which means it *was* 87 before it decayed. The element with an atomic number of 87 is Fr (francium). The loss of 2 neutrons together with the loss of 2 protons means that the mass number has decreased by (2) + (2) = 4. The mass number is now 216, which tells us that it *was* 220. Notice that choice C has the right numbers, but not the right element. Remember that the atomic number uniquely identifies an element, so an atomic number of 87 must be francium, no matter what the mass number is. This also means that an element can have several different mass numbers, collectively called isotopes.

37. A compound with a molecular weight of 56 amu has an empirical formula of CH_2. What is its molecular formula?

(A) C_2H_2
(B) C_2H_4
(C) C_4H_8
(D) C_4H_{10}
(E) C_6H_{12}

C is correct. The empirical formula tells us that the ratio of carbon to hydrogen is 1:2, so we're looking for an answer that reflects the same ratio. Only choices B, C, and E do that, so we can eliminate A and D. Now, among B, C, and E, we're looking for the one whose molecular weight is 56 amu. Look at the periodic table. Every carbon atom has an atomic weight of 12 amu, and every hydrogen atom has an atomic weight of 1 amu. Rather than pursue algebra, let's just try the three choices.

Choice B would give us a molecular weight of $(2 \times 12) + (4 \times 1) = 28$ amu.
Choice C would give us a molecular weight of $(4 \times 12) + (8 \times 1) = 56$ amu.
Choice E would give us a molecular weight of $(6 \times 12) + (12 \times 1) = 84$ amu.
C is correct.

38. The change in heat energy for a reaction is best expressed as a change in

(A) enthalpy
(B) absolute temperature
(C) specific heat
(D) entropy
(E) kinetic energy

A is correct. Don't fall into the temptation trap and pick B. Temperature differences can indicate the direction of heat flow. However, temperature is not a direct measure of heat energy. Instead, associate heat energy with enthalpy.

39. $\ldots NF_3(g) + \ldots H_2O(g) \rightarrow \ldots HF(g) + \ldots NO(g) + \ldots NO_2(g)$

When the equation for the reaction above is balanced, how many moles of NF_3 would be required to react completely with 6 moles of H_2O?

(A) 0.5 mole
(B) 1 mole
(C) 2 moles
(D) 3 moles
(E) 4 moles

E is correct. On this test, the easiest way to balance an equation is by plugging in the answers. The test writer tells you that the coefficient in front of H_2O is 6, so put that in there. Now, see which of the answer choices, if placed in front of NF_3, would result in a balanced equation. If, for instance, we try choice B, we'd have 1 mole of N on the left, which would give us 3 moles of F on the left. In order to have 3 moles of F on the right we'd have to put a 3 in front of the HF on the right. That means we'd have 3 moles of H on the right and 12 moles of H on the left. This is way out of balance.

Suppose we try option D and put a 3 in front of the NF_3 on the left. That gives us 9 moles of F on the left, which means we'd have to put a 9 in front of the HF on the right. That in turn would provide 9 moles of H on the right when we have 12 moles of H on the left. Once again, this is out of balance.

Now, let's try choice E. We put a 4 in front of NF_3 on the left, which gives us 12 F on the left and means we must put a 12 in front of the HF on the right. That gives us 12 H on the right, balanced by 12 H on the left. E is correct. The coefficients for both NO and NO_2 would be 2, which would balance both the nitrogens (N) and the oxygens (O).

40. Which characteristic is associated with bases?

    (A) React with metal to produce hydrogen gas
    (B) Donate an unshared electron pair
    (C) Always contain the hydroxide ion in their structure
    (D) Taste sour
    (E) Formed by reacting a nonmetal oxide and water

B is correct. Make sure you can distinguish between an acid and a base. A base can donate an un-shared electron pair, according to the Lewis definition, so B is correct. Choices A, D, and E are characteristics of acids. And what about C? Not all bases contain the OH^- ion in their structure—NH_3 is an example.

41. An element has the following properties: shiny, brittle, poor electrical conductivity, and high melting point. This element can be best classified as a(n)

    (A) alkali metal
    (B) halogen
    (C) metalloid
    (D) transition metal
    (E) noble gas

C is correct. The substance described has some metallic characteristics (shiny and high melting point) and some nonmetallic ones (brittle and poor electrical conductivity). It sounds like something that's between a metal and a nonmetal such as a metalloid or semimetal. This is a general description of the metalloid silicon.

42. Which of the following forward processes produces a decrease in entropy?

    I. $H_2O(g) \rightarrow H_2O(l)$
    II. $Fe^{2+}(aq) + S^{2-}(aq) \rightarrow FeS(s)$
    III. $2SO_3(g) \rightleftharpoons 2SO_2(g) + O_2(g)$

    (A) I only
    (B) III only
    (C) I and II only
    (D) II and III only
    (E) I, II, and III

C is correct. The more free that molecules are to move around, the greater the entropy of the state. In equation I we go from a gas (very high entropy) to a liquid (more ordered, less entropy). That's a decrease in entropy. Equation II also involves an entropy decrease. Here, ions go from being able to move throughout a solution to being restricted in the solid state. Equation III shows an entropy *increase* because we are increasing the moles of gas (2 on left and 3 on right). I and II illustrate an entropy decrease, and the correct answer is C.

43. Which of the following will raise the boiling point of a sample of water?

(A) Heat the water
(B) Mix gasoline into the water
(C) Bring the water sample to a higher altitude
(D) Place the water sample on a magnetic stirrer
(E) Dissolve table sugar into the water

E is correct. Choices A and D will not change water's boiling point. Remember that when a solute is dissolved in solution, the solution's boiling point will be raised (and its freezing point lowered). Only E involves dissolving a solute into water. Sugar water boils at a higher temperature than pure water under identical conditions. Why doesn't the addition of gasoline into the water have the same effect? Gasoline molecules are nonpolar and will not dissolve in water. As for C, increasing the altitude of the water will decrease its boiling point.

44. Elements H and J lie in the same period. If the atoms of H are smaller than the atoms of J, then compared to atoms of J, atoms of H are most likely to

(A) exist in a greater number of isotopes
(B) exist in a lesser number of isotopes
(C) exist in a greater number of oxidation states
(D) have a greater positive charge in their nuclei
(E) have a lesser positive charge in their nuclei

D is correct. The question concerns periodic table trends and, in particular, atomic radius. As we move from left to right across a period, atomic radius decreases. So, within a period, the higher the atomic number, the smaller the atomic radius.

This question is just a bit spiced with the camouflage trap. You might be thinking higher atomic number, and the correct answer is phrased as "greater positive charge in its nucleus." But keep the blinders off your brain. You know the answer—just remember that there's more than one way of expressing it.

45. ...$Al(s)$ + ...$O_2(g)$ → ...$Al_2O_3(s)$

When the equation representing the reaction shown above is completed and balanced and all coefficients are reduced to lowest whole-number terms, the coefficient of $O_2(g)$ is

(A) 1
(B) 2
(C) 3
(D) 4
(E) 6

C is correct. Aluminum is a metal, and oxygen is a nonmetal. They react to form an ionic compound. Aluminum (in the 3A group) forms a +3 ion. Oxygen (in the 6A group) forms a –2 ion. They will produce aluminum oxide, Al_2O_3. When the equation is balanced, we'll get: $4Al(s) + 3O_2(g) → 2Al_2O_3(s)$.

46. Which of the following solids has a brilliant blue color?

(A) $Ca(OH)_2$
(B) KCl
(C) NaBr
(D) Fe_2O_3
(E) $CuSO_4$

E is correct. Many colored compounds contain a transition metal (an element from the d region of the periodic table). Choices A, B, and C are ionic solids that possess an active metal (an element from the s region). These compounds appear white (for instance, NaCl or table salt). Choice D is rust, which is not blue. $CuSO_4$ contains the transition metal copper (Cu), and its crystals are bright blue.

47. Twenty-five percent of element X exists as ^{210}X and 75 percent of it exists as ^{214}X. What is the atomic weight of element X in amu ?

(A) 85
(B) 211
(C) 212
(D) 213
(E) 214

D is correct. Remember, the atomic weight of an element is the weighted average of all the different isotopes an element exists in. If 50 percent of element X had a mass of 210 amu and 50 percent had a mass of 214 amu, the weighted average would be 212 amu. Notice that we are told element X exists as ^{214}X more than half of the time. So the answer must exceed 212. However, since element X also exists in an isotope with a mass less than 214, we expect that its atomic weight is less than 214 amu. Only D has a mass greater than 212 amu and less than 214 amu.

48. A 600 ml container holds 2 moles of $O_2(g)$, 3 moles of $H_2(g)$, and 1 mole of He(g). Total pressure within the container is 760 torr. What is the partial pressure of O_2?

(A) 127 torr
(B) 253 torr
(C) 380 torr
(D) 507 torr
(E) 760 torr

B is correct. The container holds a total of 6 moles of gas. Oxygen (O_2) constitutes one-third of that content. If you know how to work partial pressure problems, you know that oxygen's contribution to the total 760 torr of pressure is one-third. 760 torr ÷ 3 = approximately 253 torr.

49. $$Fe(OH)_3(s) \rightleftharpoons Fe^{3+}(aq) + 3OH^-(aq)$$

The ionic solid $Fe(OH)_3$ is added to water and dissociates into its component ions, as shown above. The solubility product expression for the saturated solution is

(A) $K_{sp} = [Fe^{3+}][OH^-]$
(B) $K_{sp} = [Fe^{3+}][3OH^-]$
(C) $K_{sp} = [Fe^{3+}][3OH^-]^3$
(D) $K_{sp} = [Fe^{3+}][OH^-]^3$

(E) $K_{sp} = \dfrac{[Fe^{3+}][OH^-]^3}{[Fe(OH)_3]}$

D is correct. Since we're considering the dissolution of an ionic solid into water, we need to consider the solubility product expression. The solubility product constant, K_{sp}, will equal the product of aqueous ion concentrations raised to their coefficients. (Remember that solids are not expressed.) This is the relationship expressed in choice D.

50. Which of the following electron configurations represents an atom of magnesium in an excited state?

(A) $1s^2 2s^2 2p^6$
(B) $1s^2 2s^2 2p^6 3s^2$
(C) $1s^2 2s^2 2p^5 3s^2 3p^2$
(D) $1s^2 2s^2 2p^6 3s^1 3p^1$
(E) $1s^2 2s^2 2p^6 3s^1 3p^2$

D is correct. The normal electron configuration for magnesium would be $1s2s^2 2p^6 3s^2$. Since we're talking about an "excited" magnesium atom in which one electron has been pushed up into a higher energy state, we're looking for a configuration that shows one electron in a higher state than it should be. The total number of electrons should still be equal to magnesium's atomic number, but the location of one electron should be "elevated."

Choice D is just what we're looking for. Total number of electrons? Twelve, just as it should be. But look at the last entry. Instead of $3s^2$, we see $3p^1$. The last electron has been elevated to the $3p$ subshell.

51. All of the following when added to water will produce an electrolytic solution EXCEPT

(A) $N_2(g)$
(B) $HCl(g)$
(C) $KOH(s)$
(D) $NaI(s)$
(E) $CaCl_2(s)$

A is correct. To form an electrolytic solution, the solute must dissociate into ions. Adding $HCl(g)$ to water will produce hydrochloric acid, which ionizes into H^+ and Cl^- ions. Choices C, D, and E are all ionic solids, which will break into mobile ions upon dissolution in water. When $N_2(g)$ is dissolved into water, no ions are produced, and the resultant solution is nonelectrolytic.

52. $NH_3(aq) + H_2CO_3(aq) \rightleftharpoons NH_4^+(aq) + HCO_3^-(aq)$

In the reaction represented above, NH_4^+ acts as a(n)

(A) indicator
(B) hydrate
(C) acid
(D) base
(E) salt

C is correct. The double arrow indicates that the reaction is reversible. NH_4^+ is a reactant of the reverse reaction; if NH_4^+ donates a proton to HCO_3^-, NH_3 and H_2CO_3 are formed. Since NH_4^+ donates an H^+ ion (or proton) to another substance, it acts as an acid according to the Bronsted-Lowry definition.

53. Which species has the ground state electron configuration $1s^2\, 2s^2\, 2p^6\, 3s^2\, 3p^6$?

(A) Sulfide ion, S^{2-}
(B) Bromide ion, Br^-
(C) Neon atom, Ne
(D) Chromium ion, Cr^{3+}
(E) Potassium atom, K

A is correct. Add the superscripts to get the total number of electrons in the species: $2 + 2 + 6 + 2 + 6 = 18$. Which of the choices also has 18 electrons? A quick check of the periodic table shows that a sulfur atom has 16 electrons. Adding two more electrons gives the S^{2-} ion a total of 18 electrons.

54. Which of the following species is amphoteric?

(A) Na_3PO_4
(B) HSO_4^-
(C) KOH
(D) HNO_3
(E) $C_2O_4^{2-}$

B is correct. For a substance to be amphoteric, it must be able to donate and receive an H^+ ion. Eliminate A and E—these species don't have an H^+ ion to donate. Choice C, KOH, is a strong base. We wouldn't expect it to ever act as an acid. Likewise, HNO_3 (choice D) is a strong acid that we would not expect to behave as a base. That leaves HSO_4^-. Notice that it can act as an acid and become a sulfate ion, SO_4^{2-}, or act as a base and become sulfuric acid, H_2SO_4.

55. An ideal gas has a volume of 10 liters at 20°C and a pressure of 750 mmHg. Which of the following expressions is needed to determine the volume of the same amount of gas at STP?

(A) $10 \times \dfrac{750}{760} \times \dfrac{0}{20}$ L

(B) $10 \times \dfrac{750}{760} \times \dfrac{293}{273}$ L

(C) $10 \times \dfrac{760}{750} \times \dfrac{0}{20}$ L

(D) $10 \times \dfrac{760}{750} \times \dfrac{273}{293}$ L

(E) $10 \times \dfrac{750}{760} \times \dfrac{273}{293}$ L

E is correct. The ideal gas equation is $PV = nRT$. When the amount of gas does not change, n becomes a constant, like R. A little algebra gives us $\dfrac{PV}{T} = nR$. Since $\left(\dfrac{PV}{T}\right)$ is equal to a constant, it will not change with time. Consider that we are dealing with two points in time. At first, the gas has a volume of 10 liters at 20°C or (293 K) and 750 mmHg. So here, $\left(\dfrac{PV}{T}\right) = \dfrac{(750)(10)}{(293)}$. Later, the gas is under STP conditions, so $T = 273$ K and $P = 760$ mmHg. Now, $\left(\dfrac{PV}{T}\right) = \dfrac{(760)(V)}{(273)}$. If we set initial $\left(\dfrac{PV}{T}\right)$ = final $\left(\dfrac{PV}{T}\right)$, we get $\dfrac{(750)(10)}{(293)} = \dfrac{(760)(V)}{(273)}$. Rearranging and applying some algebra gives us $V = 10 \times \dfrac{750}{760} \times \dfrac{273}{293}$ L. This is choice E.

Questions 56–57 pertain to the accompanying phase diagram for substance Z.

56. Substance Z is at 0.5 atm and 200 K. If the pressure on substance Z is steadily increased and its temperature is kept constant, what phase change will eventually occur?

(A) Condensation
(B) Freezing
(C) Melting
(D) Sublimation
(E) Vaporization

A is correct. Use the phase diagram. At 0.5 atm and 200 K, substance Z is a gas. If we maintain this temperature and increase the pressure, we can draw a vertical line from the point (0.5 atm, 200 K). Eventually that vertical line will cross into the liquid region. This means that, under steadily increasing pressure, substance Z (starting at 0.5 atm and 200 K) will condense. Condensation is the phase change from gas to liquid.

57. The normal boiling point of substance Z is closest to

(A) 100 K
(B) 200 K
(C) 300 K
(D) 400 K
(E) 500 K

C is correct. The normal boiling point is the temperature at which the phase change from liquid to gas occurs, at a pressure of 1 atm. If you extend a horizontal line from the 1.0 atm mark on the "pressure" axis and see where it intersects the liquid-gas boundary, you'll get the normal boiling point. Doing so on this phase diagram shows a normal boiling point of about 300 K.

58. The shape of a PCl_3 molecule is described as

(A) bent
(B) trigonal pyramidal
(C) linear
(D) trigonal planar
(E) tetrahedral

B is correct. Phosphorus is the central atom in PCl_3. A phosphorus atom needs 3 electrons to complete its valence shell. It gets 3 electrons by forming covalent bonds with 3 chlorine atoms. The PCl_3 molecule has the following structure:

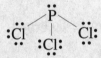

Of the four electron pair sites around phosphorus, one is a lone pair. This gives the PCl_3 molecule a trigonal pyramidal shape.

59. What volume of 0.4 M $Ba(OH)_2$ (aq) is needed to exactly neutralize 100 milliliters of 0.2 M HBr(aq)?

(A)   25 ml
(B)   50 ml
(C)   100 ml
(D)   200 ml
(E)   400 ml

A is correct. First consider the neutralization that occurs between HBr and $Ba(OH)_2$.

$$2HBr + Ba(OH)_2 \rightarrow BaBr_2 + 2H_2O$$

Notice that for every 2 moles of HBr, only 1 mole of $Ba(OH)_2$ is needed for neutralization. We have 0.1 liters (or 100 milliliters) of 0.2 M HBr. This means we have 0.1 liters × 0.2 mole/liter, or 0.02 mole of HBr. We need 0.01 mole of $Ba(OH)_2$ to neutralize 0.02 mole of HBr. Twenty-five milliliters of 0.4 M $Ba(OH)_2(aq)$ has 0.025 liters × 0.4 mole/liter, or 0.01 mole of $Ba(OH)_2$.

60. Which of the following is true regarding the aqueous dissociation of HCN, $K_a = 4.9 \times 10^{-10}$ at 25°C ?

   I. At equilibrium, $[H^+] = [CN^-]$
  II. At equilibrium, $[H^+] > [HCN]$
 III. HCN(aq) is a strong acid.

(A) I only
(B) II only
(C) I and II only
(D) II and III only
(E) I, II, and III

A is correct. A small K_a indicates a weak acid. That means statement III is false, and therefore we can eliminate choices D and E. It also means that most HCN remains as intact molecules, as opposed to H^+ and CN^- ions, so statement II is false. Process of elimination tells us that statement I must be true. And it is: $HCN \rightleftharpoons H^+ + CN^-$. Notice that the molar ratio of H^+ to CN^- is 1:1.

61. Which of the following atoms has the largest second ionization energy?

(A) Silicon, Si
(B) Calcium, Ca
(C) Chlorine, Cl
(D) Iron, Fe
(E) Sodium, Na

E is correct. Ionization energies get very large once we try to remove core electrons, which are attracted more strongly to the nucleus than valence electrons. So an atom with a very high second ionization energy would be expected to have just 1 valence electron: The second electron to be removed from such an atom would have to be a core electron. Among the choices, only sodium atoms have a single valence electron.

Question 62 refers to the overall reaction and half-reactions with standard reduction potentials below.

$$2Fe^{2+} + Cl_2 \rightarrow 2\,Fe^{3+} + 2Cl^-$$
$$Fe^{3+} + e^- \rightarrow Fe^{2+};\ E^0_{red} = 0.77\ \text{volts}$$
$$Cl_2 + 2e^- \rightarrow 2Cl^-;\ E^0_{red} = 1.36\ \text{volts}$$

62. The standard potential difference of an electrochemical cell using the overall reaction above is

(A) 0.18 volts
(B) 0.59 volts
(C) 1.05 volts
(D) 2.13 volts
(E) 2.90 volts

B is correct. Fe^{2+} is oxidized in the redox reaction. To get the standard oxidation potential for $Fe^{2+} \rightarrow Fe^{3+} + e^-$, just take the opposite of the standard reduction potential. So E^0_{ox} for $Fe^{2+} \rightarrow Fe^{3+} + e^-$ is -0.77 volts. Cl_2 is reduced for the reduction half-reaction and E^0_{red} is 1.36 volts. The potential difference for the overall reaction (E^0_{cell}) is -0.77 volts + 1.36 volts = 0.59 volts.

63. The reaction of zinc metal, Zn, and hydrochloric acid, HCl, produces which of the following?

    I. H_2 (g)
    II. Cl_2 (g)
    III. Zn^{2+} (aq)

(A) II only
(B) III only
(C) I and II only
(D) I and III only
(E) I, II and III

D is correct. Remember that many metals react with acids to produce hydrogen gas. Your first step should be to write out the reaction. Here it is: $Zn(s) + 2HCl(aq) \rightarrow ZnCl_2(aq) + H_2(g)$. Notice that the products of this reaction are $Zn^{2+}(aq)$, $Cl^-(aq)$ (from $ZnCl_2$), and $H_2(g)$.

Questions 64–65 refer to the following reaction:

$$2H_2S(g) + 3O_2(g) \rightleftharpoons 2SO_2(g) + 2H_2O(g) + heat$$

64. For the above reaction, the equilibrium concentration of $SO_2(g)$ can be increased by

(A) adding neon gas
(B) increasing the temperature
(C) adding a catalyst
(D) increasing the concentration of $H_2O(g)$
(E) increasing the concentration of $O_2(g)$

E is correct. This is a Le Chatelier's principle question. How can we produce crowding on the left side of the equation and drive equilibrium to the right (increasing the SO_2 concentration)? Don't be fooled by C: *Catalysts do not affect equilibrium,* but changing concentrations *does* influence equilibrium. Increasing the concentration of O_2 will produce crowding on the left side and lead to an increase in the concentration of SO_2.

65. Which of the following is increased by decreasing the volume of the reaction system?

    I. Rate of reaction
    II. Equilibrium concentration of reactants
    III. Value of K_{eq}

(A) I only
(B) III only
(C) I and II only
(D) II and III only
(E) I, II, and III

A is correct. Decreasing the volume of the system will increase the concentration of reactants. Why? Because the same number of molecules now exists in a smaller space, and this increases the ratio of molecules per volume. How will this affect the reaction rate? It will increase reaction rate because decreasing the volume makes it more likely that molecules will collide. What about equilibrium? Reducing the volume will force the equilibrium to shift in the direction that produces fewer moles of gas. This means the equilibrium concentration of reactants will decrease because equilibrium will shift to the right (4 moles of gas on the right versus 5 on the left). Only a temperature change will affect the value of K_{eq}, so this will stay the same. Among the three, only item I will increase, so the answer is A.

66. $Fe_2O_3(s) + 3CO(g) \rightarrow 2Fe(s) + 3CO_2(g)$

When 3 moles of Fe_2O_3 are allowed to completely react with 56 grams of CO according to the above equation, approximately how many moles of iron, Fe, are produced?

(A) 0.7
(B) 1.3
(C) 2.0
(D) 2.7
(E) 6.0

B is correct. When quantities are given for more than one reactant, you must see which is limiting. Fifty-six grams of CO (molecular weight = 28 amu) are 2 moles of CO. Since the stoichiometric ratio of Fe_2O_3 to CO is 1:3 (based on coefficients from the balanced equation), we see that CO is limiting. (We would need more than 9 moles of CO based on the 1:3 ratio for Fe_2O_3 to be limiting in this case.) The ratio of CO to Fe is 3:2. So 2 moles of CO will produce about 1.3 moles of Fe. You could quickly estimate this as between 1 and 2 to save time and still get the answer.

67. $2Na_2O_2(s) + 2H_2O(l) \rightarrow 4NaOH(aq) + O_2(g)$

Sodium peroxide, Na_2O_2, and water react in the flask at 25°C according to the equation and in the diagram above. If water levels are equal inside and outside the beaker, then the gas pressure inside the beaker is equal to the

(A) pressure of oxygen gas collected
(B) vapor pressure of water at 25°C
(C) sum of pressure of oxygen gas collected and atmospheric pressure
(D) sum of vapor pressure of water at 25°C and atmospheric pressure
(E) sum of pressure of oxygen gas collected and vapor pressure of water at 25°C

E is correct. Consider what gases are being collected in the beaker. Oxygen gas is flowing in from the reaction. Water vapor, $H_2O(g)$, is also entering the beaker from the evaporation of water. The pressure exerted by $H_2O(g)$ is equal to the vapor pressure of water. The total gas pressure in the beaker is, therefore, the sum of the pressure of oxygen gas collected and vapor pressure of water (at 25°C in this particular problem).

68. Which of the following molecules has the strongest carbon-to-carbon bond?

(A) C_2H_2
(B) C_2H_4
(C) C_2H_6
(D) C_3H_8
(E) C_4H_{10}

A is correct. If you draw the structure of acetylene, C_2H_2, you'll see that the carbon atoms must share three pairs of electrons to achieve stable octets.

$$H - C \equiv C - H$$

So C_2H_2 has a triple bond. None of the other molecules contains a triple bond. Since this is the strongest type of carbon-to-carbon bond, A is correct.

69. $N_2O_4(g) \rightleftharpoons 2\,NO_2(g)$

The following concentration data were gathered for the above reaction at 5 minute intervals from the start of an experiment:

Time After Start of Experiment	$[N_2O_4]$	$[NO_2]$
0 min (start)	0.00 M	0.50 M
5 min	0.10 M	0.33 M
10 min	0.20 M	0.20 M
15 min	0.25 M	0.15 M
20 min	0.28 M	0.13 M
25 min	0.28 M	0.13 M

If the experiment was carried out in a closed system at constant temperature, then during which time interval (from the start of the experiment) did the reaction most likely achieve equilibrium?

(A) 0 min (start) to 5 min
(B) 5 min to 10 min
(C) 10 min to 15 min
(D) 15 min to 20 min
(E) 20 min to 25 min

D is correct. Equilibrium is attained when the concentrations of all species become constant. The concentrations of N_2O_4 and NO_2 stay the same from the 20 minute mark to the 25 minute mark. This means equilibrium was achieved before the 20 minute mark. Since the concentrations of N_2O_4 and NO_2 are different from the 15 minute mark to the 20 minute mark, equilibrium was not achieved at exactly 15 minutes from the start of the reaction; equilibrium was attained between 15 and 20 minutes after the start of the reaction.

Practice SAT Chemistry
Subject Test 2

PRACTICE SAT CHEMISTRY
SUBJECT TEST 2

You are about to take the second practice SAT Chemistry Subject Test. After answering questions 1–23, which constitute Part A, you'll be directed to answer questions 101–116, which constitute Part B. Then, begin again at question 24. Questions 24–69 constitute Part C.

When you're ready to score yourself, refer to the scoring instructions and answer key on pages 224 and 225. Full explanations regarding the correct answers to all questions start on page 227.

Material in the following table may be useful in answering the questions in this examination.

PERIODIC TABLE OF THE ELEMENTS

1 H 1.0																	2 He 4.0
3 Li 6.9	4 Be 9.0											5 B 10.8	6 C 12.0	7 N 14.0	8 O 16.0	9 F 19.0	10 Ne 20.2
11 Na 23.0	12 Mg 24.3											13 Al 27.0	14 Si 28.1	15 P 31.0	16 S 32.1	17 Cl 35.5	18 Ar 39.9
19 K 39.1	20 Ca 40.1	21 Sc 45.0	22 Ti 47.9	23 V 50.9	24 Cr 52.0	25 Mn 54.9	26 Fe 55.8	27 Co 58.9	28 Ni 58.7	29 Cu 63.5	30 Zn 65.4	31 Ga 69.7	32 Ge 72.6	33 As 74.9	34 Se 79.0	35 Br 79.9	36 Kr 83.8
37 Rb 85.5	38 Sr 87.6	39 Y 88.9	40 Zr 91.2	41 Nb 92.9	42 Mo 95.9	43 Tc (98)	44 Ru 101.1	45 Rh 102.9	46 Pd 106.4	47 Ag 107.9	48 Cd 112.4	49 In 114.8	50 Sn 118.7	51 Sb 121.8	52 Te 127.6	53 I 126.9	54 Xe 131.3
55 Cs 132.9	56 Ba 137.3	57 *La 138.9	72 Hf 178.5	73 Ta 180.9	74 W 183.9	75 Re 186.2	76 Os 190.2	77 Ir 192.2	78 Pt 195.1	79 Au 197.0	80 Hg 200.6	81 Tl 204.4	82 Pb 207.2	83 Bi 209.0	84 Po (209)	85 At (210)	86 Rn (222)
87 Fr (223)	88 Ra 226.0	89 †Ac 227.0															

*Lanthanum Series

58 Ce 140.1	59 Pr 140.9	60 Nd 144.2	61 Pm (145)	62 Sm 150.4	63 Eu 152.0	64 Gd 157.3	65 Tb 158.9	66 Dy 162.5	67 Ho 164.9	68 Er 167.3	69 Tm 168.9	70 Yb 173.0	71 Lu 175.0

†Actinium Series

90 Th 232.0	91 Pa 231.0	92 U 238.0	93 Np 237.0	94 Pu (244)	95 Am (243)	96 Cm (247)	97 Bk (247)	98 Cf (251)	99 Es (252)	100 Fm (258)	101 Md (258)	102 No (259)	103 Lr (260)

DO NOT DETACH FROM BOOK.

CHEMISTRY SUBJECT TEST 2

<u>Note:</u> For all questions involving solutions and/or chemical equations, assume that the system is in pure water unless otherwise stated.

Part A

<u>Directions:</u> Each set of lettered choices below refers to the numbered statements or questions immediately following it. Select the one lettered choice that best fits each statement or answers each question, and then fill in the corresponding oval on the answer sheet. <u>A choice may be used once, more than once, or not at all in each set.</u>

Questions 1–4

 (A) Molarity
 (B) Molality
 (C) Mole fraction
 (D) Density
 (E) Partial pressure

1. Is measured in units of atmospheres or millimeters of mercury E

2. Is measured in units of moles/kilogram B

3. Is a measure of mass per unit volume D

4. Is the quantity used in the calculation of boiling point elevation E
    B

Questions 5–9

 (A) Hydrogen bonding
 (B) Ionic bonding
 (C) Network bonding
 (D) London dispersion force
 (E) Metallic bonding

5. Chiefly responsible for the relatively high boiling point of water A

6. Is present in liquid oxygen D

7. Is primarily responsible for the hardness of diamond C

8. Allows copper to conduct electricity E

9. Is present in solid KCl B

GO ON TO THE NEXT PAGE

Questions 10–13

   (A) Na$^+$
   (B) Al
   (C) F
   (D) Ti
   (E) Br$^-$

10. Has 7 valence electrons

11. Has the electron configuration $1s^22s^22p^63s^23p^1$

12. Has the same electron configuration as neon atom

13. Has valence electrons in *d* orbitals

Questions 14–17

   (A) A 0.01-molar solution of HNO_3
   (B) A 0.01-molar solution of $HC_2H_3O_2$
   (C) A 0.01-molar solution of $Cu(NO_3)_2$
   (D) A 0.01-molar solution of $NaNO_3$
   (E) A 0.01-molar solution of NaOH

14. Will be colored blue

15. Will have a pH of 2

16. Will have the lowest freezing point

17. Will contain undissociated aqueous particles

GO ON TO THE NEXT PAGE

Questions 18–20

(A) Enthalpy change
(B) Entropy change
(C) Gibbs free energy change
(D) Activation energy
(E) Specific heat capacity

18. Is the amount of energy that must be added to raise the temperature of 1 gram of a substance 1°C

E

19. Its value indicates the spontaneity of a reaction

C

20. Its value indicates whether a reaction is endothermic or exothermic

A

Questions 21–23

(A) Ionization energy
(B) Electronegativity
(C) Atomic radius
(D) Atomic number
(E) Mass number

21. Is the measure of the pull of the nucleus of an atom on the electrons of other atoms bonded to it

A

22. Is the energy required to remove an electron from an atom

B

23. Is equal to the number of protons in an atom

D

GO ON TO THE NEXT PAGE

CHEMISTRY SUBJECT TEST 2—*Continued*

PLEASE GO TO THE SPECIAL SECTION AT THE LOWER RIGHT-HAND CORNER OF PAGE 2 OF YOUR ANSWER SHEET LABELED CHEMISTRY AND ANSWER QUESTIONS 101–116 ACCORDING TO THE FOLLOWING DIRECTIONS.

Part B

<u>Directions:</u> Each question below consists of two statements, I in the left-hand column and II in the right-hand column. For each question, determine whether statement I is true or false <u>and</u> whether statement II is true or false and fill in the corresponding T or F ovals on your answer sheet. <u>Fill in oval CE only if statement II is a correct explanation of statement I.</u>

EXAMPLES:

	I		II
EX 1.	H_2SO_4 is a strong acid	BECAUSE	H_2SO_4 contains sulfur.
EX 2.	An atom of oxygen is electrically neutral	BECAUSE	an oxygen atom contains an equal number of protons and electrons.

SAMPLE ANSWERS

	I		II		CE
EX 1	●	F	●	F	
EX 2	●	F	●	F	

	I		II
101.	An ionic solid is a good conductor of electricity	BECAUSE	an ionic solid is composed of positive and negative ions joined together in a lattice structure held together by electrostatic forces.
102.	The bond in an O_2 molecule is nonpolar	BECAUSE	the oxygen atoms in an O_2 molecule share the bonding electrons equally.
103.	When a sample of water freezes, the process is exothermic	BECAUSE	ice is at a lower potential energy state than water.
104.	At 25°C, an aqueous solution with a pH of 5 will have a pOH of 9	BECAUSE	the pH of a buffered solution is not greatly affected by the addition of a relatively small amount of acid or base.
105.	When a chlorine atom gains an electron, it becomes a positively charged ion	BECAUSE	a neutral atom has equal numbers of protons and electrons.
106.	Lithium has a larger first ionization energy than oxygen	BECAUSE	oxygen atoms have larger atomic radii than lithium atoms.
107.	Potassium chloride dissolves readily in water	BECAUSE	water is a polar solvent.
108.	Ammonia is a Lewis base	BECAUSE	ammonia can donate an electron pair to a bond.

	I		**II**
109.	Elemental fluorine is more reactive than elemental neon	BECAUSE	neon has a larger atomic weight than fluorine.
110.	The addition of a catalyst will decrease the ΔH for a reaction	BECAUSE	a catalyst provides an alternate reaction pathway with a lower activation energy.
111.	The oxygen atom in a water molecule has a –2 oxidation state	BECAUSE	water molecules exhibit hydrogen bonding.
112.	When a salt sample dissolves in water, ΔS for the process is positive	BECAUSE	for a salt sample, aqueous ions have greater entropy than ions in a solid.
113.	When the temperature of a reaction at equilibrium is increased, the equilibrium will shift to favor the endothermic direction	BECAUSE	at equilibrium, all reactants have been converted into products.
114.	An atom of ^{12}C contains 12 protons	BECAUSE	the identity of an element is determined by the number of protons in the nuclei of its atoms.
115.	Water boils at a lower temperature at high altitude than at low altitude	BECAUSE	the vapor pressure of water is lower at higher altitude.
116.	Elemental sodium is a strong reducing agent	BECAUSE	an atom of elemental sodium gives up its valence electron readily.

RETURN TO THE SECTION OF YOUR ANSWER SHEET YOU STARTED FOR CHEMISTRY AND ANSWER QUESTIONS 24–69.

GO ON TO THE NEXT PAGE

Part C

Directions: Each of the questions or incomplete statements below is followed by five suggested answers or completions. Select the one that is best in each case and then fill in the corresponding oval on the answer sheet.

24. What is the oxidation state of bromine in $HBrO_3$?

    (A) –3
    (B) –1
    (C) +1
    (D) +3
    (E) +5

25. What is the percent by mass of silicon in a sample of silicon dioxide?

    (A) 21%
    (B) 33%
    (C) 47%
    (D) 54%
    (E) 78%

26. How many electrons does a ^{37}Cl ion with a charge of –1 contain?

    (A) 16
    (B) 17
    (C) 18
    (D) 37
    (E) 38

27. $CH_4(g) + 2\,O_2(g) \rightarrow CO_2(g) + 2\,H_2O(g) + 800\text{ kJ}$

    If 1 mole of $O_2(g)$ is consumed in the reaction given above, how much energy is produced?

    (A) 200 kJ
    (B) 400 kJ
    (C) 800 kJ
    (D) 1200 kJ
    (E) 1600 kJ

28. Which of the following is NOT true of the element sodium?

    (A) It takes the oxidation state +1.
    (B) It reacts with water to form a basic solution.
    (C) It forms metallic bonds in its solid uncombined form.
    (D) It is found in nature as a diatomic gas.
    (E) It reacts with a halogen to form an ionic salt.

29. What volume of a 0.200-molar solution of sodium hydroxide is required to neutralize 40 liters of a 0.300-molar hydrochloric acid solution?

    (A) 10 liters
    (B) 20 liters
    (C) 40 liters
    (D) 60 liters
    (E) 120 liters

30. $\ldots\,PH_3 + \ldots\,O_2 \rightarrow \ldots\,P_2O_5 + \ldots\,H_2O$

    When the equation above is balanced and the coefficients are reduced to the lowest whole numbers, the coefficient for H_2O is

    (A) 1
    (B) 2
    (C) 3
    (D) 4
    (E) 5

31. $H_2SO_4(aq) + \ldots\,Ba(OH)_2(aq) \rightarrow$

    Which of the following are products of the reaction shown above?

    I. $O_2(g)$
    II. $H_2O(l)$
    III. $BaSO_4(s)$

    (A) I only
    (B) III only
    (C) I and II only
    (D) I and III only
    (E) II and III only

GO ON TO THE NEXT PAGE

32. $2 Mg(s) + O_2(g) \rightarrow 2 MgO(s)$

    If 48.6 grams of magnesium are placed in a container with 64 grams of oxygen gas and the reaction above proceeds to completion, what is the mass of $MgO(s)$ produced?

    (A) 15.4 grams
    (B) 32.0 grams
    (C) 80.6 grams
    (D) 96.3 grams
    (E) 112 grams

33. An ideal gas in a closed inflexible container has a pressure of 6 atmospheres and a temperature of $27°C$. What will be the new pressure of the gas if the temperature is decreased to $-73°C$?

    (A) 2 atm
    (B) 3 atm
    (C) 4 atm
    (D) 8 atm
    (E) 9 atm

34. Equal molar quantities of hydrogen gas and oxygen gas are present in a closed container at a constant temperature. Which of the following quantities will be the same for the two gases?

    I. Partial pressure
    II. Average kinetic energy
    III. Average molecular velocity

    (A) I only
    (B) I and II only
    (C) I and III only
    (D) II and III only
    (E) I, II, and III

35. Which of the following is a nonpolar molecule?

    (A) CO_2
    (B) H_2O
    (C) NH_3
    (D) NO
    (E) HI

36. What is the molar concentration of a 500-milliliter solution that contains 20 grams of $CaBr_2$ (formula weight = 200)?

    (A) 0.1 molar
    (B) 0.2 molar
    (C) 0.5 molar
    (D) 1 molar
    (E) 5 molar

37. The structure of $BeCl_2$ can best be described as

    (A) linear
    (B) bent
    (C) trigonal
    (D) tetrahedral
    (E) square

38. $2 NO(g) + 2 H_2(g) \rightarrow N_2(g) + 2 H_2O(g)$

    Which of the following statements is true regarding the reaction given above?

    (A) If 1 mole of H_2 is consumed, 0.5 mole of N_2 is produced.
    (B) If 1 mole of H_2 is consumed, 0.5 mole of H_2O is produced.
    (C) If 0.5 mole of H_2 is consumed, 1 mole of N_2 is produced.
    (D) If 0.5 mole of H_2 is consumed, 1 mole of NO is consumed.
    (E) If 0.5 mole of H_2 is consumed, 1 mole of H_2O is produced.

GO ON TO THE NEXT PAGE

Questions 39–40 pertain to the reaction represented by the following equation:

$$\ldots Cu(s) + \ldots NO_3^-(aq) + \ldots H^+(aq) \rightarrow$$
$$\ldots Cu^{2+}(aq) + \ldots NO_2(g) + \ldots H_2O(l)$$

39. When the equation above is balanced with lowest whole number coefficients, the coefficient for $H^+(aq)$ will be

    (A) 1
    (B) 2
    (C) 3
    (D) 4
    (E) 5

40. Which of the following takes place during the reaction above?

    (A) $Cu(s)$ is oxidized.
    (B) $Cu(s)$ is reduced.
    (C) $H^+(aq)$ is oxidized.
    (D) $H^+(aq)$ is reduced.
    (E) $NO_3^-(aq)$ is oxidized.

41. Which of the following could be the molecular formula for a molecule with an empirical formula of CH_2?

    (A) CH
    (B) CH_4
    (C) C_2H_2
    (D) C_2H_6
    (E) C_3H_6

42. When CO_2 is bubbled through distilled water at 25°C, which of the following is most likely to occur?

    (A) Solid carbon will precipitate.
    (B) An electrical current will be produced in an oxidation-reduction reaction.
    (C) The pH of the solution will be reduced.
    (D) The water will boil.
    (E) Methane (CH_4) gas will be formed.

43. In which of the following processes is entropy increasing?

    (A) $N_2(g) + 3 Cl_2(g) \rightarrow 2 NCl_3(g)$
    (B) $H_2O(g) \rightarrow H_2O(l)$
    (C) $2 H_2O(l) \rightarrow 2 H_2(g) + O_2(g)$
    (D) $CO(g) + 2 H_2(g) \rightarrow CH_3OH(l)$
    (E) $2 NO_2(g) \rightarrow N_2O_4(g)$

44.

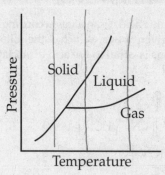

Based on the phase diagram above, which series of phase changes could take place as pressure is decreased at a constant temperature?

    (A) solid to liquid to gas
    (B) solid to gas to liquid
    (C) gas to liquid to solid
    (D) gas to solid to liquid
    (E) liquid to gas to solid

45. Which of the following forms of radioactive decay has (have) no electrical charge?

    I. Alpha decay
    II. Beta decay
    III. Gamma decay

    (A) II only
    (B) III only
    (C) I and II only
    (D) I and III only
    (E) II and III only

46. Based on the solubility products given below, which of the following salts is the most soluble?

    (A) $BaCO_3$ $K_{sp} = 5.1 \times 10^{-9}$
    (B) $PbCrO_4$ $K_{sp} = 2.8 \times 10^{-13}$
    (C) $AgCl$ $K_{sp} = 1.8 \times 10^{-10}$
    (D) $CaSO_4$ $K_{sp} = 9.1 \times 10^{-6}$
    (E) ZnC_2O_4 $K_{sp} = 2.7 \times 10^{-8}$

GO ON TO THE NEXT PAGE

47. $HCN(aq) \rightarrow H^+(aq) + CN^-(aq)$

    Hydrocyanic acid dissociates according to the reaction given above. Which of the following expressions is equal to the acid dissociation constant for HCN?

    (A) $\left[H^+\right]\left[CN^-\right]$

    (B) $\left[H^+\right]\left[CN^-\right]\left[HCN\right]$

    (C) $\dfrac{\left[HCN\right]}{\left[H^+\right]\left[CN^-\right]}$

    (D) $\dfrac{\left[H^+\right]\left[CN^-\right]}{\left[HCN\right]}$

    (E) $\dfrac{1}{\left[H^+\right]\left[CN^-\right]\left[HCN\right]}$

48. The reaction progress diagram of an uncatalyzed reaction is shown by the solid line. Which dotted line presents the same reaction in the presence of a catalyst?

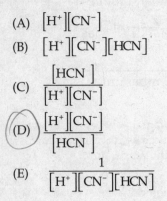

49. In a hydrogen atom, when an electron jumps from an excited energy state to a more stable energy state

    (A) electromagnetic radiation is emitted by the atom
    (B) electromagnetic radiation is absorbed by the atom
    (C) the atom becomes a positively charged ion
    (D) the atom becomes a negatively charged ion
    (E) the atom undergoes nuclear decay

Questions 50–52 pertain to the following situation:

A closed 5-liter vessel contains a sample of neon gas. The temperature inside the container is 25°C, and the pressure is 1.5 atmospheres. (The gas constant, *R*, is equal to 0.08 L-atm/mol-K.)

50. Which of the following expressions is equal to the molar quantity of gas in the sample?

    (A) $\dfrac{(1.5)(5.0)}{(0.08)(25)}$ moles

    (B) $\dfrac{(0.08)(25)}{(1.5)(5.0)}$ moles

    (C) $\dfrac{(1.5)(25)}{(0.08)(5.0)}$ moles

    (D) $\dfrac{(0.08)(298)}{(1.5)(5.0)}$ moles

    (E) $\dfrac{(1.5)(5.0)}{(0.08)(298)}$ moles

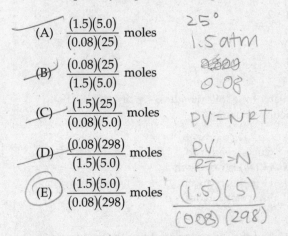

51. If the neon gas in the vessel is replaced with an equal molar quantity of helium gas, which of the following properties of the gas in the container will be changed?

    I. Pressure
    II. Temperature
    III. Density

    (A) I only
    (B) II only
    (C) III only
    (D) I and II only
    (E) II and III only

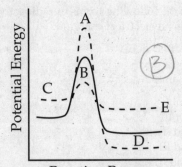

GO ON TO THE NEXT PAGE

52. The volume of the vessel was gradually changed while temperature was held constant until the pressure was measured at 1.6 atmospheres. Which of the following expressions is equal to the new volume?

(A) $5.0 \times \dfrac{1.5}{1.6}$ liters

(B) $5.0 \times \dfrac{1.6}{1.5}$ liters

(C) $25 \times \dfrac{1.5}{1.6}$ liters

(D) $0.08 \times \dfrac{1.6}{1.5}$ liters

(E) $0.08 \times \dfrac{1.5}{1.6}$ liters

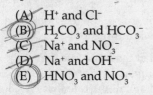

53. An oxidation-reduction reaction takes place in a chemical cell, and the flow of electrons is used to provide energy for a light bulb. Which of the following statements is true of the reaction?

(A) The reaction is nonspontaneous and has a positive voltage.
(B) The reaction is nonspontaneous and has a negative voltage.
(C) The reaction is at equilibrium and has a voltage of zero.
(D) The reaction is spontaneous and has a positive voltage.
(E) The reaction is spontaneous and has a negative voltage.

54. A solution containing which of the following pairs of species could be a buffer?

(A) H^+ and Cl^-
(B) H_2CO_3 and HCO_3^-
(C) Na^+ and NO_3^-
(D) Na^+ and OH^-
(E) HNO_3 and NO_3^-

55. Which of the following species is the conjugate acid of ammonia (NH_3)?

(A) N_2
(B) H_2
(C) NH^{2-}
(D) NH_2^-
(E) NH_4^+

56. A solution of H_2SO_3 is found to have a hydrogen ion concentration of 1×10^{-3} molar at 25°C. What is the hydroxide ion concentration in the solution?

(A) 1×10^{-13} molar
(B) 1×10^{-11} molar
(C) 1×10^{-7} molar
(D) 1×10^{-4} molar
(E) 1×10^{-3} molar

57. Which of the following expressions is equal to the number of iron (Fe) atoms present in a pure sample of solid iron with a mass of 10 grams? (The atomic mass of iron is 55.9.)

(A) $(10.0)(55.9)(6.02 \times 10^{23})$ atoms

(B) $\dfrac{\left(6.02 \times 10^{23}\right)}{(10.0)(55.9)}$ atoms

(C) $\dfrac{(10.0)\left(6.02 \times 10^{23}\right)}{(55.9)}$ atoms

(D) $\dfrac{(55.9)}{(10.0)\left(6.02 \times 10^{23}\right)}$ atoms

(E) $\dfrac{(10.0)}{(55.9)\left(6.02 \times 10^{23}\right)}$ atoms

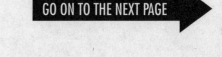

GO ON TO THE NEXT PAGE

58. A radioactive material is undergoing nuclear decay. After 40 minutes, 25 percent of the sample remains. What is the half-life of the sample?

    (A) 10 minutes
    (B) 20 minutes
    (C) 40 minutes
    (D) 80 minutes
    (E) 160 minutes

40 min

20min

10 min

59.

Element	First Ionization Energy (kJ/mol)
Lithium	520
Sodium	496
Rubidium	403
Cesium	376

Based on the table above, which of the following is most likely to be the first ionization energy for potassium?

(A) 536 kJ/mol
(B) 504 kJ/mol
(C) 419 kJ/mol
(D) 391 kJ/mol
(E) 358 kJ/mol

Questions 60–62 pertain to the reaction represented by the following equation:

$$2 NOCl(g) \leftrightarrow 2 NO(g) + Cl_2(g)$$

60. Which of the following expressions gives the equilibrium constant for the reaction above?

    (A) $\dfrac{[NOCl]}{[NO][Cl_2]}$

    (B) $\dfrac{[NO][Cl_2]}{[NOCl]}$

    (C) $\dfrac{[NOCl]^2}{[NO]^2[Cl_2]}$

    (D) $\dfrac{[NO]^2[Cl_2]}{[NOCl]^2}$

    (E) $\dfrac{[NOCl]^2}{[NO]^2[Cl_2]^2}$

61. Which of the following changes to the equilibrium above would serve to decrease the concentration of Cl_2?

    I. The addition of $NOCl(g)$ to the reaction vessel
    II. The addition of $NO(g)$ to the reaction vessel
    III. A decrease in the volume of the reaction vessel

    (A) I only
    (B) II only
    (C) I and II only
    (D) I and III only
    (E) II and III only

62. Which of the following is true of the reaction above as it proceeds in the forward direction?

    (A) $NO(g)$ is produced at the same rate that $NOCl(g)$ is consumed.
    (B) $NO(g)$ is produced at half the rate that $NOCl(g)$ is consumed.
    (C) $NO(g)$ is produced at twice the rate that $NOCl(g)$ is consumed.
    (D) $Cl_2(g)$ is produced at the same rate that $NOCl(g)$ is consumed.
    (E) $Cl_2(g)$ is produced at twice the rate that $NOCl(g)$ is consumed.

GO ON TO THE NEXT PAGE

63. Which of the following is an organic molecule?

    (A) SiO_2
    (B) NH_3
    (C) H_2O
    (D) CH_4
    (E) BeF_2

64.

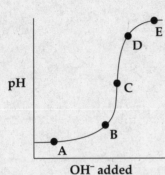

OH⁻ added

The graph above represents the titration of a strong acid with a strong base. Which of the points shown on the graph indicates the equivalence point in the titration?

    (A) A
    (B) B
    (C) C
    (D) D
    (E) E

65. Which of the following statements about fluorine is NOT true?

    (A) It is the most electronegative element.
    (B) It contains 19 protons in its nucleus.
    (C) Its compounds can engage in hydrogen bonding.
    (D) It takes the oxidation state –1.
    (E) It is found in nature as a diatomic gas.

66. The reactivity and chemical behavior of an atom is governed by many factors. The most important factor is

    (A) the number of protons in the atom's nucleus
    (B) the number of neutrons in the atom's nucleus
    (C) the number of protons and neutrons in the atom's nucleus
    (D) the ratio of protons to neutrons in the atom's nucleus
    (E) the number of electrons in the atom's valence shell

67. A beaker contains a saturated solution of copper(I) chloride, a slightly soluble salt with a solubility product of 1.2×10^{-6}. The addition of which of the salts listed below to the solution would cause the precipitation of copper(I) chloride?

    (A) Sodium chloride
    (B) Potassium bromide
    (C) Silver(I) nitrate
    (D) Lead(II) acetate
    (E) Magnesium iodide

68. Bromothymol blue is an acid/base indicator with a pK_a of 6.8. Therefore, at approximately what pH will bromothymol blue undergo a color change during an acid/base titration?

    (A) 1
    (B) 3
    (C) 5
    (D) 7
    (E) 13

69. Which of the following is necessarily true of a nonionic substance with a high boiling point?

    (A) It has a large vapor pressure.
    (B) It has strong intermolecular attractive forces.
    (C) It has a low freezing point.
    (D) It has a low heat of vaporization.
    (E) It will be present in gas phase at very low temperatures.

STOP

IF YOU FINISH BEFORE TIME IS CALLED, YOU MAY CHECK YOUR WORK ON THIS TEST ONLY.
DO NOT TURN TO ANY OTHER TEST IN THIS BOOK.

HOW TO SCORE THE PRINCETON REVIEW
PRACTICE SAT CHEMISTRY SUBJECT TEST

When you take the real exam, the proctors will collect your test booklet and bubble sheet and send your answer sheet to New Jersey where a computer looks at the pattern of filled-in ovals on your answer sheet and gives you a score. We couldn't include even a small computer with this book, so we are providing this more primitive way of scoring your exam.

DETERMINING YOUR SCORE

STEP 1 Using the answer key on the next page, determine how many questions you got right and how many you got wrong on the test. Remember, questions that you do not answer don't count as either right or wrong answers.

STEP 2 List the number of right answers here.

STEP 3 List the number of wrong answers here. Now divide that number by 4. (Use a calculator if you're feeling particularly lazy.)

STEP 4 Subtract the number of wrong answers divided by 4 from the number of correct answers. Round this score to the nearest whole number. This is your raw score.

STEP 5 To determine your real score, take the number from Step 4 above, and look it up in the left column of the Score Conversion Table on page 226; the corresponding score on the right is your score on the exam.

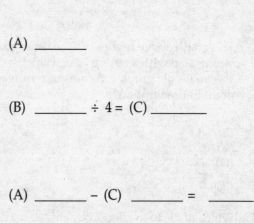

(A) _____

(B) _____ ÷ 4 = (C) _____

(A) _____ – (C) _____ = _____

ANSWERS TO THE PRINCETON REVIEW
PRACTICE SAT CHEMISTRY SUBJECT TEST 2

Question Number	Correct Answer	Right	Wrong	Question Number	Correct Answer	Right	Wrong
1.	E	___	___	46.	D	___	___
2.	B	___	___	47.	D	___	___
3.	D	___	___	48.	B	___	___
4.	B	___	___	49.	A	___	___
5.	A	___	___	50.	E	___	___
6.	D	___	___	51.	C	___	___
7.	C	___	___	52.	A	___	___
8.	E	___	___	53.	D	___	___
9.	B	___	___	54.	B	___	___
10.	C	___	___	55.	E	___	___
11.	B	___	___	56.	B	___	___
12.	A	___	___	57.	C	___	___
13.	D	___	___	58.	B	___	___
14.	C	___	___	59.	C	___	___
15.	A	___	___	60.	D	___	___
16.	C	___	___	61.	E	___	___
17.	B	___	___	62.	A	___	___
18.	E	___	___	63.	D	___	___
19.	C	___	___	64.	C	___	___
20.	A	___	___	65.	B	___	___
21.	B	___	___	66.	E	___	___
22.	A	___	___	67.	A	___	___
23.	D	___	___	68.	D	___	___
24.	E	___	___	69.	B	___	___
25.	C	___	___				
26.	C	___	___				
27.	B	___	___	101.	F, T		
28.	D	___	___	102.	T, T, CE		
29.	D	___	___	103.	T, T, CE		
30.	C	___	___	104.	T, T		
31.	E	___	___	105.	F, T		
32.	C	___	___	106.	F, F		
33.	C	___	___	107.	T, T, CE		
34.	B	___	___	108.	T, T, CE		
35.	A	___	___	109.	T, T		
36.	B	___	___	110.	F, T		
37.	A	___	___	111.	T, T		
38.	A	___	___	112.	T, T, CE		
39.	B	___	___	113.	T, F		
40.	A	___	___	114.	F, T		
41.	E	___	___	115.	T, F		
42.	C	___	___	116.	T, T, CE		
43.	C	___	___				
44.	A	___	___				
45.	B	___	___				

4.5

THE PRINCETON REVIEW PRACTICE SAT CHEMISTRY
SUBJECT TEST SCORE CONVERSION TABLE

Raw Score	Scaled Score	Raw Score	Scaled Score	Raw Score	Scaled Score
85	800	45	620	5	390
84	800	44	620	4	390
83	800	43	610	3	380
82	800	42	610	2	380
81	800	41	600	1	370
80	800	40	590	0	370
79	800	39	590	−1	370
78	790	38	580	−2	360
77	780	37	580	−3	360
76	780	36	570	−4	350
75	780	35	560	−5	340
74	780	34	560	−6	340
73	780	33	550	−7	330
72	770	32	550	−8	330
71	770	31	540	−9	320
70	750	30	530	−10	310
69	750	29	530	−11	310
68	740	28	520	−12	300
67	740	27	520	−13	300
66	740	26	520	−14	290
65	730	25	510	−15	280
64	730	24	510	−16	280
63	710	23	500	−17	270
62	710	22	500	−18	270
61	710	21	490	−19	260
60	700	20	480	−20	250
59	700	19	480	−21	250
58	690	18	470		
57	690	17	470		
56	680	16	460		
55	680	15	450		
54	680	14	450		
53	670	13	440		
52	670	12	440		
51	660	11	430		
50	650	10	420		
49	650	9	420		
48	630	8	410		
47	630	7	410		
46	630	6	400		

18

Practice SAT Chemistry Subject Test 2: Answers and Explanations

PART A

QUESTIONS 1–4

(A) Molarity
(B) Molality
(C) Mole fraction
(D) Density
(E) Partial pressure

1. Is measured in units of atmospheres or millimeters of mercury

E is correct. Atmospheres and millimeters of mercury (also written as mmHg or torr) are units of pressure used in the measurement of gas properties. Partial pressure is the only property listed that is measured in units of pressure.

2. Is measured in units of moles/kilogram

B is correct. Molality (m) is the measure of moles of solute present per kilogram of solvent. It is the only answer choice that measures moles per kilogram. Molality differs from molarity (M) in that molarity is the measure of moles of solute per liter of solution.

3. Is a measure of mass per unit volume

D is correct. Density is the measure of the mass of gas, liquid, or solid within a given volume. The densities of liquids and solids are relatively independent of their surroundings, while the density of a gas depends on the size of the container in which it is confined.

4. Is the quantity used in the calculation of boiling point elevation

B is correct. Molality (m) is used in the calculation of boiling point elevation according to the formula: $\Delta T = k_b m i$, where k_b is the boiling point elevation constant for a solvent, m is the molality of the solution and i is the van Hoff factor, which tells how many particles 1 unit of the solute will create when it dissociates. Molality is also used in the calculation of freezing point depression.

QUESTIONS 5–9

(A) Hydrogen bonding
(B) Ionic bonding
(C) Network bonding
(D) London dispersion force
(E) Metallic bonding

5. Chiefly responsible for the relatively high boiling point of water

A is correct. Liquid water (H_2O) contains hydrogen bonds between the hydrogen atoms of each molecule and the oxygen atoms of neighboring molecules. Many of water's distinctive properties, such as the fact that it has a lower density as a solid than as a liquid and that it has a relatively high boiling point, are due to hydrogen bonding.

6. Is present in liquid oxygen

D is correct. Liquid oxygen is held together by London dispersion forces, which are very weak attractions between molecules. London dispersion forces are the only type of intermolecular attractions that exist in nonpolar molecules, such as O_2. London dispersion forces occur because of instantaneous charge imbalances in molecules. Most substances that experience only London dispersion forces are gases at room temperature.

7. Is primarily responsible for the hardness of diamond

C is correct. Diamond owes its great strength to the fact that its carbon atoms are bonded together in a tetrahedral network of covalent bonds. This tetrahedral structure means that diamonds have no natural breaking points and are thus very difficult to shatter.

8. Allows copper to conduct electricity

E is correct. Solid copper is held together by metallic bonding. When elements are held together by metallic bonds, positively charged nuclei float in a sea of mobile electrons. The electrons move freely from nucleus to nucleus. This electron mobility is responsible for the distinctive properties of metals such as conductivity and malleability.

9. Is present in solid KCl

B is correct. Solid KCl (potassium chloride) salt is held together by ionic bonds. The positively charged potassium ions and the negatively charged chloride ions are held together by the electrostatic force between them. Remember, the electrostatic force comes from the attraction between two atoms that differ very significantly in electronegativity and is very strong.

QUESTIONS 10–13

(A) Na^+
(B) Al
(C) F
(D) Ti
(E) Br^-

10. Has 7 valence electrons

C is correct. Fluorine (F) has 7 electrons in its second shell, 1 short of a complete stable octet.

11. Has the electron configuration $1s^22s^22p^63s^23p^1$

B is correct. Aluminum (Al) has 3 electrons in its third shell, 2 in the s subshell, and 1 in the p subshell.

12. Has the same electron configuration as a neon
    atom

A is correct. A positively charged sodium ion (Na^+) has given up the 1 electron from its third shell, so it has the same electron configuration as a neon atom, which has a completed second shell.

13. Has valence electrons in *d* orbitals

D is correct. Titanium (Ti) is a transition metal and has 2 electrons in its $3d$ subshell.

QUESTIONS 14–17

(A) A 0.01-molar solution of HNO_3
(B) A 0.01-molar solution of $HC_2H_3O_2$
(C) A 0.01-molar solution of $Cu(NO_3)_2$
(D) A 0.01-molar solution of $NaNO_3$
(E) A 0.01-molar solution of $NaOH$

14. Will be colored blue

C is correct. The solution containing Cu^{2+} ion will be blue. Most solutions containing salts of transition metals are distinctly colored because the *d* subshell electrons of transition metals absorb and emit electromagnetic radiation in the visible spectrum.

15. Will have a pH of 2

A is correct. HNO_3 is a strong acid, so it will dissociate completely in solution. That means that a 0.01-molar solution of HNO_3 will have a hydrogen ion concentration of 0.01-molar. pH is $-\log[H^+]$, and $-\log(0.01) = 2$, so the pH of the solution will be 2.

16. Will have the lowest freezing point

C is correct. Freezing point depression is a colligative property, which means that it depends only on the number of particles in a solution, not on their identities. For every unit of $Cu(NO_3)_2$ in a solution, 3 particles are produced: 1 Cu^{2+} and 2 NO_3^-. For all of the other choices, each unit in solution produces only 2 particles.

17. Will contain undissociated aqueous particles

B is correct. $HC_2H_3O_2$ (acetic acid) is a weak acid, which means that it does not dissociate significantly in solution. That means that most of the particles present in the acetic acid solution will be undissociated $HC_2H_3O_2$. All of the other solutions listed contain solutes that dissociate completely.

QUESTIONS 18–20

(A) Enthalpy change
(B) Entropy change
(C) Gibbs free energy change
(D) Activation energy
(E) Specific heat capacity

18. Is the amount of energy that must be added to raise the temperature of 1 gram of a substance 1°C

E is correct. The specific heat capacity is the amount of energy that must be added to raise the temperature of 1 gram of a substance 1°C. If a substance has a large specific heat capacity, it can absorb a large amount of heat while undergoing a small temperature change.

19. Its value indicates the spontaneity of a reaction

C is correct. The value of the Gibbs free energy change (ΔG) for a reaction indicates the spontaneity of the reaction. If ΔG is negative, then the forward reaction is spontaneous. If ΔG is positive, then the reaction is not spontaneous. If ΔG is zero, then the forward reaction is at equilibrium.

20. Its value indicates whether a reaction is endothermic or exothermic

A is correct. The value of the enthalpy change (ΔH) for a reaction indicates whether the reaction is endothermic or exothermic. If ΔH is positive, energy is absorbed over the course of the reaction, and the reaction is endothermic. If ΔH is negative, energy is released over the course of the reaction, and the reaction is exothermic.

QUESTIONS 21–23

(A) Ionization energy
(B) Electronegativity
(C) Atomic radius
(D) Atomic number
(E) Mass number

21. Is the measure of the pull of the nucleus of an atom on the electrons of other atoms bonded to it

B is correct. Electronegativity indicates how strongly an atom will attract the electrons of another atom in a bond. The larger the electronegativity difference between two atoms in a bond, the more polar the bond will be.

22. Is the energy required to remove an electron from an atom

A is correct. Ionization energy is the energy required to remove an electron from an atom or ion. The larger the ionization energy, the more difficult it is to remove the electron.

23. Is equal to the number of protons in an atom

D is correct. The atomic number, which determines the identity of an element, is equal to the number of protons in the atom's nucleus. The mass number is equal to the sum of the protons and neutrons in an atom's nucleus. Atoms with the same atomic number and different mass numbers are isotopes.

PART B

101. An ionic solid is a good   BECAUSE   an ionic solid is composed of
      conductor of electricity   positive and negative ions joined
                                                       together in a lattice structure held
                                                       together by electrostatic forces.

F, T Divide and conquer. The first statement is false. Neither the electrons nor the ions in an ionic solid are free to move about, so an ionic solid will not conduct electricity. The second statement is true. An ionic solid is composed of positive and negative ions joined in a lattice structure by electrostatic forces. The first statement is false and the second statement is true.

102. The bond in an O_2 molecule   BECAUSE   the oxygen atoms in an O_2
      is nonpolar   molecule share the bonding
                                                         electrons equally.

T, T, CE Divide and conquer. Both statements are true. Since the oxygen atoms are identical to each other, they will have equal attraction for the bonding electrons. The second statement is a correct explanation for the first statement, so we fill in the CE oval.

103. When a sample of water freezes,   BECAUSE   ice is at a lower potential energy
      the process is exothermic   state than water.

T, T, CE Divide and conquer. Both statements are true. Ice has stronger intermolecular forces and more stability than water, so when water freezes, energy is released. The second statement is a correct explanation of the first statement, so fill in the CE oval.

104. At 25°C, an aqueous solution   BECAUSE   the pH of a buffered solution is not
      with a pH of 5 will have a pOH of 9   greatly affected by the addition of a
                                                         relatively small amount of
                                                         acid or base.

T, T Divide and conquer: The first statement is true. For an aqueous solution at 25°C, pH + pOH = 14. The second statement is also true. The definition of a buffer is *a solution whose pH is not easily changed by the addition of an acid or base.* Now, ask yourself if the word "because" relates the two statements. The second statement does not explain the first statement, so do not fill in the CE oval.

105. When a chlorine atom gains an electron, it becomes a positively charged ion   BECAUSE   a neutral atom has equal numbers of protons and electrons.

F, T Divide and conquer. The first statement is false. When an atom gains an electron, it becomes a negatively charged ion. The second statement is true. Protons are positively charged and electrons are negatively charged, so an atom that has equal numbers of protons and electrons will be electrically neutral. The first statement is false and the second statement is true.

106. Lithium has a larger first ionization energy than oxygen   BECAUSE   oxygen atoms have larger atomic radii than lithium atoms.

F, F Divide and conquer. The first statement is false. As you travel across a period on the periodic table, from left to right, ionization energy increases. That's because as we move across a period, we are adding protons to the nucleus, which increases the pull of the nucleus on the valence electrons, making them more difficult to remove. The second statement is also false. The same reasoning applies here; oxygen's nucleus has more protons, so oxygen exerts a greater pull on its electrons. As a result, oxygen's valence electrons will be closer to the nucleus than lithium's, making its atomic radius smaller. Both statements are false.

107. Potassium chloride dissolves readily in water   BECAUSE   water is a polar solvent.

T, T, CE Divide and conquer. The first statement is true; potassium chloride (KCl) is a soluble salt. The second statement is also true. The second statement is a correct explanation of the first statement because we know that like dissolves like, so ionic solids are best dissolved by polar solvents. Both statements are true and we fill in the CE oval.

108. Ammonia is a Lewis base   BECAUSE   ammonia can donate an electron pair to a bond.

T, T, CE Divide and conquer. Both statements are true; we know that ammonia (NH_3) is a Lewis base and that a Lewis base is an electron pair *donor*. The second statement is a correct explanation of the first statement—the statements together give us the definition of a Lewis base. We fill in the CE oval.

109. Elemental fluorine is more reactive than elemental neon   BECAUSE   neon has a larger atomic weight than fluorine.

T, T Divide and conquer. The first statement is true. Fluorine is more reactive than neon because it needs 1 electron to complete its valence shell, while neon has a complete stable octet of electrons in its valence shell. The second statement is true. Neon has an atomic weight of 20.2 g/mol, while fluorine has an atomic weight of 19.0 g/mol. Now see if the second statement explains the first. Fluorine is more reactive than neon for the reason given above, *not* because of its atomic weight, so the second statement does *not* explain the first. Both statements are true, and we do *not* fill in the CE oval.

110. The addition of a catalyst will   BECAUSE   a catalyst provides an alternate
      decrease the ΔH for a reaction   reaction pathway with a
                                                                lower activation energy.

F, T Divide and conquer. The first statement is false. The enthalpy change (ΔH) for a reaction is unaffected by the addition of a catalyst. The second statement is true: A catalyst increases the rate of a reaction by decreasing the activation energy of the reaction. The first statement is false and the second statement is true.

111. The oxygen atom in a water   BECAUSE   water molecules exhibit
      molecule has a –2 oxidation   hydrogen bonding.
      state

T, T Divide and conquer. The first statement is true. In water (H_2O), the oxygen atom gains 2 electrons and takes the –2 oxidation state while each of the 2 hydrogen atoms gives up an electron and takes the +1 oxidation state. The second statement is also true. Water does exhibit hydrogen bonding. Now, ask yourself whether the second statement is an explanation of the first. The two statements are not related. Both statements are true, and we do not fill in the CE oval.

112. When a salt sample dissolves   BECAUSE   for a salt sample, aqueous ions
      in water, ΔS for the process   have greater entropy than
      is positive   ions in a solid.

T, T, CE Divide and conquer. Entropy is a measure of disorder, and aqueous ions have greater disorder than ions in a solid, so both statements are true. The second statement is a good explanation of the first statement because knowing that aqueous ions have greater entropy than ions in a solid, we can see why entropy increases in solution. Both statements are true, and we fill in the CE oval.

113. When the temperature of a   BECAUSE   at equilibrium, all reactants have
      reaction at equilibrium is   been converted into products.
      increased, the equilibrium will
      shift to favor the endothermic
      direction

T, F Divide and conquer. The first statement is true. From Le Chatelier's principle we know that when temperature is increased, an equilibrium will move in the direction that will absorb the excess heat; that's the endothermic direction. The second statement is false. A reaction reaches equilibrium when the rate of the forward reaction is equal to the rate of the reverse reaction, not when all the reactants have been converted to products. The first statement is true and the second statement is false.

114. An atom of ^{12}C contains   BECAUSE   the identity of an element is
      12 protons   determined by the number of
                                                              protons in the nuclei of its atoms.

F, T Divide and conquer. The first statement is false. A carbon atom always contains 6 protons. The number 12 is the mass number, which is the sum of the protons and neutrons in the nucleus. The second statement is true. The number of protons in an atom is the atomic number and gives the element its identity. The first statement is false and the second statement is true.

115. Water boils at a lower   BECAUSE   the vapor pressure of water
     temperature at high altitude   is lower at higher altitude.
     than at low altitude

T, F Divide and conquer. The first statement is true. Water's vapor pressure increases when heat is added, and water boils when its vapor pressure is equal to the atmospheric pressure. At high altitudes, atmospheric pressure is decreased, so water will boil at a lower temperature. The second statement is false. The vapor pressure of water is unaffected by altitude. The first statement is true and the second statement is false.

116. Elemental sodium is a strong   BECAUSE   an atom of elemental sodium gives
     reducing agent   up its valence electron readily.

T, T, CE Divide and conquer. Both statements are true. A strong reducing agent is readily oxidized. Remember LEO says GER: when something is oxidized, it loses electrons. A sodium atom has only 1 valence electron, which it gives up readily, so it is easily oxidized. Therefore, elemental sodium is a strong reducing agent. The second statement is a good explanation of the first statement. Both statements are true, so fill in the CE oval.

PART C

24. What is the oxidation state of bromine in $HBrO_3$?
    (A) −3
    (B) −1
    (C) +1
    (D) +3
    (E) +5

E is correct. The oxidation states of all of the atoms in a neutral molecule must add up to zero. We know that oxygen almost always takes the oxidation state −2 and that hydrogen is almost always +1, so we know that $(+1) + (Br) + (3)(-2) = 0$. This makes the oxidation state of bromine +5.

25. What is the percent by mass of silicon in a sample
    of silicon dioxide?
    (A) 21%
    (B) 33%
    (C) 47%
    (D) 54%
    (E) 78%

C is correct. The molecular formula of silicon dioxide is SiO_2, so the molecular weight is $(28) + (2)(16)$ $= (28) + (32) = 60$. The percent by mass of silicon is equal to $\frac{28}{60} \times 100$, which is slightly less than 50 percent, or 47 percent to be exact.

26. How many electrons does a ^{37}Cl ion with a charge of –1 contain?

(A) 16
(B) 17
(C) 18
(D) 37
(E) 38

C is correct. The number of electrons in a chloride ion with a –1 charge will be one greater than the number of its protons. A chlorine atom or ion always contains 17 protons, so a chloride ion with a –1 charge will possess 18 electrons.

27. $CH_4(g) + 2\,O_2(g) \rightarrow CO_2(g) + 2\,H_2O(g) + 800\ kJ$

If 1 mole of $O_2(g)$ is consumed in the reaction given above, how much energy is produced?

(A) 200 kJ
(B) 400 kJ
(C) 800 kJ
(D) 1200 kJ
(E) 1600 kJ

B is correct. From the balanced equation, we can see that when 2 moles of $O_2(g)$ are consumed, 800 kJ of energy are produced. So when half that number of moles of $O_2(g)$(1 mole) are consumed, half as much energy is produced (400 kJ).

28. Which of the following is NOT true of the element sodium?

(A) It takes the oxidation state +1.
(B) It reacts with water to form a basic solution.
(C) It forms metallic bonds in its solid
    uncombined form.
(D) It is found in nature as a diatomic gas.
(E) It reacts with a halogen to form an ionic salt.

D is correct. All of the statements are true except choice D. Sodium is not found in nature as a diatomic gas; it is usually seen in nature in ionic salts.

29. What volume of a 0.200-molar solution of sodium hydroxide is required to neutralize 40.0 liters of a 0.300-molar hydrochloric acid solution?

(A)   10 liters
(B)   20 liters
(C)   40 liters
(D)   60 liters
(E)   120 liters

D is correct. To neutralize the HCl solution, we need to add as many moles of hydroxide ions as there are moles of hydrogen ions in the solution. Use the relationship moles = (molarity)(liters). We know that we have a strong acid and a strong base that will dissociate completely in solution and that 1 unit of HCl gives 1 hydrogen ion and 1 unit of NaOH gives 1 hydroxide ion upon dissociation. So, we can just set moles of hydroxide ion equal to moles of hydrogen ion, and use the following equation:

$$(M_{HCl})(L_{HCl}) = (M_{NaOH})(L_{NaOH})$$

$$(0.300\ M)(40.0\ L) = (0.200\ M)(x)$$

$$x = 60.0\ L$$

30. $\ldots PH_3 + \ldots O_2 \rightarrow \ldots P_2O_5 + \ldots H_2O$

When the equation above is balanced and the coefficients are reduced to the lowest whole numbers the coefficient for H_2O is

(A) 1
(B) 2
(C) 3
(D) 4
(E) 5

C is correct. Plug the answers into the equation. If the coefficient for H_2O is 3, then there are 6 hydrogens and the coefficient for PH_3 must be 2. That makes 1 the coefficient for P_2O_5. Now we have 8 oxygens on the right, so the coefficient for O_2 on the left must be 4. Since we have 1 as a coefficient for one of the species in the reaction, these must be the lowest whole number coefficients, and C is correct.

31. $H_2SO_4(aq) + Ba(OH)_2(aq) \rightarrow$

Which of the following are products of the reaction shown above?

  I. $O_2(g)$
  II. $H_2O(l)$
  III. $BaSO_4(s)$

(A) I only
(B) III only
(C) I and II only
(D) I and III only
(E) II and III only

E is correct. First, look at your reactants: You have an acid and a base, so you know that they will neutralize one another. Now write out the products.

$$H_2SO_4(aq) + Ba(OH)_2(aq) \rightarrow BaSO_4 + H_2O$$

Note that in this problem, you don't need to balance anything, just figure out the type of reaction and the products. The products of an acid-base neutralization (when the base is a metal hydroxide) are water and salt. In this case, the salt is barium sulfate.

32. $2 \text{ Mg}(s) + \text{O}_2(g) \rightarrow 2 \text{ MgO}(s)$

If 48.6 grams of magnesium are placed in a container with 64 grams of oxygen gas and the reaction above proceeds to completion, what is the mass of MgO(s) produced?

(A)   15.4 grams
(B)   32.0 grams
(C)   80.6 grams
(D)   96.3 grams
(E)   112 grams

C is correct. We need to determine the limiting reagent. Magnesium has an atomic weight of about 24 g/mol, so 48 grams of magnesium is 2 moles. O_2 has a molecular weight of 32 g/mol, so 64 grams of O_2 is about 2 moles. We need twice as much Mg for the reaction, so we'll run out of it first; magnesium is the limiting reagant. Two moles of Mg will produce 2 moles of MgO, which has a molecular weight of 40.3 g/mol, so we end up with 80.6 grams of MgO.

33. An ideal gas in a closed inflexible container has a pressure of 6 atmospheres and a temperature of 27°C. What will be the new pressure of the gas if the temperature is decreased to –73°C?

(A) 2 atm
(B) 3 atm
(C) 4 atm
(D) 8 atm
(E) 9 atm

C is correct. We know that the pressure and temperature of an ideal gas are related by the following equation (when the amount of gas and volume are held constant): $\dfrac{P_1}{T_1} = \dfrac{P_2}{T_2}$. We also know that we need to convert Celsius to Kelvin, so 27°C = 300 K and –73°C = 200 K. Now we can calculate:

$$\frac{(6 \text{ atm})}{(300 \text{ K})} = \frac{x}{(200 \text{ K})}$$

$$x = 4 \text{ atm}$$

34. Equal molar quantities of hydrogen gas and oxygen gas are present in a closed container at a constant temperature. Which of the following quantities will be the same for the two gases?

    I. Partial pressure
   II. Average kinetic energy
  III. Average molecular velocity

(A) I only
(B) I and II only
(C) I and III only
(D) II and III only
(E) I, II, and III

B is correct. The partial pressures of the two gases will be the same because partial pressure of a gas is directly proportional to the number of moles of the gas present, and we have equal numbers of moles of the two gases. The average kinetic energies of the two gases will be the same because the average kinetic energy of a gas is directly proportional to absolute temperature and the two gases are at the same temperature. The average molecular velocities will differ because when two gases have equal kinetic energies, the molecules of the gas with lower molecular weight must be moving faster on average.

35. Which of the following is a nonpolar molecule?

(A) CO_2
(B) H_2O
(C) NH_3
(D) NO
(E) HI

A is correct. CO_2 is a nonpolar molecule although it contains polar bonds. That's because carbon dioxide has its 3 atoms arranged in linear fashion, with its negatively charged oxygen atoms on the ends. There is a partial positive charge on the carbon atom. Due to the symmetrical arrangement of 2 equivalent polar bonds, the overall molecule has no net charge.

$$O=C=O$$
$$\delta^-\ \ \delta^+\ \ \delta^-$$

36. What is the molar concentration of a 500-milliliter solution that contains 20 grams of $CaBr_2$ (formula weight = 200)?

(A) 0.1 molar
(B) 0.2 molar
(C) 0.5 molar
(D) 1 molar
(E) 5 molar

B is correct. Knowing that moles = $\dfrac{grams}{formula\ weight}$, we can calculate the number of moles of $CaBr_2$ in the solution.

$$Moles\ of\ CaBr_2 = \frac{(20\,g)}{(200\ g/mol)}\ 0.1\ mole.$$

Now we can calculate the molarity of the solution (don't forget to convert milliliters to liters):

$$\text{Molarity} = \frac{\text{moles}}{\text{liters}} = \frac{(0.1 \text{ mol})}{(0.5 \text{ L})} = 0.2 \text{ molar.}$$

37. The structure of $BeCl_2$ can best be described as

 (A) linear
 (B) bent
 (C) trigonal
 (D) tetrahedral
 (E) square

A is correct. Be has 2 valence electrons to give up to Cl, so the 2 Cl atoms align themselves opposite each other and the molecule is linear. [Cl–Be–Cl]

38. $2 NO(g) + 2 H_2(g) \rightarrow N_2(g) + 2 H_2O(g)$

 Which of the following statements is true regarding the reaction given above?

 (A) If 1 mole of H_2 is consumed, 0.5 mole of N_2 is produced.
 (B) If 1 mole of H_2 is consumed, 0.5 mole of H_2O is produced.
 (C) If 0.5 mole of H_2 is consumed, 1 mole of N_2 is produced.
 (D) If 0.5 mole of H_2 is consumed, 1 mole of NO is consumed.
 (E) If 0.5 mole of H_2 is consumed, 1 mole of H_2O is produced.

A is correct. From the balanced equation, we can see that there will be twice as much H_2 consumed as there is N_2 produced.

Questions 39–40 pertain to the reaction represented by the following equation:

$$\ldots Cu(s) + \ldots NO_3^-(aq) + \ldots H^+(aq) \rightarrow$$
$$\ldots Cu^{2+}(aq) + \ldots NO_2(g) + \ldots H_2O(l)$$

39. When the equation above is balanced with lowest whole number coefficients, the coefficient for $H^+(aq)$ will be

 (A) 1
 (B) 2
 (C) 3
 (D) 4
 (E) 5

B is correct. Plug the answers into the reaction, and see which one works. Let's start at choice C because it's in the middle. If there are 3 H$^+$, then there can't be a whole number coefficient for H$_2$O, so the answer can't be an odd number. So the answer must be B or D. Try D. If there are 4 H$^+$, then there are 2 H$_2$O. The coppers are in balance if each has a coefficient of 1. Notice that this makes the net charge on the right side +2. With 4 H$^+$, the charge on the left is +4. Since charges must be in balance, the charge on the left must be reduced. If the coefficient of NO$_3^-$ is 2, this will balance charges. NO$_2$ will need a coefficient of 2 to balance nitrogens and oxygens. The equation is now balanced with the lowest whole number terms.

40. Which of the following takes place during the re-
    action above?

    (A) Cu(s) is oxidized.
    (B) Cu(s) is reduced.
    (C) H$^+$(aq) is oxidized.
    (D) H$^+$(aq) is reduced.
    (E) NO$_3^-$(aq) is oxidized.

A is correct. In the course of this reaction, Cu^0 is converted to Cu^{2+}. Remember LEO says GER; Cu has lost electrons, so it has been oxidized. By the way, NO$_3^-$ is reduced in the reaction, and the oxidation state of H$^+$ is not changed.

41. Which of the following could be the molecular
    formula for a molecule with an empirical formula
    of CH$_2$?

    (A) CH
    (B) CH$_4$
    (C) C$_2$H$_2$
    (D) C$_2$H$_6$
    (E) C$_3$H$_6$

E is correct. A molecule's empirical formula is its molecular formula with numbers reduced to lowest whole numbers, so if the empirical formula is CH$_2$, then its molecular formula must be C$_3$H$_6$.

42. When CO$_2$ is bubbled through distilled water at
    25°C, which of the following is most likely to occur?

    (A) Solid carbon will precipitate.
    (B) An electrical current will be produced in an
        oxidation-reduction reaction.
    (C) The pH of the solution will be reduced.
    (D) The water will boil.
    (E) Methane (CH$_4$) gas will be formed.

C is correct. CO$_2$ combines with water to form carbonic acid (H$_2$CO$_3$).

$$CO_2 + H_2O \leftrightharpoons H_2CO_3 \leftrightharpoons H^+ + HCO_3^-$$

Carbonic acid is a weak acid, so it will release H$^+$ ions into the solution. When the concentration of H$^+$ increases, the pH decreases.

43. In which of the following processes is entropy increasing?

(A) $N_2(g) + 3 Cl_2(g) \rightarrow 2 NCl_3(g)$
(B) $H_2O(g) \rightarrow H_2O(l)$
(C) $2 H_2O(l) \rightarrow 2 H_2(g) + O_2(g)$
(D) $CO(g) + 2 H_2(g) \rightarrow CH_3OH(l)$
(E) $2 NO_2(g) \rightarrow N_2O_4(g)$

C is correct. Entropy is the measure of a system's randomness, and gases are more random than liquids. Also, the more molecules, the greater the randomness. In choice C, a liquid is converted into two gases, and the number of molecules is increasing, so entropy must be increasing.

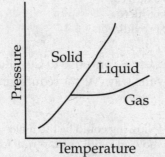

44. Based on the phase diagram above, which series of phase changes could take place as pressure is decreased at a constant temperature?

(A) solid to liquid to gas
(B) solid to gas to liquid
(C) gas to liquid to solid
(D) gas to solid to liquid
(E) liquid to gas to solid

A is correct. As pressure is decreased at constant temperature, phase changes could occur as shown in the diagram below:

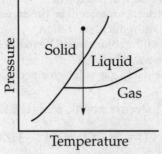

45. Which of the following forms of radioactive decay has (have) no electrical charge?

    I. Alpha decay
   II. Beta decay
  III. Gamma decay

(A) II only
(B) III only
(C) I and II only
(D) I and III only
(E) II and III only

B is correct. Gamma decay involves the release of electromagnetic radiation, which has no electrical charge. Alpha particles are positively charged, and beta particles are negatively charged.

46. Based on the solubility products given below, which of the following salts is the most soluble?

(A) $BaCO_3$ $K_{sp} = 5.1 \times 10^{-9}$
(B) $PbCrO_4$ $K_{sp} = 2.8 \times 10^{-13}$
(C) $AgCl$ $K_{sp} = 1.8 \times 10^{-10}$
(D) $CaSO_4$ $K_{sp} = 9.1 \times 10^{-6}$
(E) ZnC_2O_4 $K_{sp} = 2.7 \times 10^{-8}$

D is correct. The solubility product (K_{sp}) of a molecule is a measure of the concentrations of the particles into which it dissociates in solution at equilibrium. Since all of these salts will ionize into two ions per unit, the salt with the largest value of K_{sp} will be the most soluble.

47. $HCN(aq) \rightarrow H^+(aq) + CN^-(aq)$

Hydrocyanic acid dissociates according to the reaction given above. Which of the following expressions is equal to the acid dissociation constant for HCN?

(A) $\left[H^+ \right]\left[CN^- \right]$

(B) $\left[H^+ \right]\left[CN^- \right]\left[HCN \right]$

(C) $\dfrac{\left[HCN \right]}{\left[H^+ \right]\left[CN^- \right]}$

(D) $\dfrac{\left[H^+ \right]\left[CN^- \right]}{\left[HCN \right]}$

(E) $\dfrac{1}{\left[H^+ \right]\left[CN^- \right]\left[HCN \right]}$

D is correct. The acid dissociation constant (K_a) is an equilibrium constant, with the concentrations of the products in the numerator and the concentrations of the reactants in the denominator.

48. The reaction progress diagram of an uncatalyzed reaction is shown by the solid line. Which dotted line presents the same reaction in the presence of a catalyst?

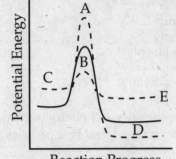

B is correct. A catalyst lowers the activation energy of a reaction but does not change the potential energy of the starting materials or products. Choice A actually raises the activation energy, and C, D, and E change the energies of the reactant or product. Choice B is correct.

49. In a hydrogen atom, when an electron jumps from an excited energy state to a more stable energy state

   (A) electromagnetic radiation is emitted by the atom
   (B) electromagnetic radiation is absorbed by the atom
   (C) the atom becomes a positively charged ion
   (D) the atom becomes a negatively charged ion
   (E) the atom undergoes nuclear decay

A is correct. When an electron jumps from an excited state to a more stable state, energy is released by the atom. This energy is released in the form of electromagnetic radiation. In the reverse process, an atom may absorb electromagnetic radiation, and its electrons may jump to excited energy levels.

Questions 50–52 pertain to the following situation:

A closed 5-liter vessel contains a sample of neon gas. The temperature inside the container is 25°C, and the pressure is 1.5 atmospheres. (The gas constant, R, is equal to 0.08 L-atm/mol-K.)

50. Which of the following expressions is equal to the molar quantity of gas in the sample?

(A) $\dfrac{(1.5)(5.0)}{(0.08)(25)}$ moles

(B) $\dfrac{(0.08)(25)}{(1.5)(5.0)}$ moles

(C) $\dfrac{(1.5)(25)}{(0.08)(5.0)}$ moles

(D) $\dfrac{(0.08)(298)}{(1.5)(5.0)}$ moles

(E) $\dfrac{(1.5)(5.0)}{(0.08)(298)}$ moles

E is correct. Use the ideal gas equation, $PV = nRT$, and solve for n, the number of moles of gas. Don't forget to convert 25°C to 298 K.

$$n = \frac{PV}{RT} = \frac{(1.5)(5.0)}{(0.08)(298)} \text{ moles}$$

51. If the neon gas in the vessel is replaced with an equal molar quantity of helium gas, which of the following properties of the gas in the container will be changed?

   I. Pressure
  II. Temperature
 III. Density

(A) I only
(B) II only
(C) III only
(D) I and II only
(E) II and III only

C is correct. Pressure and temperature will not be changed as long as the number of moles of gas in the vessel doesn't change. The density of the gas will decrease because equal numbers of moles of helium and neon will have different masses, and density is the measure of mass per unit volume.

52. The volume of the vessel was gradually changed while temperature was held constant until the pressure was measured at 1.6 atmospheres. Which of the following expressions is equal to the new volume?

(A) $5.0 \times \dfrac{1.5}{1.6}$ liters

(B) $5.0 \times \dfrac{1.6}{1.5}$ liters

(C) $25 \times \dfrac{1.5}{1.6}$ liters

(D) $0.08 \times \dfrac{1.6}{1.5}$ liters

(E) $0.08 \times \dfrac{1.5}{1.6}$ liters

A is correct. From the ideal gas equation, we can see that volume is related to pressure by the following relationship (when n and T are kept constant):

$$P_1 V_1 = P_2 V_2$$

and, by solving for the new volume, V_2, we get

$$V_2 = V_1 \frac{P_1}{P_2} = 5.0 \times \frac{1.5}{1.6} \text{ L}$$

53. An oxidation-reduction reaction takes place in a chemical cell, and the flow of electrons is used to provide energy for a light bulb. Which of the following statements is true of the reaction?

(A) The reaction is nonspontaneous and has a positive voltage.
(B) The reaction is nonspontaneous and has a negative voltage.
(C) The reaction is at equilibrium and has a voltage of zero.
(D) The reaction is spontaneous and has a positive voltage.
(E) The reaction is spontaneous and has a negative voltage.

D is correct. If the reaction is being used to provide energy to electrons, it must have a positive reaction potential or voltage. In the same way, if the reaction is being used to provide energy to a circuit, it must be spontaneous (ΔG is negative).

54. A solution containing which of the following pairs of species could be a buffer?

   (A) H^+ and Cl^-
   (B) H_2CO_3 and HCO_3^-
   (C) Na^+ and NO_3^-
   (D) Na^+ and OH^-
   (E) HNO_3 and NO_3^-

B is correct. A buffered solution is made up of a weak acid and its conjugate base (or weak base and its conjugate acid). Carbonic acid (H_2CO_3) and bicarbonate ion (HCO_3^-) are the only examples of this type of pairing in the answer choices. Choices A and E represent strong acids and their conjugates, choice C represents a salt, and choice D represents a strong base.

55. Which of the following species is the conjugate acid of ammonia (NH_3)?

   (A) N_2
   (B) H_2
   (C) NH^{2-}
   (D) NH_2^-
   (E) NH_4^+

E is correct. Ammonia (NH_3) is a base, which means it can accept a proton or H^+ ion. NH_3 accepts a proton to become NH_4^+.

56. A solution of H_2SO_3 is found to have a hydrogen ion concentration of 1×10^{-3} molar at 25°C. What is the hydroxide ion concentration in the solution?

   (A) 1×10^{-13} molar
   (B) 1×10^{-11} molar
   (C) 1×10^{-7} molar
   (D) 1×10^{-4} molar
   (E) 1×10^{-3} molar

B is correct. We know that pH + pOH = 14 and that $[H^+][OH^-] = 1 \times 10^{-14}$ at 25°C.

$$\text{So, } \left[OH^-\right] = \frac{\left(1 \times 10^{-14}\right)}{\left[H^+\right]}M = \frac{\left(1 \times 10^{-14}\right)}{1 \times 10^{-3}}M = 1 \times 10^{-11}M$$

57. Which of the following expressions is equal to the number of iron (Fe) atoms present in a pure sample of solid iron with a mass of 10 grams? (The atomic mass of iron is 55.9.)

(A) $(10.0)(55.9)(6.02 \times 10^{23})$ atoms

(B) $\dfrac{\left(6.02 \times 10^{23}\right)}{(10.0)(55.9)}$ atoms

(C) $\dfrac{(10.0)\left(6.02 \times 10^{23}\right)}{(55.9)}$ atoms

(D) $\dfrac{(55.9)}{(10.0)\left(6.02 \times 10^{23}\right)}$ atoms

(E) $\dfrac{(10.0)}{(55.9)\left(6.02 \times 10^{23}\right)}$ atoms

C is correct. The number of moles of iron in the sample is given by the following expression:

$$\text{moles} = \frac{\text{grams}}{\text{atomic mass}} = \frac{(10.0)}{(55.9)}$$

Now we use Avogadro's number (6.02×10^{23}) to find the number of atoms in the sample.

$$\text{atoms} = (\text{moles})(6.02 \ 10^{23}) = \frac{(10.0)}{(55.9)}\left(6.02 \times 10^{23}\right) = \frac{(10.0)\left(6.02 \times 10^{23}\right)}{(55.9)}$$

58. A radioactive material is undergoing nuclear decay. After 40 minutes, 25 percent of the sample remains. What is the half-life of the sample?

(A) 10 minutes
(B) 20 minutes
(C) 40 minutes
(D) 80 minutes
(E) 160 minutes

B is correct. The half-life of a radioactive material is the time that it takes for half of the sample to decay. After 1 half-life 50 percent of this sample remains, and after 2 half lives, 25 percent remains. If two half lives are 40 minutes, then 1 half-life is 20 minutes long.

59.

Element	First Ionization Energy (kJ/mol)
Lithium	520
Sodium	496
Rubidium	403
Cesium	376

Based on the table above, which of the following is most likely to be the first ionization energy for potassium?

(A) 536 kJ/mol
(B) 504 kJ/mol
(C) 419 kJ/mol
(D) 391 kJ/mol
(E) 358 kJ/mol

C is correct. Potassium (K) is in group 1A of the periodic table, between sodium (Na) and rubidium (Rb). We know from our knowledge of periodic trends that the value of potassium's first ionization energy will fall between that of sodium and rubidium.

Questions 60–62 pertain to the reaction represented by the following equation:

$$2\ NOCl(g) \leftrightarrow 2\ NO(g) + Cl_2(g)$$

60. Which of the following expressions gives the equilibrium constant for the reaction above?

(A) $\dfrac{[NOCl]}{[NO][Cl_2]}$

(B) $\dfrac{[NO][Cl_2]}{[NOCl]}$

(C) $\dfrac{[NOCl]^2}{[NO]^2[Cl_2]}$

(D) $\dfrac{[NO]^2[Cl_2]}{[NOCl]^2}$

(E) $\dfrac{[NOCl]^2}{[NO]^2[Cl_2]^2}$

D is correct. In the expression for the equilibrium constant, the products are in the numerator, the reactants are in the denominator, and the coefficients become exponents. So the correct expression is

$$K = \frac{[NO]^2[Cl_2]}{[NOCl]^2}$$

61. Which of the following changes to the equilibrium above would serve to decrease the concentration of Cl_2?

   I. The addition of NOCl(g) to the reaction vessel.

   II. The addition of NO(g) to the reaction vessel.

   III. A decrease in the volume of the reaction vessel.

(A) I only
(B) II only
(C) I and II only
(D) I and III only
(E) II and III only

E is correct. According to Le Chatelier's principle, equilibrium shifts to relieve any stresses placed on it. If NOCl is added, the equilibrium will shift to the right, and the concentration of Cl_2 will be increased, so I is wrong. If NO is added, the equilibrium will shift to the left and decrease the concentration of Cl_2, so II is correct. If the volume is decreased, the equilibrium will shift to the left, which has fewer moles of gas, and the concentration of Cl_2 will be decreased, so III is correct.

62. Which of the following is true of the reaction above as it proceeds in the forward direction?

(A) NO(g) is produced at the same rate that NOCl(g) is consumed.
(B) NO(g) is produced at half the rate that NOCl(g) is consumed.
(C) NO(g) is produced at twice the rate that NOCl(g) is consumed.
(D) Cl_2(g) is produced at the same rate that NOCl(g) is consumed.
(E) Cl_2(g) is produced at twice the rate that NOCl(g) is consumed.

A is correct. We can see from the balanced equation that for every mole of NOCl consumed, 1 mole of NO is produced, so choice A is correct.

63. Which of the following is an organic molecule?

(A) SiO_2
(B) NH_3
(C) H_2O
(D) CH_4
(E) BeF_2

D is correct. Organic chemistry is the study of carbon compounds. Methane (CH_4) is the only compound listed that contains carbon.

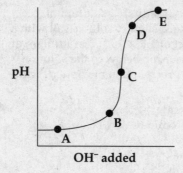

OH⁻ added

64. The graph above represents the titration of a
strong acid with a strong base. Which of the points
shown on the graph indicates the equivalence
point in the titration?

(A) A
(B) B
(C) C
(D) D
(E) E

C is correct. The equivalence point in a titration is the point when enough base has been added to neutralize all the acid that was initially present in the solution. This point is in the middle of the steep part of a titration curve. In this case, when a strong acid is titrated by a strong base, the pH at the equivalence point will be 7, and the solution will be neutral.

65. Which of the following statements about fluorine
is NOT true?

(A) It is the most electronegative element.
(B) It contains 19 protons in its nucleus.
(C) Its compounds can engage in hydrogen
bonding.
(D) It takes the oxidation state –1.
(E) It is found in nature as a diatomic gas.

B is correct. The atomic *mass* of fluorine is 19; the atomic *number*, which is the number of protons in the nucleus, 9. All of the other statements about fluorine are true.

66. The reactivity and chemical behavior of an atom
is governed by many factors. The most important
factor is

(A) the number of protons in the atom's nucleus
(B) the number of neutrons in the atom's nucleus
(C) the number of protons and neutrons in the
atom's nucleus
(D) the ratio of protons to neutrons in the atom's
nucleus
(E) the number of electrons in the atom's valence
shell

E is correct. Atoms react with other atoms to fill their valence electron shells, so the single most important factor in determining the reactivity of an atom is the makeup of its valence electron shell.

67. A beaker contains a saturated solution of copper(I) chloride, a slightly soluble salt with a solubility product of 1.2×10^{-6}. The addition of which of the salts listed below to the solution would cause the precipitation of copper(I) chloride?

(A) Sodium chloride
(B) Potassium bromide
(C) Silver(I) nitrate
(D) Lead(II) acetate
(E) Magnesium iodide

A is correct. The addition of sodium chloride (NaCl) will introduce more Cl⁻ ions to the solution. Because of the common ion effect, these Cl⁻ ions will affect the equilibrium of the copper(I) chloride (CuCl) with its dissociated ions. The addition of extra Cl⁻ ions will cause the re-formation and precipitation of CuCl.

68. Bromothymol blue is an acid/base indicator with a pK_a of 6.8. Therefore, at approximately what pH will bromothymol blue undergo a color change during an acid/base titration?

(A) 1
(B) 3
(C) 5
(D) 7
(E) 13

D is correct. The rule with chemical pH indicators is simple: They change color at a pH that's about equal to their pK_a. Therefore, if bromothymol blue has a pK_a around 7, it will change color around pH 7.

69. Which of the following is necessarily true of a nonionic substance with a high boiling point?

(A) It has a large vapor pressure.
(B) It has strong intermolecular attractive forces.
(C) It has a low freezing point.
(D) It has a low heat of vaporization.
(E) It will be present in gas phase at very low temperatures.

B is correct. If a nonionic substance has a high boiling point, that means that a large amount of energy must be put into the substance to overcome its intermolecular attractions and convert it to the gas phase. So a high boiling point is an indication of very strong intermolecular attractive forces.

Practice SAT Chemistry
Subject Test 3

PRACTICE SAT CHEMISTRY SUBJECT TEST 3

You are about to take the third practice SAT Chemistry Subject Test.
After answering questions 1–32, which constitute Part A, you'll be directed
to answer questions 101–116, which constitute Part B. Then, begin again at
question 33. Questions 33–69 constitute Part C.

When you're ready to score yourself, refer to the scoring instructions and
answer key on pages 268 and 269. Full explanations regarding the correct
answers to all questions start on page 271.

Material in the following table may be useful in answering the questions in this examination.

PERIODIC TABLE OF THE ELEMENTS

1 **H** 1.0																		2 **He** 4.0
3 **Li** 6.9	4 **Be** 9.0											5 **B** 10.8	6 **C** 12.0	7 **N** 14.0	8 **O** 16.0	9 **F** 19.0	10 **Ne** 20.2
11 **Na** 23.0	12 **Mg** 24.3											13 **Al** 27.0	14 **Si** 28.1	15 **P** 31.0	16 **S** 32.1	17 **Cl** 35.5	18 **Ar** 39.9
19 **K** 39.1	20 **Ca** 40.1	21 **Sc** 45.0	22 **Ti** 47.9	23 **V** 50.9	24 **Cr** 52.0	25 **Mn** 54.9	26 **Fe** 55.8	27 **Co** 58.9	28 **Ni** 58.7	29 **Cu** 63.5	30 **Zn** 65.4	31 **Ga** 69.7	32 **Ge** 72.6	33 **As** 74.9	34 **Se** 79.0	35 **Br** 79.9	36 **Kr** 83.8
37 **Rb** 85.5	38 **Sr** 87.6	39 **Y** 88.9	40 **Zr** 91.2	41 **Nb** 92.9	42 **Mo** 95.9	43 **Tc** (98)	44 **Ru** 101.1	45 **Rh** 102.9	46 **Pd** 106.4	47 **Ag** 107.9	48 **Cd** 112.4	49 **In** 114.8	50 **Sn** 118.7	51 **Sb** 121.8	52 **Te** 127.6	53 **I** 126.9	54 **Xe** 131.3
55 **Cs** 132.9	56 **Ba** 137.3	57 ***La** 138.9	72 **Hf** 178.5	73 **Ta** 180.9	74 **W** 183.9	75 **Re** 186.2	76 **Os** 190.2	77 **Ir** 192.2	78 **Pt** 195.1	79 **Au** 197.0	80 **Hg** 200.6	81 **Tl** 204.4	82 **Pb** 207.2	83 **Bi** 209.0	84 **Po** (209)	85 **At** (210)	86 **Rn** (222)
87 **Fr** (223)	88 **Ra** 226.0	89 **†Ac** 227.0															

*Lanthanum Series	58 **Ce** 140.1	59 **Pr** 140.9	60 **Nd** 144.2	61 **Pm** (145)	62 **Sm** 150.4	63 **Eu** 152.0	64 **Gd** 157.3	65 **Tb** 158.9	66 **Dy** 162.5	67 **Ho** 164.9	68 **Er** 167.3	69 **Tm** 168.9	70 **Yb** 173.0	71 **Lu** 175.0
†Actinium Series	90 **Th** 232.0	91 **Pa** 231.0	92 **U** 238.0	93 **Np** 237.0	94 **Pu** (244)	95 **Am** (243)	96 **Cm** (247)	97 **Bk** (247)	98 **Cf** (251)	99 **Es** (252)	100 **Fm** (258)	101 **Md** (258)	102 **No** (259)	103 **Lr** (260)

DO NOT DETACH FROM BOOK.

CHEMISTRY SUBJECT TEST 3

<u>Note:</u> For all questions involving solutions and/or chemical equations, assume that the system is in pure water unless otherwise stated.

Part A

<u>Directions:</u> Each set of lettered choices below refers to the numbered statements or questions immediately following it. Select the one lettered choice that best fits each statement or answers each question, and then fill in the corresponding oval on the answer sheet. <u>A choice may be used once, more than once, or not at all in each set.</u>

Questions 1–5

   (A) Carbon
   (B) Nitrogen
   (C) Oxygen,
   (D) Neon
   (E) Argon

1. Is the third most abundant gas in the earth's atmosphere

2. At standard conditions, has an allotrophic form that is a good electrical conductor

3. Regardless of its electron configuration, it must always be paramagnetic when it's a single, neutrally charged atom

4. The key element delivered in soil fertilizer

5. Allotrope of this element is the primary absorber of UV solar radiation in the earth's atmosphere

Questions 6–9

   (A) Chemical pH indicator
   (B) Acid/base buffer
   (C) Anhydrous solution
   (D) Hypotonic solution
   (E) Supersaturated solution

6. A conjugate acid/base pair with differing spectral absorbencies

7. An example of a solution not in equilibrium

8. Term used in reference to an aqueous solution's osmotic pressure

9. Addition of water to this solution will not change $[H_3O^+]$

GO ON TO THE NEXT PAGE

Questions 10–14

    (A) Standard voltaic potential
    (B) Entropy
    (C) Enthalpy
    (D) Reaction rate
    (E) Gibbs free energy

10. Increased with the addition of a catalyst

          D

11. Abbreviated as *"H"*

          C

12. A property that must decrease when a gas condenses into a liquid

          B

13. Is always positive for a spontaneous chemical reaction

       E   A

14. Is zero for a crystalline solid that is elementally pure at 0 K

       A   B

Questions 15–19

    (A) Alkali metals
    (B) Alkaline earth metals
    (C) Noble gases
    (D) Halogens
    (E) Transition metals

15. The most unreactive family of elements

          C

16. Form negative ions in an ionic bond

       B   D

17. Consist of atoms that have valence electrons in a *d* subshell

          E

18. Exist as diatomic molecules at room temperature

          D

19. Members possess the lowest first ionization energy in their respective period

       B   A

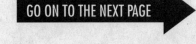

GO ON TO THE NEXT PAGE

Questions 20–24

(A) N_2
(B) KI
(C) CCl_4
(D) $AgNO_3$
(E) $CaCO_3$

20. A product of a neutralization of a strong acid with a strong base

E

21. A volatile covalent liquid at 25°C and 1 atm

D

22. Releases a gas with the addition of dilute acid

B

23. Forms a white precipitate when added to a solution of NaCl

C

24. Treatment of the dry solid with a mild oxidizing agent produces a purple solid

D

Questions 25–28

(A) Gamma decay
(B) Nuclear fusion
(C) Alpha decay
(D) Positron emission
(E) Nuclear fission

25. Is the principle reaction responsible for the energy output of the sun

D   *B*

26. Is a nuclear process that results in no change in the mass number and atomic number of a nuclide

A

27. Responsible for most helium found on Earth

C

28. The nuclear process that transmutes uranium-238 into thorium-234

D   *C*

Questions 29–32

(A) 0.1 M $MgCl_2$
(B) 0.1 M $HClO_4$
(C) 0.1 M NH_4OH
(D) 0.1 M KOH
(E) 0.1 M $LiNO_3$

29. Has a pH of 13

D

30. The solution with the lowest freezing point temperature

E   *A*

31. The solution with the highest boiling point temperature

E   *A*

32. Indicates a red flame when ionized with a Bunsen burner

D   *E*

GO ON TO THE NEXT PAGE

CHEMISTRY SUBJECT TEST 3—*Continued*

PLEASE GO TO THE SPECIAL SECTION AT THE LOWER RIGHT-HAND CORNER OF PAGE 2 OF YOUR ANSWER SHEET LABELED CHEMISTRY AND ANSWER QUESTIONS 101–116 ACCORDING TO THE FOLLOWING DIRECTIONS.

Part B

Directions: Each question below consists of two statements, I in the left-hand column and II in the right-hand column. For each question, determine whether statement I is true or false <u>and</u> whether statement II is true or false and fill in the corresponding T or F ovals on your answer sheet. <u>Fill in oval CE only if statement II is a correct explanation of statement I.</u>

EXAMPLES:

	I		II
EX 1.	H_2SO_4 is a strong acid	BECAUSE	H_2SO_4 contains sulfur.
EX 2.	An atom of oxygen is electrically neutral	BECAUSE	an oxygen atom contains an equal number of protons and electrons.

SAMPLE ANSWERS

	I	II	CE
EX 1	● F	● F	○
EX 2	● F	● F	●

	I		II
101.	Transition metal compounds are often colored	BECAUSE	they frequently possess partially-filled *d* orbitals.
102.	Chemical reactions slow down with lower temperature	BECAUSE	the energy barrier for the formation of products decreases with decreasing temperature.
103.	Exothermic reactions absorb heat	BECAUSE	breaking covalent bonds always requires energy.
104.	The solubility of gases in liquids does not depend upon pressure	BECAUSE	the vapor pressure of a substance is independent of external pressure.
105.	MgO has a high melting point	BECAUSE	highly charged ions result in strong ionic forces and high lattice energies.
106.	The ground state electron configuration of elemental Cu is $[Ar]\,4s^13d^{10}$	BECAUSE	completely half-filled and filled *d* orbitals bestow special electronic stabilization.
107.	Isotopes of a particular element have nearly identical chemical behavior	BECAUSE	they have identical electron configurations.
108.	In an electrochemical cell, the electrode that is the site of reduction is called the anode	BECAUSE	oxidation always occurs at the cathode.

GO ON TO THE NEXT PAGE

I II

109. The addition of acid to a solution buffered to pH 7 slightly lowers the pH BECAUSE the addition of acids to any neutral solution always lowers the pH.

110. Saltwater boils at a higher temperature than pure water BECAUSE the presence of salt increases the vapor pressure of water.

111. BF_3 has a tetrahedral geometry BECAUSE the central B atom does not have a complete stable octet.

112. Hydrogen peroxide, H_2O_2, is a good oxidizing agent BECAUSE the hydrogen in H_2O_2 has a +1 oxidation number.

113. Hydrogen gas (H_2) is considered a perfectly ideal gas BECAUSE hydrogen atoms interact with each other via hydrogen bonds.

114. Electrolysis of water requires the input of energy BECAUSE the products formed, H_2 and O_2, possess more chemical potential energy than H_2O.

115. By mass, oxygen is the most abundant element in the human body BECAUSE it is principally found as O_2 in the bloodstream.

116. LiOH is considered a strong base BECAUSE it undergoes neutralization reactions with acids.

RETURN TO THE SECTION OF YOUR ANSWER SHEET YOU STARTED FOR CHEMISTRY AND ANSWER QUESTIONS 33–69.

GO ON TO THE NEXT PAGE

CHEMISTRY SUBJECT TEST 3—*Continued*

Part C

Directions: Each of the questions or incomplete statements below is followed by five suggested answers or completions. Select the one that is best in each case and then fill in the corresponding oval on the answer sheet.

33. Choose the answer below that accurately describes the correct molecular shape for the molecule $XeOF_4$.

   (A) tetrahedral
   (B) trigonal pyramidal
   (C) trigonal bipyramidal
   (D) square pyramidal
   (E) flat

34. For the radioactive atom ^{99}Tc, what is the correct number of protons and neutrons?

   (A) 43 protons and 56 neutrons
   (B) 43 protons and 99 neutrons
   (C) 56 protons and 43 neutrons
   (D) 56 protons and 99 neutrons
   (E) cannot be determined

35. Which one of the following acids is not strong?

   (A) HCl
   (B) HBr
   (C) HNO_3
   (D) H_3PO_4
   (E) H_2SO_4

36. Identify the equation used to determine the amount of heat required to melt 10 grams of ice.

   (A) $Q = mC_{sp}\Delta T$

   (B) $Q = n\Delta H$

   (C) $KE = \dfrac{1}{2}mv^2$

   (D) $PE = mgh$

   (E) $PV = nRT$

37. Identify the correct ground state electron configuration for Cr.

   (A) $[Ar]\, 3s^2 3d^4$
   (B) $[Ar]\, 3s^2 3d^5$
   (C) $[Ar]\, 4s^2 3d^5$
   (D) $[Ar]\, 4s^2 3d^4$
   (E) $[Ar]\, 4s^1 3d^5$

38. What is the hydroxide concentration for a solution with a pH of 10 at 25°C?

   (A) $10^{-14}\, M$
   (B) $10^{-10}\, M$
   (C) $10^{-7}\, M$
   (D) $10^{-4}\, M$
   (E) $10^{-1}\, M$

39. Five hundred milliliters of solution of 0.1 M NaBr has how many milligrams of bromine?

   (A) 200 mg
   (B) 400 mg
   (C) 2,000 mg
   (D) 4,000 mg
   (E) 20,000 mg

40. According to the ideal gas law, what is the approximate volume that will be occupied by 0.5 mole of an ideal gas at 30°C and 3 atm pressure (gas constant R = 0.0821 L–atm/mol–K)?

   (A) less than 1 L
   (B) 5 L
   (C) 10 L
   (D) 15 L
   (E) more than 20 L

41. Given that $\Delta G = \Delta H - T\Delta S$, how is the spontaneity of an endothermic reaction expected to change with decreasing T?

   (A) becomes less spontaneous
   (B) becomes more spontaneous
   (C) does not change
   (D) decreases at first but then increases
   (E) insufficient information to make a conclusion

42. Identify the element with the greatest first ionization energy.

   (A) Ce
   (B) C
   (C) Cl
   (D) Ca
   (E) Cs

GO ON TO THE NEXT PAGE

43. Identify the molecule/ion with the greatest potential to act as a Lewis acid.

    (A) $^+CH_3$
    (B) ^-CN
    (C) NH_3
    (D) BF_4^-
    (E) CO_2

44. $2\,Ca_3(PO_4)_2 + 6\,SiO_2 + 10\,C \rightarrow P_4 + \underline{\quad}\,CaSiO_3 + 10\,CO$

    Which coefficient balances the reaction given above?

    (A) 2
    (B) 4
    (C) 5
    (D) 6
    (E) 8

45. A 100-milliliter solution containing $AgNO_3$ was treated with excess NaCl to completely precipitate the silver as AgCl. If 5.7 g AgCl was obtained, what was the concentration of Ag^+ in the original solution?

    (A) 0.03 M
    (B) 0.05 M
    (C) 0.12 M
    (D) 0.30 M
    (E) 0.40 M

46. Identify which of the following statements is FALSE.

    (A) The vapor pressure of a liquid decreases with increasing atmospheric pressure.
    (B) The value of an equilibrium constant is dependent on temperature.
    (C) The rate of a spontaneous reaction cannot solely be determined by its Gibbs free energy.
    (D) During a phase transition, the temperature of a substance must be constant.
    (E) The addition of a catalyst to a reaction at equilibrium has no net effect on the system.

47. Which of the following compounds would be expected to have the greatest lattice binding energy?

    (A) $LiNO_3$
    (B) LiF
    (C) KI
    (D) NH_4Br
    (E) $CsNO_3$

48. The daughter nucleus formed when ^{18}F undergoes positron emission is

    (A) ^{14}N
    (B) ^{16}O
    (C) ^{18}O
    (D) ^{19}F
    (E) ^{20}Ne

49. Which of the following reactions produces a yellow precipitate?

    (A) $NaOH\,(aq) + HCl\,(aq) \rightarrow NaCl\,(s) + H_2O$
    (B) $NaOH\,(aq) + BaCl\,(aq) \rightarrow BaOH\,(s) + NaCl\,(aq)$
    (C) $Pb(NO_3)_2\,(aq) + 2KI\,(aq) \rightarrow 2KNO_3\,(aq) + PbI_2\,(s)$
    (D) $CuO(s) + Mg(s) \rightarrow Cu(s) + MgO\,(s)$
    (E) $4Fe + 3O_2 \rightarrow 2Fe_2O_3$

50. $Zn(s)\,|\,ZnCl_2(aq)\,|\,|\,Cl^-(aq)\,|\,Cl_2(g)\,|\,C(s)$

    In the electrochemical cell described by the cell diagram above, what reaction occurs at the anode?

    (A) $Zn \rightarrow Zn^{2+} + 2e$
    (B) $Zn^{2+} + 2e \rightarrow Zn$
    (C) $Cl_2 + 2e \rightarrow 2Cl^-$
    (D) $2Cl^- \rightarrow Cl_2 + 2e$
    (E) $Zn + Cl_2 \rightarrow ZnCl_2$

51. Given the reaction $A \rightarrow B + C$, where ΔH_{rxn} is negative, what effect would increasing the temperature (at constant pressure) have on the system at equilibrium?

    (A) no change
    (B) cannot be determined
    (C) shift to the right
    (D) shift to the left for $K < 1$ and to the right for $K > 1$
    (E) shift to the left

GO ON TO THE NEXT PAGE

52. An unknown acid solution was presumed to be either HCl or H_2SO_4. Which one of the following salt solutions would produce a precipitate when added to H_2SO_4 but not when added to HCl?

    (A) $LiNO_3$
    (B) NH_4NO_3
    (C) $CsNO_3$
    (D) $Ba(NO_3)_2$
    (E) $AgNO_3$

53. $Ca_3(PO_4)_2(s) \rightleftharpoons 3\ Ca^{2+}(aq) + 2\ PO_4^{3-}(aq)$

    What is the equilibrium expression for the dissolution of $Ca_3(PO_4)_2$ where the above is true?

    (A) $K_{sp} = [Ca^{2+}]^3[PO_4^{3-}]^2$
    (B) $K_{sp} = [Ca^{2+}]^2[PO_4^{3-}]^3$
    (C) $K_{sp} = [Ca^{2+}][PO_4^{3-}]/[Ca_3(PO_4)_2]$
    (D) $K_{sp} = [Ca^{2+}]^3[PO_4^{3-}]^2/[Ca_3(PO_4)_2]$
    (E) $K_{sp} = [Ca^{2+}]^2[PO_4^{3-}]^3/[Ca_3(PO_4)_2]$

54. Which of the following represents a conjugate acid/base pair?

    (A) Na^+/Cl^-
    (B) HCl/H^+
    (C) H_2CO_3/CO_3^{2-}
    (D) NH_3/NH_4^+
    (E) K^+/OH^-

55. An unknown solution having a pH of 3.5 was titrated with 0.1 M NaOH. Analysis of the resulting titration curve showed a single equivalence point at pH 7. Therefore, which of the following could be the unknown solute in the initial solution?

    (A) HF
    (B) HCl
    (C) LiOH
    (D) NH_3
    (E) H_2SO_4

56. Acid/base titration experiments could be used to determine all of the following directly EXCEPT

    (A) the acid concentration of an acidic solution
    (B) the alkalinity of a basic solution
    (C) the pK_a of an unknown weak acid
    (D) whether an unknown acid is monoprotic or polyprotic
    (E) the molecular weight of an unknown acid or base

57. What is the correct term for the phase change from gas directly to solid?

    (A) deposition
    (B) sublimation
    (C) liquefaction
    (D) fusion
    (E) vaporization

58. What is the correct name for a straight-chained organic compound with the molecular formula C_3H_8?

    (A) methane
    (B) ethane
    (C) methylethane
    (D) propane
    (E) isopropane

59. If the pH of a solution is changed from 1 to 3 with the addition of an antacid, what percentage of $[H^+]$ was neutralized?

    (A) 2%
    (B) 10%
    (C) 20%
    (D) 90%
    (E) 99%

60. Which of the following statements is the most accurate with regard to the significance of Avogadro's number, 6.02×10^{23}?

    (A) It is the conversion factor between grams and atomic mass units.
    (B) It is a universal physical constant just as the speed of light.
    (C) It is the number of particles that are required to fill a 1-liter container.
    (D) It is the inverse diameter of an H atom.
    (E) It is the number of electrons in the universe.

GO ON TO THE NEXT PAGE

Questions 61–64 refer to the following data at standard conditions:

	Appearance	Reaction with dilute HCl	Reaction with dilute HNO$_3$
Unknown metal #1	Dull gray solid with white oxide coating	Dissolved with bubbles of clear gas	Dissolved with bubbles of clear gas
Unknown metal #2	Solid; lustrous, smooth silver-gray surface	No reaction	Dissolved with bubbles of orange gas

61. Unknown metal #1 could be

    (A) mercury
    (B) copper
    (C) zinc
    (D) iron
    (E) silver

62. Unknown metal #2 could be

    (A) carbon
    (B) copper
    (C) zinc
    (D) sodium
    (E) silver

63. The addition of dilute HCl to unknown metal #1 produced a transparent gas. What is the likely identity of this gas?

    (A) Cl$_2$
    (B) H$_2$
    (C) O$_2$
    (D) CO$_2$
    (E) NO$_2$

64. The addition of dilute HNO$_3$ to unknown metal #2 produced an orange gas. What is the likely identity of this gas?

    (A) Cl$_2$
    (B) H$_2$
    (C) O$_2$
    (D) CO$_2$
    (E) NO$_2$

65. Which of the following solutions is the product of the neutralization reaction between 10 mL 0.2 M KOH and 10 mL 0.2 M HI?

    (A) 0.1 M KI$_3$
    (B) 0.1 M KI
    (C) 0.2 M KI
    (D) 0.4 M KI
    (E) 0.4 M HOH

66. Which of the following is true regarding an Ne atom with a mass number of 20 and an O^{2-} ion with a mass number of 16?

    (A) They contain the same number of protons.
    (B) They contain the same number of neutrons.
    (C) They contain the same number of protons plus neutrons.
    (D) They are isoelectronic.
    (E) They are isomers.

67. Which of the following statements is NOT correct regarding chemical catalysts?

    (A) They are not consumed during the chemical reaction.
    (B) They cannot make nonspontaneous reactions occur.
    (C) They do not have to be the same phase as the reactant molecules.
    (D) They shift equilibrated reactions to the product's side.
    (E) Enzymes are biological catalysts.

GO ON TO THE NEXT PAGE

68. Most elements are solids at 25°C and 1 atm pressure, the exception being the 11 elements that are gases and 2 that are liquids. What 2 elements are liquids?

   (A) Hg and Br
   (B) Hg and I
   (C) Ag and Kr
   (D) Au and Kr
   (E) Pt and Co

69. A student conducted an experiment and obtained three values during three repetitive trials: 1.65, 1.68, 1.71. Later, the student discovered that the true value was 2.37. In contrast to the real value, the experimental results should be characterized as

   (A) not accurate and not precise
   (B) accurate but not precise
   (C) not accurate but precise
   (D) accurate and precise
   (E) accurate, precise, but unreliable

STOP
IF YOU FINISH BEFORE TIME IS CALLED, YOU MAY CHECK YOUR WORK ON THIS TEST ONLY.
DO NOT TURN TO ANY OTHER TEST IN THIS BOOK.

HOW TO SCORE THE PRINCETON REVIEW
PRACTICE SAT CHEMISTRY SUBJECT TEST

When you take the real exam, the proctors will collect your test booklet and bubble sheet and send your answer sheet to New Jersey where a computer looks at the pattern of filled-in ovals on your answer sheet and gives you a score. We couldn't include even a small computer with this book, so we are providing this more primitive way of scoring your exam.

DETERMINING YOUR SCORE

STEP 1   Using the answer key on the next page, determine how many questions you got right and how many you got wrong on the test. Remember, questions that you do not answer don't count as either right or wrong answers.

STEP 2   List the number of right answers here.

(A) _____

STEP 3   List the number of wrong answers here. Now divide that number by 4. (Use a calculator if you're feeling particularly lazy.)

(B) _____ ÷ 4 = (C)_____

STEP 4   Subtract the number of wrong answers divided by 4 from the number of correct answers. Round this score to the nearest whole number. This is your raw score.

(A) _____ – (C) _____ = _____

STEP 5   To determine your real score, take the number from Step 4 above, and look it up in the left column of the Score Conversion Table on page 270; the corresponding score on the right is your score on the exam.

ANSWERS TO THE PRINCETON REVIEW
PRACTICE SAT CHEMISTRY SUBJECT TEST 3

Question Number	Correct Answer	Right	Wrong
1.	E	⎯⎯	⎯⎯
2.	A	⎯⎯	⎯⎯
3.	B	⎯⎯	⎯⎯
4.	B	⎯⎯	⎯⎯
5.	C	⎯⎯	⎯⎯
6.	A	⎯⎯	⎯⎯
7.	E	⎯⎯	⎯⎯
8.	D	⎯⎯	⎯⎯
9.	B	⎯⎯	⎯⎯
10.	D	⎯⎯	⎯⎯
11.	C	⎯⎯	⎯⎯
12.	B	⎯⎯	⎯⎯
13.	A	⎯⎯	⎯⎯
14.	B	⎯⎯	⎯⎯
15.	C	⎯⎯	⎯⎯
16.	D	⎯⎯	⎯⎯
17.	E	⎯⎯	⎯⎯
18.	D	⎯⎯	⎯⎯
19.	A	⎯⎯	⎯⎯
20.	B	⎯⎯	⎯⎯
21.	C	⎯⎯	⎯⎯
22.	E	⎯⎯	⎯⎯
23.	D	⎯⎯	⎯⎯
24.	B	⎯⎯	⎯⎯
25.	B	⎯⎯	⎯⎯
26.	A	⎯⎯	⎯⎯
27.	C	⎯⎯	⎯⎯
28.	C	⎯⎯	⎯⎯
29.	D	⎯⎯	⎯⎯
30.	A	⎯⎯	⎯⎯
31.	A	⎯⎯	⎯⎯
32.	E	⎯⎯	⎯⎯
33.	D	⎯⎯	⎯⎯
34.	A	⎯⎯	⎯⎯
35.	D	⎯⎯	⎯⎯
36.	B	⎯⎯	⎯⎯
37.	E	⎯⎯	⎯⎯
38.	D	⎯⎯	⎯⎯
39.	D	⎯⎯	⎯⎯
40.	B	⎯⎯	⎯⎯
41.	E	⎯⎯	⎯⎯
42.	B	⎯⎯	⎯⎯
43.	A		
44.	D		
45.	E		

Question Number	Correct Answer	Right	Wrong
46.	A	⎯⎯	⎯⎯
47.	B	⎯⎯	⎯⎯
48.	C	⎯⎯	⎯⎯
49.	A	⎯⎯	⎯⎯
50.	A	⎯⎯	⎯⎯
51.	E	⎯⎯	⎯⎯
52.	D	⎯⎯	⎯⎯
53.	A	⎯⎯	⎯⎯
54.	D	⎯⎯	⎯⎯
55.	B	⎯⎯	⎯⎯
56.	E	⎯⎯	⎯⎯
57.	A	⎯⎯	⎯⎯
58.	D	⎯⎯	⎯⎯
59.	E	⎯⎯	⎯⎯
60.	A	⎯⎯	⎯⎯
61.	C	⎯⎯	⎯⎯
62.	E	⎯⎯	⎯⎯
63.	B	⎯⎯	⎯⎯
64.	E	⎯⎯	⎯⎯
65.	B	⎯⎯	⎯⎯
66.	D	⎯⎯	⎯⎯
67.	D	⎯⎯	⎯⎯
68.	A	⎯⎯	⎯⎯
69.	C	⎯⎯	⎯⎯

101.	T, T, CE
102.	T, F
103.	F, T
104.	F, T
105.	T, T, CE
106.	T, T, CE
107.	T, T, CE
108.	F, F
109.	T, T, CE
110.	T, F
111.	F, T
112.	T, T
113.	F, F
114.	T, T, CE
115.	T, F
116.	T, T

THE PRINCETON REVIEW PRACTICE SAT CHEMISTRY SUBJECT TEST SCORE CONVERSION TABLE

Raw Score	Scaled Score	Raw Score	Scaled Score	Raw Score	Scaled Score
85	800	45	620	5	390
84	800	44	620	4	390
83	800	43	610	3	380
82	800	42	610	2	380
81	800	41	600	1	370
80	800	40	590	0	370
79	800	39	590	−1	370
78	790	38	580	−2	360
77	780	37	580	−3	360
76	780	36	570	−4	350
75	780	35	560	−5	340
74	780	34	560	−6	340
73	780	33	550	−7	330
72	770	32	550	−8	330
71	770	31	540	−9	320
70	750	30	530	−10	310
69	750	29	530	−11	310
68	740	28	520	−12	300
67	740	27	520	−13	300
66	740	26	520	−14	290
65	730	25	510	−15	280
64	730	24	510	−16	280
63	710	23	500	−17	270
62	710	22	500	−18	270
61	710	21	490	−19	260
60	700	20	480	−20	250
59	700	19	480	−21	250
58	690	18	470		
57	690	17	470		
56	680	16	460		
55	680	15	450		
54	680	14	450		
53	670	13	440		
52	670	12	440		
51	660	11	430		
50	650	10	420		
49	650	9	420		
48	630	8	410		
47	630	7	410		
46	630	6	400		

Practice SAT Chemistry Subject Test 3: Answers and Explanations

PART A

QUESTIONS 1–5

(A) Carbon
(B) Nitrogen
(C) Oxygen
(D) Neon
(E) Argon

1. Is the third most abundant gas in the earth's atmosphere

E is correct. The composition of earth's atmosphere is approximately: 78% N_2, 20% O_2, 1% Ar, 0.5% H_2O, 0.4% CO_2, and 0.1% other trace gases.

2. At standard conditions, has an allotrophic form that is a good electrical conductor

A is correct. Allotropes are different forms or molecular arrangements of the same element. Carbon has three common allotrophic forms at standard conditions (25°C and 1 atm): amorphous carbon (charcoal), graphite, and diamond. Graphite is unique among nonmetals in that it conducts electricity.

3. Regardless of its electron configuration, it must always be paramagnetic when it's a single, neutrally charged atom

B is correct. Paramagnetic means that the atom or molecule has at least one unpaired electron. Since it is impossible to completely pair up an odd number of electrons, atomic nitrogen must always be paramagnetic because it has an odd number of electrons (7).

4. The key element delivered in soil fertilizer

B is correct. Two elements that are essential to plant growth but are depleted in most soils are nitrogen and phosphorous. Phosphorous is not given as a choice, but nitrogen is. Plants cannot utilize atmospheric nitrogen gas because the strong triple bond in N_2 makes it virtually inert to biological processing.

5. Allotrope of this element is the primary absorber of UV solar radiation in the earth's atmosphere

C is correct. Again, **allotropes** are different forms or molecular arrangements of the pure element. Oxygen has two allotropic forms at standard conditions: molecular oxygen, O_2, and ozone, O_3. Ozone (and to a lesser extent, molecular oxygen) is the primary absorber of UV light in the earth's atmosphere.

Questions 6–9

    (A) Chemical pH indicator
    (B) Acid/base buffer
    (C) Anhydrous solution
    (D) Hypotonic solution
    (E) Supersaturated solution

6. A conjugate acid/base pair with differing spectral absorbances

A is correct. This is the definition of chemical pH indicators.

7. An example of a solution not in equilibrium

E is correct. Supersaturated solutions are solutions that have an amount of dissolved solute (the solute can be a solid, liquid, or gas) greater than they should at that particular temperature and pressure. Therefore, these solutions are not in equilibrium with their environment. For example, a glass of soda that's just been poured is supersaturated with CO_2. The soda tries to reach equilibrium with its environment by ejecting excess CO_2 as bubbles of CO_2. If left alone for a while, the soda will eventually release all of the excess CO_2 and stop forming bubbles because it's reached equilibrium—at that point we say the soda has gone flat.

8. Term used in reference to an aqueous solution's osmotic pressure

D is correct. Biologists use the terms *hypotonic*, *isotonic*, and *hypertonic* to contrast the osmotic pressure of a cell's cytoplasm with that of the surrounding extracellular solution.

9. Addition of water to this solution will not change [H_3O+]

B is correct. One of the most important intrinsic properties of a buffer is that *the addition or removal of water in no way alters the pH of a buffer*. In contrast, diluting any of the other solutions is likely to alter their pH—i.e., [H_3O^+].

Questions 10–14

    (A) Standard voltaic potential
    (B) Entropy
    (C) Enthalpy
    (D) Reaction rate
    (E) Gibbs free energy

10. Increased with the addition of a catalyst

D is correct. A catalyst decreases the activation energy, or energy barrier, that must be overcome for reactants to become products. In this way, catalysts increase the rate of chemical reactions.

11. Abbreviated as "*H*"

C is correct. Enthalpy is the fancy word for *heat of reaction*; it is abbreviated with an "*H*". The abbreviations for the other properties listed above are standard voltaic potential: $E°$, entropy: S, reaction rate, and Gibb's free energy: G.

12. A property that must decrease when a gas
    condenses into a liquid

B is correct. Entropy, S, is the measure of the amount of disorder in a molecular system. When a gas condenses into a liquid, the molecules become more organized, so the entropy of the system decreases.

13. Is always positive for a spontaneous chemical
    reaction

A is correct. It may be tempting to choose E, but remember that by definition, the change in Gibbs free energy, ΔG, must be negative for a reaction to be spontaneous. Standard voltaic potential, $E°$, is related to $\Delta G°$ by the equation

$$E° = -nF\Delta G°$$

where n is the number of transferred electrons and F is Faraday's constant. Since n and F are always positive numbers, you can see that for a spontaneous reaction—where $\Delta G°$ is negative—$E°$ will always be positive.

14. Is zero for a crystalline solid that is elementally
    pure at 0 K.

B is correct. By definition, entropy for a pure element in crystalline form at absolute zero (0 K) is zero.

QUESTIONS 15–19

    (A) Alkali metals
    (B) Alkaline earth metals
    (C) Noble gases
    (D) Halogens
    (E) Transition metals

15. The most unreactive family of elements

C is correct. The atoms of noble gas elements have filled valence shells and, therefore, are extremely unreactive—more so than any other family.

16. Form negative ions in an ionic bond

D is correct. To form a negative ion, an atom needs to *acquire* electrons. This sounds like a nonmetal, not a metal. Eliminate A, B, and E. Noble gases are essentially inert, so that leaves the halogens. Halogens need 1 valence electron to complete their valence shell and so will readily gain an electron and form an anion.

17. Consist of atoms that have valence electrons
    in a d subshell

E is correct. When the test writers start talking about the "d" subshell, think "transition metals."

18. Exist as diatomic molecules at room temperature

D is correct. Did you remember: **H**ave **N**o **F**ear **O**f **I**ce **C**old **B**ears? If so, you'd realize that some of the most common diatomic molecules are halogens—F_2, Cl_2, Br_2, and I_2.

19. Members possess the lowest first ionization energy in their respective period

A is correct. Ionization energy is needed to remove an electron from an atom. Which kind of elements tend to give up electrons? Metals, of course. Of the metals, alkali metals, having only 1 valence electron per atom, will lose an electron most easily because this allows an alkali metal atom to assume a stable noble gas electron configuration.

QUESTIONS 20–24

(A) N_2
(B) KI
(C) CCl_4
(D) $AgNO_3$
(E) $CaCO_3$

20. A product of a neutralization of a strong acid with a strong base

B is correct. Given that the strong acids are HCl, HBr, HI, HNO_3, H_2SO_4, and $HClO_4$ and the strong bases are LiOH, NaOH, KOH, RbOH, and CsOH, the only compound that could result from a neutralization between a strong acid and strong base is KI.

21. A volatile covalent liquid at 25°C and 1 atm

C is correct. Compounds composed of only nonmetal elements tend to form covalent bonds, while compounds composed of metals and nonmetals tend to form ionic bonds. Therefore, N_2 and CCl_4 are expected to be covalent compounds. However, N_2 is a gas at standard conditions; only CCl_4 is a liquid.

22. Releases a gas with the addition of dilute acid

E is correct. Carbonates, CO_3^{2-}, and bicarbonates, HCO_3^-, form CO_2 gas when mixed with acid. That's why baking soda ($NaHCO_3$) fizzes when added to vinegar (acetic acid).

23. Forms a white precipitate when added to a solution of NaCl

D is correct. Precipitation reactions most often involve single or double displacement reactions between two ionic compounds. Therefore, compounds A and C are eliminated because they are not ionic compounds. Recall the basic solubility rules for ionic compounds.

- All group 1 and ammonium salts are soluble.

- All nitrate and perchlorate salts are soluble.

- All silver, lead, and mercury salts are insoluble (except for their nitrates and perchlorates).

Therefore, mixing $AgNO_3$ with NaCl should produce the insoluble compound $AgCl$.

24. Treatment of the dry solid with a mild oxidizing
    agent produces a purple solid

B is correct. There are only two purple solids commonly found in a general chemistry lab: iodine, I_2, and potassium permanganate, $KMnO_4$. Considering that element Mn is not present in any of the answer choices, but I is (in KI), it is likely the purple solid formed here is iodine. In fact, the iodide ion, I^-, is easily oxidized to form I_2.

QUESTIONS 25–28

(A) Gamma decay
(B) Nuclear fusion
(C) Alpha decay
(D) Positron emission
(E) Nuclear fission

25. Is the principle reaction responsible for the energy
    output of the sun

B is correct. The primary source of solar energy is energy released by the nuclear fusion of hydrogen at high pressure and temperature to form helium. $4^1H \rightarrow {}^4He + 2$ electrons + lots of energy

26. Is a nuclear process that results in no change in the
    mass number and atomic number of a nuclide

A is correct. The only nuclear process that does not change the number of protons and neutrons of a nucleus is gamma decay. Gamma decay involves stabilization of a nucleus by loss of energy in the form of a gamma ray photon.

27. Responsible for most helium found on Earth

C is correct. Although nuclear fusion of hydrogen is the chief source of helium in the universe, most of the helium originally caught up in the earth as it formed 4.5 billion years ago has escaped into space because Earth's gravity is too weak to retain helium atoms once they find their way into the atmosphere. However, new helium atoms are constantly being formed as a product of the alpha decay of heavy elements such as uranium and thorium present in the earth's crust. Therefore, oddly enough, people in the helium business actually mine for pockets of helium trapped in underground caverns and fissures; they don't extract it from the air.

28. The nuclear process that transmutes uranium-238
    into thorium-234

C is correct. Given the nuclear reaction

$$^{238}_{92}U \rightarrow {}^{234}_{90}Th + \;?$$

When conserving mass and charge, the missing particle must be ^4_2He. Therefore, the nuclear process responsible for this transmutation is alpha decay.

Questions 29–32

(A) 0.1 M $MgCl_2$
(B) 0.1 M $HClO_4$
(C) 0.1 M NH_4OH
(D) 0.1 M KOH
(E) 0.1 M $LiNO_3$

29. Has a pH of 13

D is correct. A pH of 13 indicates a basic solution; therefore, there must be a base in solution in the first place. NH_4OH and KOH are bases. However, a pH of 13 means that the pOH is 1, i.e., $[OH^-]$ = 0.1 M. For the $[OH^-]$ to be the same as the base, that base must completely dissociate and be strong. KOH is the only strong base given.

30. The solution with the lowest freezing point temperature

A is correct. This is a question about the colligative property freezing point depression. Remember that for all colligative properties, the greater the number of dissolved particles, the greater the effect. Therefore, this question is really asking which solution has the greatest number of dissolved particles. Since all of them have the same molar concentration, this is really just a contest of which compound breaks up into the most individual particles.

$$MgCl_2 \rightarrow Mg^{2+} + Cl^- + Cl^- \quad \text{(3 particles)}$$
$$HClO_4 \rightarrow H^+ + ClO_4^- \quad \text{(2 particles)}$$
$$NH_4OH \rightarrow NH_4^+ + OH^- \quad \text{(2 particles)}$$
$$KOH \rightarrow K^+ + OH^- \quad \text{(2 particles)}$$
$$LiNO_3 \rightarrow Li^+ + NO_3^- \quad \text{(2 particles)}$$

Therefore, the winner is $MgCl_2$.

31. The solution with the highest boiling point temperature

A is correct. This is a question about the colligative property boiling point elevation. As in question 30, recall that for all colligative properties, the greater the number of dissolved particles, the greater the effect. Therefore, this question is really asking which solution has the greatest number of dissolved particles. Since all of them have the same molar concentration, this too is a contest of which compound breaks up into the most individual particles.

$$MgCl_2 \rightarrow Mg^{2+} + Cl^- + Cl^- \quad \text{(3 particles)}$$
$$HClO_4 \rightarrow H^+ + ClO_4^- \quad \text{(2 particles)}$$
$$NH_4OH \rightarrow NH_4^+ + OH^- \quad \text{(2 particles)}$$
$$KOH \rightarrow K^+ + OH^- \quad \text{(2 particles)}$$
$$LiNO_3 \rightarrow Li^+ + NO_3^- \quad \text{(2 particles)}$$

Again, the winner is $MgCl_2$.

32. Indicates a red flame when ionized with a Bunsen
    burner

E is correct. Certain metal ions produce characteristic colors when ionized in a flame—that's how fireworks are made to have different colors. Here are the most common ions, and the color they produce.

Red:	Lithium, strontium
Orange:	Calcium
Yellow:	Sodium
Green:	Barium, copper
Violet:	Potassium

Therefore, lithium ions, Li^+, will produce a red flame—choice E.

PART B

101. Transitionmetal compounds are   BECAUSE   they frequently possess partially-filled *d*
     often colored   orbitals.

T, T, CE Divide and conquer. Both statements are true. Nearly all colored compounds fall into two categories: 1) those that are colored because they are organic molecules that have conjugation and 2) those that are colored because they have transition metal atoms with partially-filled *d* subshells. That's why sodium oxide is colorless, but iron(II) oxide is orange.

102. Chemical reactions slow down   BECAUSE   the energy barrier for the formation of
     with lower temperature   products decreases with decreasing
                                                     temperature.

T, T Divide and conquer. The first statement is true. It is a fundamental law of chemical kinetics that all chemical processes slow down at lower temperatures—that's why refrigerating food retards the growth of microbes. At lower temperatures, reactant molecules have less kinetic energy to use to overcome the energy barrier for the formation of products, called the activation energy. The second statement is false. The only way to lower activation energy is to add a catalyst.

103. Exothermic reactions absorb heat   BECAUSE   breaking covalent bonds always requires
                                                         energy.

F, T Divide and conquer. Exothermic reactions *release* heat energy (notice *exo*– looks like *exit*), endothermic reactions *absorb* energy (notice *endo*– looks like *enter*), so the first statement is false. The second statement is true and is an important law in chemistry.

104. The solubility of gases in liquids   BECAUSE   the vapor pressure of a substance is
     does not depend upon pressure   independent of external pressure.

F, T Divide and conquer. The first statement is false. The solubility of a gas in a liquid is very sensitive to pressure, such that the solubility of gases in liquids increases with increasing pressure. That's why when we release the pressure trapped in a bottle of soda by opening it, a sudden surge of carbon dioxide bubbles races to get out of the container. The second statement is true but has no relevance to the solubility of gases.

105. MgO has a high melting point   BECAUSE   highly-charged ions result in strong ionic forces and high lattice energies.

T, T, CE Divide and conquer. Exactly true. All ionic compounds have relatively high melting points (all are solids at room temperature) because ionic forces between ions are very strong. In the case of MgO, the +2 and –2 charges on Mg and O, respectively, result in very strong intermolecular forces. Not surprisingly, MgO has a melting point—it's about 2,000°C.

106. The ground state electron configuration of elemental Cu is [Ar] $4s^13d^{10}$ BECAUSE   completely half-filled and filled d orbitals bestow special electronic stabilization.

T, T, CE Divide and conquer. According to the Aufbau principle, we completely fill subshells before moving up to the next higher one. However, completely half-filled and filled d subshells bestow extra stabilization to an atom. Therefore, Cr and Cu actually violate the Aufbau principle and promote a $4s$ electron to become [Ar] $4s^13d^5$ and [Ar] $4s^13d^{10}$, respectively. Remember this important exception.

107. Isotopes of a particular element have nearly identical chemical behavior   BECAUSE   they have identical electron configurations.

T, T, CE Divide and conquer. Isotopes are atoms of the same element that have differing numbers of neutrons. They have nearly identical chemical behavior because the number of protons and electrons in an atom (two quantities that are identical between isotopes) govern an atom's chemical properties.

108. In an electrochemical cell, the electrode that is the site of reduction is called the anode   BECAUSE   oxidation always occurs at the cathode.

F, F Divide and conquer. Both statements are false. For any electrochemical or electrolytic cell, **oxidation** occurs at the **an**ode and **reduction** occurs at the **cathode** (remember: **AN OX** and **RED CAT**). Therefore, both statements are false.

109. The addition of acid to a solution buffered to pH 7 lowers the pH   BECAUSE   the addition of acids to any neutral solution always lowers the pH.

T, T, CE Divide and conquer. No matter how complicated acid/base chemistry can appear, never forget that *adding acid to any solution, buffered or not, always lowers the pH; adding base to any solution, always raises the pH.* A buffer does *not* prevent the pH from changing in these cases; it simply lessens by how much the pH changes.

110. Saltwater boils at a higher   BECAUSE   the presence of salt increases the vapor
       temperature than pure water   pressure of water.

T, F Divide and conquer. The first statement is true. Remember the colligative properties: Adding any solute to a liquid always raises the boiling point temperature of the resulting solution—that's called boiling point elevation. This occurs because adding a solute to a liquid always lowers the vapor pressure of the solution—vapor pressure depression. Recall two more things: 1) the vapor pressure of a liquid always gets higher with higher temperature and 2) a liquid boils when its vapor pressure is equal to the atmospheric pressure. So if the vapor pressure of a solution is lowered by the addition of a solute, we have to heat the solution to a higher temperature before the vapor pressure equals the atmospheric pressure and the solution will boil again.

111. BF_3 has a tetrahedral geometry   BECAUSE   the central B atom does not have a
                                                                 complete stable octet.

F, T Divide and conquer. The Lewis dot structure for BF_3 is

$$:\ddot{F}:$$
$$|$$
$$B$$
$$\diagup \quad \diagdown$$
$$:\ddot{F} \qquad :\ddot{F}:$$

Now, count the groups of electrons around the central atom (B), keeping in mind that every pair of nonbonding electrons, every single bond, every double bond, and every triple bond counts as one group. So here, boron is surrounded by three groups of electrons. Any atom that is surrounded by three groups of electrons has an sp^2 hybridization and a *trigonal planar* geometry. Of course, the second statement is true because this B doesn't have a stable octet—it has only 6 electrons.

112. Hydrogen peroxide, H_2O_2, is a   BECAUSE   the hydrogen in H_2O_2 has a +1 oxidation
       good oxidizing agent   number.

T, T Divide and conquer. Like all peroxides, hydrogen peroxide is a good oxidizing agent. It is also true that the hydrogen atoms in H_2O_2 have a +1 oxidation number. However, the oxidizing tendency of this molecule is not due to the H, but rather to the fact that each O has a –1 oxidation number, instead of the usual –2.

113. Hydrogen gas (H_2) is considered a   BECAUSE   hydrogen atoms interact with each other
       perfectly ideal gas   via hydrogen bonds.

F, F Divide and conquer. Both statements are false. There are no ideal gases—end of story. Furthermore, H's in H_2 are bonded together via a covalent bond. Hydrogen bonding refers to a specific dipole interaction between two or more different molecules where an H covalently bonded to an F, O, or N is electrostatically attracted to an F, O, or N on another molecule.

114. Electrolysis of water requires   BECAUSE   the products formed, H_2 and O_2, possess
       the input of energy   more chemical potential energy than H_2O.

T, T, CE Divide and conquer. Both statements are true. In an ordinary electrochemical cell, chemical reactions produce electricity (like in a battery). In contrast, in an electrolytic cell, electrical energy is added to produce a chemical reaction (like a battery being recharged). This is because the chemical energy of the products is greater than that of the reactants.

115. By mass, oxygen is the most   BECAUSE   it is principally found as O_2 in the
     abundant element in the human   bloodstream.
     body

T, F Divide and conquer. Over $\frac{3}{4}$ of the mass of the average human is oxygen. However, most oxygen atoms in the bloodstream, over 99.99 percent of them, are in the form of H_2O, not as O_2. The first statement is true but the second is false.

116. LiOH is considered a strong base   BECAUSE   it undergoes neutralization reactions
                                                       with acids.

T, T Divide and conquer. Strong acids and strong bases are those that undergo 100 percent dissociation in water.

The strong acids are: HCl, HBr, HI, HNO_3, H_2SO_4, and $HClO_4$

The strong bases are: LiOH, NaOH, KOH, RbOH, CsOH

Mixing any acid with any base will produce a neutralization reaction, regardless of whether the acid and base are strong or weak.

PART C

33. Choose the answer below that accurately describes the correct molecular shape for the molecule $XeOF_4$

    (A) tetrahedral
    (B) trigonal pyramidal
    (C) trigonal bipyramidal
    (D) square pyramidal
    (E) flat

D is correct. First, draw the Lewis dot structure for $XeOF_4$.

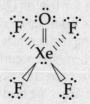

Now, count the groups of electrons around the central atom (Xe) keeping in mind that every pair of nonbonding electrons, every single bond, every double bond, and every triple bond counts as one group. So here, Xe is surrounded by six groups of electrons. Any atom that is surrounded by six groups of electrons has an sp^3d^2 hybridization and an octahedral geometry. However, the question asks about the molecular shape (as opposed to the geometry), we look at the arrangement of the surrounding atoms. In this case, the F would make a flat square around the Xe with the oxygen atom lying directly above. This traces out a square pyramid (choice D).

34. For the radionuclide ^{99}Tc, what is the correct number of protons and neutrons?

    (A) 43 protons and 56 neutrons
    (B) 43 protons and 99 neutrons
    (C) 56 protons and 43 neutrons
    (D) 56 protons and 99 neutrons
    (E) cannot be determined

A is correct. After examining the periodic table, realize that the full atomic symbol for this isotope of technicium is

$$^{99}_{43}\text{Tc}$$

Remembering that the superscript (the mass number) represents the total number of protons and neutrons, and the subscript (the atomic number) represents just the number of protons, $^{99}_{43}\text{Tc}$ has 43 protons and 99 − 43 = 56 neutrons—choice A.

35. Which one of the following acids is not strong?

    (A) HCl
    (B) HBr
    (C) HNO_3
    (D) H_3PO_4
    (E) H_2SO_4

D is correct. Recall that the six strong acids are: HCl, HBr, HI, HNO_3, $HClO_4$, and H_2SO_4. Phosphoric acid, H_3PO_4, is a weak acid.

36. Identify the equation used to determine the amount of heat required to melt 10 grams of ice:

    (A) $Q = mC_{sp}\Delta T$
    (B) $Q = n\Delta H$
    (C) $KE = \dfrac{1}{2}mv^2$
    (D) $PE = mgh$
    (E) $PV = nRT$

B is correct. First, the correct abbreviation for heat is Q. So we can eliminate choices C, D, and E. During a phase change, the temperature of a substance remains constant. Therefore, choice A must be wrong because it has a term for changing temperature, ΔT. In fact, choice A is the equation used to determine the change in temperature when heat is added or removed from a substance that isn't undergoing a phase change. Choice B is the correct choice, where Q is the heat added or removed, n is the number of moles of substance, and ΔH is the heat of phase change, a quantity that is unique for every substance.

37. Identify the correct ground state electron configuration for Cr.

(A) $[Ar] 3s^2 3d^4$
(B) $[Ar] 3s^2 3d^5$
(C) $[Ar] 4s^2 3d^5$
(D) $[Ar] 4s^2 3d^4$
(E) $[Ar] 4s^1 3d^5$

E is correct. First, according to the periodic table, Cr has 24 electrons. We can eliminate choices B and C because those configurations have 25 electrons. Choice A is wrong because the $3s$ subshell is already accounted for in the [Ar] core—i.e., [Ar] stands for $1s^2$, $2s^2$, $2p^6$, $3s^2$, $3p^6$. Now, according to the Aufbau principle, we completely fill subshells before moving up to the next higher one. So the best answer would appear to be choice D. However, remember that completely half-filled and filled d subshells bestow extra stabilization to an atom. Therefore, Cr and Cu actually violate the Aufbau principle and promote a $4s$ electron to become $[Ar] 4s^1 3d^5$ and $[Ar] 4s^1 3d^{10}$, respectively. Choice E is the correct ground state configuration for Cr.

38. What is the hydroxide concentration for a solution with a pH of 10 at 25°C?

(A) $10^{-14} M$
(B) $10^{-10} M$
(C) $10^{-7} M$
(D) $10^{-4} M$
(E) $10^{-1} M$

D is correct. At 25°C, pH + pOH = 14 for any solution. Therefore, if the pH is 10 for this solution, the pOH is 14 − 10 = 4. Taking the negative antilog of 4 gives 10^{-4}, choice D.

39. Five hundred milliliters of solution of 0.1 M NaBr has how many milligrams of bromine?

(A) 200 mg
(B) 400 mg
(C) 2,000 mg
(D) 4,000 mg
(E) 20,000 mg

D is correct. First, find the number of moles of Br⁻.

$$molarity = moles \,/\, volume \text{ or } moles = molarity \times volume$$
$$= 0.1\ M \times 0.5\ L$$
$$= 0.05\ moles$$

Then figure out how much 0.05 moles of Br⁻ weighs.

$$grams = molecular\ weight \times moles$$
$$= 80\ g/mole \times 0.05\ moles$$
$$= 4\ grams\ or\ 4,000\ mg\ (choice\ D)$$

40. According to the ideal gas law, what is the approximate volume that will be occupied by 0.5 mole of
an ideal gas at 30°C and 3 atm pressure (gas constant $R = 0.0821$ L-atm/mol–K)?

(A) less than 1 L
(B) 5 L
(C) 10 L
(D) 15 L
(E) more than 20 L

B is correct. This is another math problem, but this one involves the ideal gas law. A couple of things first: 1) since we don't have a calculator, let's round off the value of R to 0.1 L-atm/mol–K and 2) remember that T must be in K, not °C, for $PV = nRT$ to work correctly. So

$$PV = nRT \text{ or } V = nRT/P$$
$$= (0.5 \text{ moles} \times 0.1 \text{ L-atm/mol–K} \times 300 \text{ K}) / 3 \text{ atm}$$
$$= (15 \text{ L-atm}) / 3 \text{ atm}$$
$$= 5 \text{ (choice B)}$$

41. Given that $\Delta G = \Delta H - T\Delta S$, how is the spontaneity of an endothermic reaction expected to change
with decreasing T?

(A) becomes less spontaneous
(B) becomes more spontaneous
(C) does not change
(D) decreases at first but then increases
(E) insufficient information to make a conclusion

E is correct. Recall that when ΔG is negative, a reaction is spontaneous, and when ΔG is positive, a reaction is nonspontaneous. The question indicates that the reaction in question is endothermic—i.e., ΔH is positive. Looking at the equation provided, the effect that decreasing T has will depend on the sign of ΔS. But the question doesn't tell us the sign of ΔS, nor can we figure it out on our own. Therefore, there is no way to make any conclusions—choice E.

42. Identify the element with the greatest first ionization
energy.

(A) Ce
(B) C
(C) Cl
(D) Ca
(E) Cs

B is correct. First ionization energy is a periodic trend that increases up and to the right on the periodic table. After looking at the position of these elements on the periodic table, carbon is clearly the best answer—choice B.

43. Identify the molecule/ion with the greatest potential to act as a Lewis acid.

   (A) $^+CH_3$
   (B) ^-CN
   (C) NH_3
   (D) BF_4^-
   (E) CO_2

A is correct. Lewis acids are molecules/ions that can accept a pair of nonbonding electrons to form a covalent bond. Not surprisingly, molecules/ions that contain an atom with an incomplete octet are good Lewis acids. The only choice that has an atom without a stable octet (or bitet in the case of H) is the carbon in choice A.

44. $2 Ca_3(PO_4)_2 + 6 SiO_2 + 10 C \rightarrow P_4 + \ldots CaSiO_3 + 10 CO$

   Which coefficient balances the reaction give above?

   (A) 2
   (B) 4
   (C) 5
   (D) 6
   (E) 8

D is correct. Looking at the reaction, 6 Ca atoms are present in the reactants. Therefore, 6 $CaSiO_3$ must be present as products (choice D).

45. A 100-milliliter solution containing $AgNO_3$ was treated with excess NaCl to completely precipitate the silver as AgCl. If 5.70 g AgCl was obtained, what was the concentration of Ag^+ in the original solution?

   (A) 0.03 M
   (B) 0.05 M
   (C) 0.12 M
   (D) 0.30 M
   (E) 0.40 M

E is correct. Given that the molecular weight of AgCl is 143.4 g/mol, the number of moles of AgCl precipitated is

$$\text{Moles AgCl} = 5.70 \text{ g} / 143.4 \text{ g/mol}$$
$$= 0.040 \text{ moles}$$

Since the molar ratio of Ag^+ in AgCl is 1, the number of moles of Ag^+ in the original solution was also 0.040. Therefore, the concentration of the original solution was

$$\text{Molarity Ag}^+ = \text{moles Ag}^+ / \text{volume (L)}$$
$$= 0.040 \text{ moles} / 0.100 \text{ L}$$
$$= 0.40 \text{ } M \text{ (choice E)}$$

46. Identify which of the following statements is FALSE.

    (A) The vapor pressure of a liquid decreases with increasing atmospheric pressure.

    (B) The value of an equilibrium constant is dependent on temperature.

    (C) The rate of a spontaneous reaction cannot solely be determined by its Gibbs free energy.

    (D) During a phase transition, the temperature of a substance must be constant.

    (E) The addition of a catalyst to a reaction at equilibrium has no net effect on the system.

A is correct. Choices B, C, D, and E are all true statements. Choice A is a false statement—the vapor pressure of a substance depends only upon: 1) the substance's temperature and 2) its mole fraction when it's in solution (see the colligative property of vapor pressure depression).

47. Which of the following compounds would be expected to have the greatest lattice binding energy?

    (A) $LiNO_3$
    (B) LiF
    (C) KI
    (D) NH_4Br
    (E) $CsNO_3$

B is correct. Since these are all ionic compounds, electrostatic forces can be assumed to be entirely responsible for the cohesive forces on the lattice. According to Coulomb's law

$$F = Kq_1q_2/r^2 \text{ where } Energy = Kq_1q_2/r$$

Since the charges for all of the ion pairs given in the choices (q_1 and q_2) are ±1, it is the internuclear distance, r, of each ion pair that is the determinant factor. According to the equations above, the smaller the r, the greater the energy. So using the periodic trend in atomic/ion size, LiF (choice B) is the ion pair with the smallest internuclear distance.

48. The daughter nucleus formed when ^{18}F undergoes positron emission is

    (A) ^{14}N
    (B) ^{16}O
    (C) ^{18}O
    (D) ^{19}F
    (E) ^{20}Ne

C is correct. Positron emission is a type of beta decay. During beta decay, nuclear mass remains constant. Therefore, choice C is the only possible answer.

$$^{18}_{9}F \rightarrow ^{?}_{?}? + ^{0}_{+1}e$$

Conserving mass (superscript) and charge (subscript) gives choice C.

49. Which of the following reactions produces a yellow precipitate?

(A) $NaOH(aq) + HCl(aq) \rightarrow NaCl(s) + H_2O$
(B) $NaOH(aq) + BaCl(aq) \rightarrow BaOH(s) + NaCl(aq)$
(C) $Pb(NO_3)_2(aq) + 2KI(aq) \rightarrow 2KNO_3(aq) + PbI_2(s)$
(D) $CuO(s) + Mg(s) \rightarrow Cu(s) + MgO(s)$
(E) $4Fe + 3O_2 \rightarrow 2Fe_2O_3$

C is correct. Recall the solubility rules. A and B are incorrect because neither NaCl nor BaOH are insoluble and therefore would not precipitate out of the aqueous solution. Because lead salts are insoluble except for their nitrates and perchlorates, lead iodide would precipitate out of solution as C depicts. Answer choices D and E are examples of oxidation-reduction reactions.

50. $Zn(s)\,|\,ZnCl_2(aq)\,|\,|\,Cl^-(aq)\,|\,Cl_2(g)\,|\,C(s)$

In the electrochemical cell described by the cell diagram above, what reaction occurs at the anode?

(A) $Zn \rightarrow Zn^{2+} + 2e$
(B) $Zn^{2+} + 2e \rightarrow Zn$
(C) $Cl_2 + 2e \rightarrow 2Cl^-$
(D) $2Cl^- \rightarrow Cl_2 + 2e$
(E) $Zn + Cl_2 \rightarrow ZnCl_2$

A is correct. Cell diagrams are read as

$$\text{Anode}\,|\,\text{Anodic Solution}\,|\,|\,\text{Cathodic Solution}\,|\,\text{Cathode}$$

For any electrochemical or electrolytic cell, *ox*idation occurs at the *an*ode and *red*uction occurs at the *cat*hode (remember *AN OX* and *RED CAT*). Therefore, the correct choice must be an oxidation. This eliminates choices B and C. We can also eliminate choices D and E because Cl is never allowed to enter the anodic side of the cell. Therefore, choice A is the correct answer.

51. Given the reaction $A \rightarrow B + C$, where $\Delta H_{r \times n}$ is negative, what effect would increasing the temperature (at constant pressure) have on the system at equilibrium?

(A) no change
(B) cannot be determined
(C) shift to the right
(D) shift to the left for $K < 1$ and to the right for $K > 1$
(E) shift to the left

E is correct. According to Le Chatelier's principle, the direction in which an equilibrium is disturbed can be predicted if $\Delta H_{r \times n}$ is known (eliminate choice B). A straightforward way of solving this is to write "HEAT" into the reaction either as a reactant for endothermic reactions or as a product for exothermic reactions. Here, the reaction is exothermic, so

$$A \rightleftharpoons B + C + \text{"HEAT"}$$

Then, since temperature is a measure of "HEAT," increasing T, or "HEAT," would be expected to shift the system to the left. Choice E is the answer.

52. An unknown acid solution was presumed to be either HCl or H_2SO_4. Which one of the following salt solutions would produce a precipitate when added to H_2SO_4 but not when added to HCl?

   (A) $LiNO_3$
   (B) NH_4NO_3
   (C) $CsNO_3$
   (D) $Ba(NO_3)_2$
   (E) $AgNO_3$

D is correct. Recall some fundamental solubility rules.

- All group 1 metals and NH_4^+ salts are *soluble*.
- All NO_3^- and ClO_4^- salts are *soluble*.
- All silver, lead, and mercury salts are *insoluble*.

Therefore, the addition of Li^+, NH_4^+, or Cs^+ would not produce a precipitate with either acid (eliminate choices A, B, and C). Silver, Ag^+, would form precipitates with both acids (eliminate choice E). Ba^{2+} is somewhat unique, even among other group 2 elements, because $BaCl_2$ is soluble while $BaSO_4$ is not (choice D).

53. $Ca_3(PO_4)_2(s) \leftrightharpoons 3\,Ca^{2+}(aq) + 2\,PO_4^{3-}(aq)$

   What is the equilibrium expression for the dissolution of $Ca_3(PO_4)_2$ where the above is true?

   (A) $K_{sp} = [Ca^{2+}]^3[PO_4^{3-}]^2$
   (B) $K_{sp} = [Ca^{2+}]^2[PO_4^{3-}]^3$
   (C) $K_{sp} = [Ca^{2+}][PO_4^{3-}]/[Ca_3(PO_4)_2]$
   (D) $K_{sp} = [Ca^{2+}]^3[PO_4^{3-}]^2/[Ca_3(PO_4)_2]$
   (E) $K_{sp} = [Ca^{2+}]^2[PO_4^{3-}]^3/[Ca_3(PO_4)_2]$

A is correct. Writing equilibrium expressions is a three-step process.

1. First, ignore any molecule that is in the solid (s) or liquid (l) phases.

2. Second, write $K = [products] / [reactants]$

3. Third, all coefficients in front of molecules become exponents in the equilibrium expression.

Therefore, the correct choice is A.

54. Which of the following represents a conjugate acid/base pair?

(A) Na^+/Cl^-
(B) HCl/H^+
(C) H_2CO_3/CO_3^{2-}
(D) NH_3/NH_4^+
(E) K^+/OH^-

D is correct. A conjugate acid/base pair is a set of 2 molecules/ions that have identical molecular formulas, except that one of them has one more H^+ than the other. Only choice D represents a true pair of conjugates.

55. An unknown solution having a pH of 3.5 was titrated with 0.1 M NaOH. Analysis of the resulting titration curve showed a single equivalence point at pH 7. Therefore, which of the following could be the unknown solute in the initial solution?

(A) HF
(B) HCl
(C) LiOH
(D) NH_3
(E) H_2SO_4

B is correct. The starting solution has a pH of 3.5. Therefore, the starting solution must be acidic. We can eliminate choices C and D because they are bases. The subsequent titration experiment revealed a single equivalence point, so the acid in question must be monoprotic—eliminate choice E. Since the equivalence point comes at pH 7, the unknown acid must be *strong*. HCl is the only monoprotic strong acid given (choice B).

56. Acid/base titration experiments could be used to determine all of the following directly EXCEPT

(A) the acid concentration of an acidic solution
(B) the alkalinity of a basic solution
(C) the pK_a of an unknown weak acid
(D) whether an unknown acid is monoprotic or polyprotic
(E) the molecular weight of an unknown acid or base

E is correct. Statements A through D can all be determined with data obtained from a titration experiment.

57. What is the correct term for the phase change from gas directly to solid?

(A) deposition
(B) sublimation
(C) liquefaction
(D) fusion
(E) vaporization

A is correct. The phase changes associated with the terms on the previous page are

deposition (gas → solid)
sublimation (solid → gas)
liquefaction (gas→ liquid)
fusion (solid → liquid)
vaporization (liquid → gas)

58. What is the correct IUPAC name for a straight-chained organic compound with the molecular formula C_3H_8?

(A) methane
(B) ethane
(C) methylethane
(D) propane
(E) isopropane

D is correct. The molecular formulas associated with the IUPAC names for organic molecules above are

methane:	CH_4
ethane:	CH_3CH_3
methylethane:	does not exist in the IUPAC system
propane:	$CH_3CH_2CH_3$
isopropane:	does not exist in the IUPAC system

59. If the pH of a solution is changed from 1 to 3 with the addition of an antacid, what percentage of $[H^+]$ was neutralized?

(A) 2%
(B) 10%
(C) 20%
(D) 90%
(E) 99%

E is correct. First, figure out the concentration of $[H^+]$ at pH 1 and pH 3.

$$pH = 1; [H^+] = 0.1\ M \qquad\qquad pH = 3; [H^+] = 0.001\ M$$

Then realize that $0.001\ M$ is 1 percent of (or 100 times smaller than) $0.1\ M$. Therefore, 99 percent of the H^+ is neutralized when going from pH 1 to pH 3.

60. Which of the following statements is the most accurate with regard to the significance of Avogadro's number, 6.02×10^{23}?

(A) It is the conversion factor between grams and atomic mass units.
(B) It is a universal physical constant just as the speed of light.
(C) It is the number of particles that are required to fill a 1-liter container.
(D) It is the inverse diameter of an H atom.
(E) It is the number of electrons in the universe.

A is correct. Avogadro's number is nothing more than the conversion faction among two measures of mass, atomic mass units, and grams. Just as you can say that there are 2.54 centimeters in an inch, so too can you say there are 6.02×10^{23} amu in a gram.

Questions 61–64 refer to the following data at standard conditions.

	Appearance	Reaction with dilute HCl	Reaction with dilute HNO$_3$
Unknown metal #1	Dull gray solid with white oxide coating	Dissolved with bubbles of clear gas	Dissolved with bubbles of clear gas
Unknown metal #2	Solid; lustrous, smooth silver-gray surface	No reaction	Dissolved with bubbles of orange gas

61. Unknown metal #1 could be

(A) mercury
(B) copper
(C) zinc
(D) iron
(E) silver

C is correct. Process of elimination is the best tool to use here. First, we can eliminate mercury (choice A) because mercury metal is a liquid at standard conditions, yet the table indicates that unknown metal #1 is a solid. Second, we can eliminate copper (choice B) because copper metal is brownish, yet the table says unknown metal #1 is dull gray. Now, consider the presence of the white oxide coat. The oxide of iron, better known as rust, is orange brown, not white, so eliminate choice D. Last, the oxide of silver is gray-black, better known as tarnish, so eliminate choice E. Therefore, zinc is the best choice—choice C.

62. Unknown metal #2 could be

(A) carbon
(B) copper
(C) zinc
(D) sodium
(E) silver

E is correct. Again, process of elimination is the best tool to use here. First, we can eliminate carbon (choice A) because carbon is not a metal. Second, we can again eliminate copper (choice B) because copper metal is brownish, yet the table says unknown metal #2 is silver-gray. Third, we can eliminate zinc (choice C) because it is a fairly reactive metal that always has a whitish oxide coat in air. Fourth, we can definitely eliminate sodium because sodium metal explodes with yellow flame on contact with even plain water, let alone acidic solutions—the table doesn't report any explosions! Finally, the best choice is silver, a relatively inert metal along with copper, gold, and platinum (it's no accident that these metals are used for jewelry and coinage)—choice E.

63. The addition of dilute HCl to unknown metal #1 produced a transparent gas. What is the likely identity of this gas?

(A) Cl_2
(B) H_2
(C) O_2
(D) CO_2
(E) NO_2

B is correct. There are several ways to approach this one. Again, process of elimination is very useful here. Chlorine (choice A) and nitrogen dioxide (choice E) gases are colored—greenish and orange, respectively. Therefore, they cannot be the gas in question. Furthermore, it's difficult to choose carbon dioxide (choice D) because there are no carbon atoms anywhere in this experiment. Finally, as a rule of thumb, a colorless gas produced from reactions between metals and acids is hydrogen—choice B.

64. The addition of dilute HNO_3 to unknown metal #2 produced an orange gas. What is the likely identity of this gas?

(A) Cl_2
(B) H_2
(C) O_2
(D) CO_2
(E) NO_2

E is correct. This requires a bit of general chemistry knowledge. The colors of the gases above are

$$Cl_2\text{—green}$$
$$H_2\text{—colorless}$$
$$O_2\text{—colorless}$$
$$CO_2\text{—colorless}$$
$$NO_2\text{—orange/brown}$$

Choice E is the best choice.

65. Which of the following solutions is the product of the neutralization reaction between 10 mL 0.2 M KOH and 10 mL 0.2 M HI?

(A) 0.1 M KI_3
(B) 0.1 M KI
(C) 0.2 M KI
(D) 0.4 M KI
(E) 0.4 M HOH

B is correct. First, the neutralization reaction that occurs here is

$$KOH + HI \rightarrow KI + H_2O$$

The trick is to realize that the number of K's and I's are not changing during the reaction; but since the solutions are being added, the volume is doubling. If the volume doubles, then the initial solution concentrations (0.2 M) are halved (0.1 M).

66. Which of the following is true regarding a Ne atom with a mass number of 20 and an O^{2-} ion with a mass number of 16?

(A) They contain the same number of protons.
(B) They contain the same number of neutrons.
(C) They contain the same number of protons plus neutrons.
(D) They are isoelectronic.
(E) They are isomers.

D is correct. An O_2^- ion has gained 2 electrons to fill its outer shell. This gives an O^{2-} ion the same electron configuration as Ne. That is, the 2 are isoelectronic.

67. Which of the following statements is NOT correct regarding chemical catalysts?

(A) They are not consumed during the chemical reaction.
(B) They cannot make nonspontaneous reactions occur.
(C) They do not have to be the same phase as the reactant molecules.
(D) They shift equilibrated reactions to the product's side.
(E) Enzymes are biological catalysts.

D is correct. The addition of a catalyst to a system at equilibrium has NO effect. That's because all a catalyst does is increase the rate at which a nonequilibrated system reaches equilibrium.

68. Most elements are solids at 25°C and 1 atm pressure, the exception being the 11 elements that are gases and 2 that are liquids. What 2 elements are liquids?

(A) Hg and Br
(B) Hg and I
(C) Ag and Kr
(D) Au and Kr
(E) Pt and Co

A is correct. It's important to know the phase of the elements at standard conditions (25°C at 1 atm)

Gases: hydrogen, helium, nitrogen, oxygen, fluorine, neon, chlorine, argon, krypton, xenon, and radon
Liquids: mercury and bromine (choice A)
Solids: the rest of the elements

69. A student conducted an experiment and obtained three values during three repetitive trials: 1.65, 1.68, 1.71. Later, the student discovered that the true value was 2.37. In contrast to the real value, the experimental results should be characterized as

(A) not accurate and not precise
(B) accurate but not precise
(C) not accurate but precise
(D) accurate and precise
(E) accurate, precise, but unreliable

C is correct. By definition, **accuracy** is the measure of how close experimental data are to true data, while **precision** is the measure of how similar experimental data are to one another. Clearly, the student's data is very precise, the values of 1.65, 1.68, 1.71 vary by no more than 4 percent. However, the average value of the experimental data is over 50 percent off the true value, meaning these results are not very accurate—choice C.

ABOUT THE AUTHOR

Theodore Silver holds a medical degree from the Yale University School of Medicine, a bachelor's degree from Yale University, and a law degree from the University of Connecticut.

Dr. Silver has been intensely involved in the field of education, testing, and test preparation since 1976 and has written several books and computer tutorials pertaining to those fields. He became affiliated with The Princeton Review in 1988 and is chief author and architect of The Princeton Review MCAT preparatory course.

Dr. Silver is Associate Professor of Law at Touro College Jacob D. Fuchsberg Law Center where he teaches the law of medical practice and malpractice, contracts, and federal income taxation.

The Princeton Review

1.

YOUR NAME: _____
(Print)   Last   First   M.I.

SIGNATURE: _____ DATE: __/__/__

HOME ADDRESS: _____
(Print)   Number and Street

_____
City   State   Zip Code

PHONE NO.: _____
(Print)

IMPORTANT: Please fill in these boxes exactly as shown on the back cover of your test book.

2. TEST FORM

3. TEST CODE

4. REGISTRATION NUMBER

5. YOUR NAME

First 4 letters of last name				FIRST INIT	MID INIT
⊂A⊃	⊂A⊃	⊂A⊃	⊂A⊃	⊂A⊃	⊂A⊃
⊂B⊃	⊂B⊃	⊂B⊃	⊂B⊃	⊂B⊃	⊂B⊃
⊂C⊃	⊂C⊃	⊂C⊃	⊂C⊃	⊂C⊃	⊂C⊃
⊂D⊃	⊂D⊃	⊂D⊃	⊂D⊃	⊂D⊃	⊂D⊃
⊂E⊃	⊂E⊃	⊂E⊃	⊂E⊃	⊂E⊃	⊂E⊃
⊂F⊃	⊂F⊃	⊂F⊃	⊂F⊃	⊂F⊃	⊂F⊃
⊂G⊃	⊂G⊃	⊂G⊃	⊂G⊃	⊂G⊃	⊂G⊃
⊂H⊃	⊂H⊃	⊂H⊃	⊂H⊃	⊂H⊃	⊂H⊃
⊂I⊃	⊂I⊃	⊂I⊃	⊂I⊃	⊂I⊃	⊂I⊃
⊂J⊃	⊂J⊃	⊂J⊃	⊂J⊃	⊂J⊃	⊂J⊃
⊂K⊃	⊂K⊃	⊂K⊃	⊂K⊃	⊂K⊃	⊂K⊃
⊂L⊃	⊂L⊃	⊂L⊃	⊂L⊃	⊂L⊃	⊂L⊃
⊂M⊃	⊂M⊃	⊂M⊃	⊂M⊃	⊂M⊃	⊂M⊃
⊂N⊃	⊂N⊃	⊂N⊃	⊂N⊃	⊂N⊃	⊂N⊃
⊂O⊃	⊂O⊃	⊂O⊃	⊂O⊃	⊂O⊃	⊂O⊃
⊂P⊃	⊂P⊃	⊂P⊃	⊂P⊃	⊂P⊃	⊂P⊃
⊂Q⊃	⊂Q⊃	⊂Q⊃	⊂Q⊃	⊂Q⊃	⊂Q⊃
⊂R⊃	⊂R⊃	⊂R⊃	⊂R⊃	⊂R⊃	⊂R⊃
⊂S⊃	⊂S⊃	⊂S⊃	⊂S⊃	⊂S⊃	⊂S⊃
⊂T⊃	⊂T⊃	⊂T⊃	⊂T⊃	⊂T⊃	⊂T⊃
⊂U⊃	⊂U⊃	⊂U⊃	⊂U⊃	⊂U⊃	⊂U⊃
⊂V⊃	⊂V⊃	⊂V⊃	⊂V⊃	⊂V⊃	⊂V⊃
⊂W⊃	⊂W⊃	⊂W⊃	⊂W⊃	⊂W⊃	⊂W⊃
⊂X⊃	⊂X⊃	⊂X⊃	⊂X⊃	⊂X⊃	⊂X⊃
⊂Y⊃	⊂Y⊃	⊂Y⊃	⊂Y⊃	⊂Y⊃	⊂Y⊃
⊂Z⊃	⊂Z⊃	⊂Z⊃	⊂Z⊃	⊂Z⊃	⊂Z⊃

TEST CODE bubbles: ⊂A⊃ ⊂B⊃ ⊂C⊃ ⊂D⊃ ⊂E⊃ ⊂F⊃ ⊂G⊃

Number columns (0–9): ⊂0⊃ ⊂1⊃ ⊂2⊃ ⊂3⊃ ⊂4⊃ ⊂5⊃ ⊂6⊃ ⊂7⊃ ⊂8⊃ ⊂9⊃

6. DATE OF BIRTH

Month	Day	Year
⊂ ⊃ JAN		
⊂ ⊃ FEB		
⊂ ⊃ MAR	⊂0⊃ ⊂0⊃	⊂0⊃ ⊂0⊃
⊂ ⊃ APR	⊂1⊃ ⊂1⊃	⊂1⊃ ⊂1⊃
⊂ ⊃ MAY	⊂2⊃ ⊂2⊃	⊂2⊃ ⊂2⊃
⊂ ⊃ JUN	⊂3⊃ ⊂3⊃	⊂3⊃ ⊂3⊃
⊂ ⊃ JUL	⊂4⊃	⊂4⊃ ⊂4⊃
⊂ ⊃ AUG	⊂5⊃	⊂5⊃ ⊂5⊃
⊂ ⊃ SEP	⊂6⊃	⊂6⊃ ⊂6⊃
⊂ ⊃ OCT	⊂7⊃	⊂7⊃ ⊂7⊃
⊂ ⊃ NOV	⊂8⊃	⊂8⊃ ⊂8⊃
⊂ ⊃ DEC	⊂9⊃	⊂9⊃ ⊂9⊃

7. SEX

⊂ ⊃ MALE
⊂ ⊃ FEMALE

The Princeton Review

1 ⊂A⊃ ⊂B⊃ ⊂C⊃ ⊂D⊃ ⊂E⊃
2 ⊂A⊃ ⊂B⊃ ⊂C⊃ ⊂D⊃ ⊂E⊃
3 ⊂A⊃ ⊂B⊃ ⊂C⊃ ⊂D⊃ ⊂E⊃
4 ⊂A⊃ ⊂B⊃ ⊂C⊃ ⊂D⊃ ⊂E⊃
5 ⊂A⊃ ⊂B⊃ ⊂C⊃ ⊂D⊃ ⊂E⊃
6 ⊂A⊃ ⊂B⊃ ⊂C⊃ ⊂D⊃ ⊂E⊃
7 ⊂A⊃ ⊂B⊃ ⊂C⊃ ⊂D⊃ ⊂E⊃
8 ⊂A⊃ ⊂B⊃ ⊂C⊃ ⊂D⊃ ⊂E⊃
9 ⊂A⊃ ⊂B⊃ ⊂C⊃ ⊂D⊃ ⊂E⊃
10 ⊂A⊃ ⊂B⊃ ⊂C⊃ ⊂D⊃ ⊂E⊃
11 ⊂A⊃ ⊂B⊃ ⊂C⊃ ⊂D⊃ ⊂E⊃
12 ⊂A⊃ ⊂B⊃ ⊂C⊃ ⊂D⊃ ⊂E⊃
13 ⊂A⊃ ⊂B⊃ ⊂C⊃ ⊂D⊃ ⊂E⊃
14 ⊂A⊃ ⊂B⊃ ⊂C⊃ ⊂D⊃ ⊂E⊃
15 ⊂A⊃ ⊂B⊃ ⊂C⊃ ⊂D⊃ ⊂E⊃
16 ⊂A⊃ ⊂B⊃ ⊂C⊃ ⊂D⊃ ⊂E⊃
17 ⊂A⊃ ⊂B⊃ ⊂C⊃ ⊂D⊃ ⊂E⊃
18 ⊂A⊃ ⊂B⊃ ⊂C⊃ ⊂D⊃ ⊂E⊃
19 ⊂A⊃ ⊂B⊃ ⊂C⊃ ⊂D⊃ ⊂E⊃
20 ⊂A⊃ ⊂B⊃ ⊂C⊃ ⊂D⊃ ⊂E⊃
21 ⊂A⊃ ⊂B⊃ ⊂C⊃ ⊂D⊃ ⊂E⊃
22 ⊂A⊃ ⊂B⊃ ⊂C⊃ ⊂D⊃ ⊂E⊃
23 ⊂A⊃ ⊂B⊃ ⊂C⊃ ⊂D⊃ ⊂E⊃

24 ⊂A⊃ ⊂B⊃ ⊂C⊃ ⊂D⊃ ⊂E⊃
25 ⊂A⊃ ⊂B⊃ ⊂C⊃ ⊂D⊃ ⊂E⊃
26 ⊂A⊃ ⊂B⊃ ⊂C⊃ ⊂D⊃ ⊂E⊃
27 ⊂A⊃ ⊂B⊃ ⊂C⊃ ⊂D⊃ ⊂E⊃
28 ⊂A⊃ ⊂B⊃ ⊂C⊃ ⊂D⊃ ⊂E⊃
29 ⊂A⊃ ⊂B⊃ ⊂C⊃ ⊂D⊃ ⊂E⊃
30 ⊂A⊃ ⊂B⊃ ⊂C⊃ ⊂D⊃ ⊂E⊃
31 ⊂A⊃ ⊂B⊃ ⊂C⊃ ⊂D⊃ ⊂E⊃
32 ⊂A⊃ ⊂B⊃ ⊂C⊃ ⊂D⊃ ⊂E⊃
33 ⊂A⊃ ⊂B⊃ ⊂C⊃ ⊂D⊃ ⊂E⊃
34 ⊂A⊃ ⊂B⊃ ⊂C⊃ ⊂D⊃ ⊂E⊃
35 ⊂A⊃ ⊂B⊃ ⊂C⊃ ⊂D⊃ ⊂E⊃
36 ⊂A⊃ ⊂B⊃ ⊂C⊃ ⊂D⊃ ⊂E⊃
37 ⊂A⊃ ⊂B⊃ ⊂C⊃ ⊂D⊃ ⊂E⊃
38 ⊂A⊃ ⊂B⊃ ⊂C⊃ ⊂D⊃ ⊂E⊃
39 ⊂A⊃ ⊂B⊃ ⊂C⊃ ⊂D⊃ ⊂E⊃
40 ⊂A⊃ ⊂B⊃ ⊂C⊃ ⊂D⊃ ⊂E⊃
41 ⊂A⊃ ⊂B⊃ ⊂C⊃ ⊂D⊃ ⊂E⊃
42 ⊂A⊃ ⊂B⊃ ⊂C⊃ ⊂D⊃ ⊂E⊃
43 ⊂A⊃ ⊂B⊃ ⊂C⊃ ⊂D⊃ ⊂E⊃
44 ⊂A⊃ ⊂B⊃ ⊂C⊃ ⊂D⊃ ⊂E⊃
45 ⊂A⊃ ⊂B⊃ ⊂C⊃ ⊂D⊃ ⊂E⊃
46 ⊂A⊃ ⊂B⊃ ⊂C⊃ ⊂D⊃ ⊂E⊃

47 ⊂A⊃ ⊂B⊃ ⊂C⊃ ⊂D⊃ ⊂E⊃
48 ⊂A⊃ ⊂B⊃ ⊂C⊃ ⊂D⊃ ⊂E⊃
49 ⊂A⊃ ⊂B⊃ ⊂C⊃ ⊂D⊃ ⊂E⊃
50 ⊂A⊃ ⊂B⊃ ⊂C⊃ ⊂D⊃ ⊂E⊃
51 ⊂A⊃ B ⊂C⊃ ⊂D⊃ ⊂E⊃
52 ⊂A⊃ ⊂B⊃ ⊂C⊃ ⊂D⊃ ⊂E⊃
53 ⊂A⊃ ⊂B⊃ ⊂C⊃ ⊂D⊃ ⊂E⊃
54 ⊂A⊃ ⊂B⊃ ⊂C⊃ ⊂D⊃ ⊂E⊃
55 ⊂A⊃ ⊂B⊃ ⊂C⊃ ⊂D⊃ ⊂E⊃
56 ⊂A⊃ ⊂B⊃ ⊂C⊃ ⊂D⊃ ⊂E⊃
57 ⊂A⊃ ⊂B⊃ ⊂C⊃ ⊂D⊃ ⊂E⊃
58 ⊂A⊃ ⊂B⊃ ⊂C⊃ ⊂D⊃ ⊂E⊃
59 ⊂A⊃ ⊂B⊃ ⊂C⊃ ⊂D⊃ ⊂E⊃
60 ⊂A⊃ ⊂B⊃ ⊂C⊃ ⊂D⊃ ⊂E⊃
61 ⊂A⊃ ⊂B⊃ ⊂C⊃ ⊂D⊃ ⊂E⊃
62 ⊂A⊃ ⊂B⊃ ⊂C⊃ ⊂D⊃ ⊂E⊃
63 ⊂A⊃ ⊂B⊃ ⊂C⊃ ⊂D⊃ ⊂E⊃
64 ⊂A⊃ ⊂B⊃ ⊂C⊃ ⊂D⊃ ⊂E⊃
65 ⊂A⊃ ⊂B⊃ ⊂C⊃ ⊂D⊃ ⊂E⊃
66 ⊂A⊃ ⊂B⊃ ⊂C⊃ ⊂D⊃ ⊂E⊃
67 ⊂A⊃ ⊂B⊃ ⊂C⊃ ⊂D⊃ ⊂E⊃
68 ⊂A⊃ ⊂B⊃ ⊂C⊃ ⊂D⊃ ⊂E⊃
69 ⊂A⊃ ⊂B⊃ ⊂C⊃ ⊂D⊃ ⊂E⊃

Part B

	I	II	CE
101	⊂T⊃ ⊂F⊃	⊂T⊃ ⊂F⊃	⊂ ⊃
102	⊂T⊃ ⊂F⊃	⊂T⊃ ⊂F⊃	⊂ ⊃
103	⊂T⊃ ⊂F⊃	⊂T⊃ ⊂F⊃	⊂ ⊃
104	⊂T⊃ ⊂F⊃	⊂T⊃ ⊂F⊃	⊂ ⊃
105	⊂T⊃ ⊂F⊃	⊂T⊃ ⊂F⊃	⊂ ⊃
106	⊂T⊃ ⊂F⊃	⊂T⊃ ⊂F⊃	⊂ ⊃
107	⊂T⊃ ⊂F⊃	⊂T⊃ ⊂F⊃	⊂ ⊃
108	⊂T⊃ ⊂F⊃	⊂T⊃ ⊂F⊃	⊂ ⊃
109	⊂T⊃ ⊂F⊃	⊂T⊃ ⊂F⊃	⊂ ⊃
110	⊂T⊃ ⊂F⊃	⊂T⊃ ⊂F⊃	⊂ ⊃
111	⊂T⊃ ⊂F⊃	⊂T⊃ ⊂F⊃	⊂ ⊃
112	⊂T⊃ ⊂F⊃	⊂T⊃ ⊂F⊃	⊂ ⊃
113	⊂T⊃ ⊂F⊃	⊂T⊃ ⊂F⊃	⊂ ⊃
114	⊂T⊃ ⊂F⊃	⊂T⊃ ⊂F⊃	⊂ ⊃
115	⊂T⊃ ⊂F⊃	⊂T⊃ ⊂F⊃	⊂ ⊃
116	⊂T⊃ ⊂F⊃	⊂T⊃ ⊂F⊃	⊂ ⊃

The Princeton Review

1.

YOUR NAME: _____
(Print)   Last   First   M.I.

SIGNATURE: _____   DATE: __/__/__

HOME ADDRESS: _____
(Print)   Number and Street

City   State   Zip Code

PHONE NO.: _____
(Print)

IMPORTANT: Please fill in these boxes exactly as shown on the back cover of your test book.

2. TEST FORM

_____

6. DATE OF BIRTH

Month		Day		Year	
⊂ ⊃ JAN					
⊂ ⊃ FEB					
⊂ ⊃ MAR	⊂0⊃	⊂0⊃	⊂0⊃	⊂0⊃	
⊂ ⊃ APR	⊂1⊃	⊂1⊃	⊂1⊃	⊂1⊃	
⊂ ⊃ MAY	⊂2⊃	⊂2⊃	⊂2⊃	⊂2⊃	
⊂ ⊃ JUN	⊂3⊃	⊂3⊃	⊂3⊃	⊂3⊃	
⊂ ⊃ JUL		⊂4⊃	⊂4⊃	⊂4⊃	
⊂ ⊃ AUG		⊂5⊃	⊂5⊃	⊂5⊃	
⊂ ⊃ SEP		⊂6⊃	⊂6⊃	⊂6⊃	
⊂ ⊃ OCT		⊂7⊃	⊂7⊃	⊂7⊃	
⊂ ⊃ NOV		⊂8⊃	⊂8⊃	⊂8⊃	
⊂ ⊃ DEC		⊂9⊃	⊂9⊃	⊂9⊃	

3. TEST CODE

⊂0⊃ ⊂A⊃ ⊂0⊃ ⊂0⊃ ⊂0⊃
⊂1⊃ ⊂B⊃ ⊂1⊃ ⊂1⊃ ⊂1⊃
⊂2⊃ ⊂C⊃ ⊂2⊃ ⊂2⊃ ⊂2⊃
⊂3⊃ ⊂D⊃ ⊂3⊃ ⊂3⊃ ⊂3⊃
⊂4⊃ ⊂E⊃ ⊂4⊃ ⊂4⊃ ⊂4⊃
⊂5⊃ ⊂F⊃ ⊂5⊃ ⊂5⊃ ⊂5⊃
⊂6⊃ ⊂G⊃ ⊂6⊃ ⊂6⊃ ⊂6⊃
⊂7⊃ ⊂7⊃ ⊂7⊃ ⊂7⊃
⊂8⊃ ⊂8⊃ ⊂8⊃ ⊂8⊃
⊂9⊃ ⊂9⊃ ⊂9⊃ ⊂9⊃

4. REGISTRATION NUMBER

⊂0⊃ ⊂0⊃ ⊂0⊃ ⊂0⊃ ⊂0⊃ ⊂0⊃ ⊂0⊃
⊂1⊃ ⊂1⊃ ⊂1⊃ ⊂1⊃ ⊂1⊃ ⊂1⊃ ⊂1⊃
⊂2⊃ ⊂2⊃ ⊂2⊃ ⊂2⊃ ⊂2⊃ ⊂2⊃ ⊂2⊃
⊂3⊃ ⊂3⊃ ⊂3⊃ ⊂3⊃ ⊂3⊃ ⊂3⊃ ⊂3⊃
⊂4⊃ ⊂4⊃ ⊂4⊃ ⊂4⊃ ⊂4⊃ ⊂4⊃ ⊂4⊃
⊂5⊃ ⊂5⊃ ⊂5⊃ ⊂5⊃ ⊂5⊃ ⊂5⊃ ⊂5⊃
⊂6⊃ ⊂6⊃ ⊂6⊃ ⊂6⊃ ⊂6⊃ ⊂6⊃ ⊂6⊃
⊂7⊃ ⊂7⊃ ⊂7⊃ ⊂7⊃ ⊂7⊃ ⊂7⊃ ⊂7⊃
⊂8⊃ ⊂8⊃ ⊂8⊃ ⊂8⊃ ⊂8⊃ ⊂8⊃ ⊂8⊃
⊂9⊃ ⊂9⊃ ⊂9⊃ ⊂9⊃ ⊂9⊃ ⊂9⊃ ⊂9⊃

7. SEX

⊂ ⊃ MALE
⊂ ⊃ FEMALE

The Princeton Review

5. YOUR NAME

First 4 letters of last name				FIRST INIT	MID INIT
⊂A⊃	⊂A⊃	⊂A⊃	⊂A⊃	⊂A⊃	⊂A⊃
⊂B⊃	⊂B⊃	⊂B⊃	⊂B⊃	⊂B⊃	⊂B⊃
⊂C⊃	⊂C⊃	⊂C⊃	⊂C⊃	⊂C⊃	⊂C⊃
⊂D⊃	⊂D⊃	⊂D⊃	⊂D⊃	⊂D⊃	⊂D⊃
⊂E⊃	⊂E⊃	⊂E⊃	⊂E⊃	⊂E⊃	⊂E⊃
⊂F⊃	⊂F⊃	⊂F⊃	⊂F⊃	⊂F⊃	⊂F⊃
⊂G⊃	⊂G⊃	⊂G⊃	⊂G⊃	⊂G⊃	⊂G⊃
⊂H⊃	⊂H⊃	⊂H⊃	⊂H⊃	⊂H⊃	⊂H⊃
⊂I⊃	⊂I⊃	⊂I⊃	⊂I⊃	⊂I⊃	⊂I⊃
⊂J⊃	⊂J⊃	⊂J⊃	⊂J⊃	⊂J⊃	⊂J⊃
⊂K⊃	⊂K⊃	⊂K⊃	⊂K⊃	⊂K⊃	⊂K⊃
⊂L⊃	⊂L⊃	⊂L⊃	⊂L⊃	⊂L⊃	⊂L⊃
⊂M⊃	⊂M⊃	⊂M⊃	⊂M⊃	⊂M⊃	⊂M⊃
⊂N⊃	⊂N⊃	⊂N⊃	⊂N⊃	⊂N⊃	⊂N⊃
⊂O⊃	⊂O⊃	⊂O⊃	⊂O⊃	⊂O⊃	⊂O⊃
⊂P⊃	⊂P⊃	⊂P⊃	⊂P⊃	⊂P⊃	⊂P⊃
⊂Q⊃	⊂Q⊃	⊂Q⊃	⊂Q⊃	⊂Q⊃	⊂Q⊃
⊂R⊃	⊂R⊃	⊂R⊃	⊂R⊃	⊂R⊃	⊂R⊃
⊂S⊃	⊂S⊃	⊂S⊃	⊂S⊃	⊂S⊃	⊂S⊃
⊂T⊃	⊂T⊃	⊂T⊃	⊂T⊃	⊂T⊃	⊂T⊃
⊂U⊃	⊂U⊃	⊂U⊃	⊂U⊃	⊂U⊃	⊂U⊃
⊂V⊃	⊂V⊃	⊂V⊃	⊂V⊃	⊂V⊃	⊂V⊃
⊂W⊃	⊂W⊃	⊂W⊃	⊂W⊃	⊂W⊃	⊂W⊃
⊂X⊃	⊂X⊃	⊂X⊃	⊂X⊃	⊂X⊃	⊂X⊃
⊂Y⊃	⊂Y⊃	⊂Y⊃	⊂Y⊃	⊂Y⊃	⊂Y⊃
⊂Z⊃	⊂Z⊃	⊂Z⊃	⊂Z⊃	⊂Z⊃	⊂Z⊃

1 ⊂A⊃ ⊂B⊃ ⊂C⊃ ⊂D⊃ ⊂E⊃
2 ⊂A⊃ ⊂B⊃ ⊂C⊃ ⊂D⊃ ⊂E⊃
3 ⊂A⊃ ⊂B⊃ ⊂C⊃ ⊂D⊃ ⊂E⊃
4 ⊂A⊃ ⊂B⊃ ⊂C⊃ ⊂D⊃ ⊂E⊃
5 ⊂A⊃ ⊂B⊃ ⊂C⊃ ⊂D⊃ ⊂E⊃
6 ⊂A⊃ ⊂B⊃ ⊂C⊃ ⊂D⊃ ⊂E⊃
7 ⊂A⊃ ⊂B⊃ ⊂C⊃ ⊂D⊃ ⊂E⊃
8 ⊂A⊃ ⊂B⊃ ⊂C⊃ ⊂D⊃ ⊂E⊃
9 ⊂A⊃ ⊂B⊃ ⊂C⊃ ⊂D⊃ ⊂E⊃
10 ⊂A⊃ ⊂B⊃ ⊂C⊃ ⊂D⊃ ⊂E⊃
11 ⊂A⊃ ⊂B⊃ ⊂C⊃ ⊂D⊃ ⊂E⊃
12 ⊂A⊃ ⊂B⊃ ⊂C⊃ ⊂D⊃ ⊂E⊃
13 ⊂A⊃ ⊂B⊃ ⊂C⊃ ⊂D⊃ ⊂E⊃
14 ⊂A⊃ ⊂B⊃ ⊂C⊃ ⊂D⊃ ⊂E⊃
15 ⊂A⊃ ⊂B⊃ ⊂C⊃ ⊂D⊃ ⊂E⊃
16 ⊂A⊃ ⊂B⊃ ⊂C⊃ ⊂D⊃ ⊂E⊃
17 ⊂A⊃ ⊂B⊃ ⊂C⊃ ⊂D⊃ ⊂E⊃
18 ⊂A⊃ ⊂B⊃ ⊂C⊃ ⊂D⊃ ⊂E⊃
19 ⊂A⊃ ⊂B⊃ ⊂C⊃ ⊂D⊃ ⊂E⊃
20 ⊂A⊃ ⊂B⊃ ⊂C⊃ ⊂D⊃ ⊂E⊃
21 ⊂A⊃ ⊂B⊃ ⊂C⊃ ⊂D⊃ ⊂E⊃
22 ⊂A⊃ ⊂B⊃ ⊂C⊃ ⊂D⊃ ⊂E⊃
23 ⊂A⊃ ⊂B⊃ ⊂C⊃ ⊂D⊃ ⊂E⊃

24 ⊂A⊃ ⊂B⊃ ⊂C⊃ ⊂D⊃ ⊂E⊃
25 ⊂A⊃ ⊂B⊃ ⊂C⊃ ⊂D⊃ ⊂E⊃
26 ⊂A⊃ ⊂B⊃ ⊂C⊃ ⊂D⊃ ⊂E⊃
27 ⊂A⊃ ⊂B⊃ ⊂C⊃ ⊂D⊃ ⊂E⊃
28 ⊂A⊃ ⊂B⊃ ⊂C⊃ ⊂D⊃ ⊂E⊃
29 ⊂A⊃ ⊂B⊃ ⊂C⊃ ⊂D⊃ ⊂E⊃
30 ⊂A⊃ ⊂B⊃ ⊂C⊃ ⊂D⊃ ⊂E⊃
31 ⊂A⊃ ⊂B⊃ ⊂C⊃ ⊂D⊃ ⊂E⊃
32 ⊂A⊃ ⊂B⊃ ⊂C⊃ ⊂D⊃ ⊂E⊃
33 ⊂A⊃ ⊂B⊃ ⊂C⊃ ⊂D⊃ ⊂E⊃
34 ⊂A⊃ ⊂B⊃ ⊂C⊃ ⊂D⊃ ⊂E⊃
35 ⊂A⊃ ⊂B⊃ ⊂C⊃ ⊂D⊃ ⊂E⊃
36 ⊂A⊃ ⊂B⊃ ⊂C⊃ ⊂D⊃ ⊂E⊃
37 ⊂A⊃ ⊂B⊃ ⊂C⊃ ⊂D⊃ ⊂E⊃
38 ⊂A⊃ ⊂B⊃ ⊂C⊃ ⊂D⊃ ⊂E⊃
39 ⊂A⊃ ⊂B⊃ ⊂C⊃ ⊂D⊃ ⊂E⊃
40 ⊂A⊃ ⊂B⊃ ⊂C⊃ ⊂D⊃ ⊂E⊃
41 ⊂A⊃ ⊂B⊃ ⊂C⊃ ⊂D⊃ ⊂E⊃
42 ⊂A⊃ ⊂B⊃ ⊂C⊃ ⊂D⊃ ⊂E⊃
43 ⊂A⊃ ⊂B⊃ ⊂C⊃ ⊂D⊃ ⊂E⊃
44 ⊂A⊃ ⊂B⊃ ⊂C⊃ ⊂D⊃ ⊂E⊃
45 ⊂A⊃ ⊂B⊃ ⊂C⊃ ⊂D⊃ ⊂E⊃
46 ⊂A⊃ ⊂B⊃ ⊂C⊃ ⊂D⊃ ⊂E⊃

47 ⊂A⊃ ⊂B⊃ ⊂C⊃ ⊂D⊃ ⊂E⊃
48 ⊂A⊃ ⊂B⊃ ⊂C⊃ ⊂D⊃ ⊂E⊃
49 ⊂A⊃ ⊂B⊃ ⊂C⊃ ⊂D⊃ ⊂E⊃
50 ⊂A⊃ ⊂B⊃ ⊂C⊃ ⊂D⊃ ⊂E⊃
51 ⊂A⊃ B ⊂C⊃ ⊂D⊃ ⊂E⊃
52 ⊂A⊃ ⊂B⊃ ⊂C⊃ ⊂D⊃ ⊂E⊃
53 ⊂A⊃ ⊂B⊃ ⊂C⊃ ⊂D⊃ ⊂E⊃
54 ⊂A⊃ ⊂B⊃ ⊂C⊃ ⊂D⊃ ⊂E⊃
55 ⊂A⊃ ⊂B⊃ ⊂C⊃ ⊂D⊃ ⊂E⊃
56 ⊂A⊃ ⊂B⊃ ⊂C⊃ ⊂D⊃ ⊂E⊃
57 ⊂A⊃ ⊂B⊃ ⊂C⊃ ⊂D⊃ ⊂E⊃
58 ⊂A⊃ ⊂B⊃ ⊂C⊃ ⊂D⊃ ⊂E⊃
59 ⊂A⊃ ⊂B⊃ ⊂C⊃ ⊂D⊃ ⊂E⊃
60 ⊂A⊃ ⊂B⊃ ⊂C⊃ ⊂D⊃ ⊂E⊃
61 ⊂A⊃ ⊂B⊃ ⊂C⊃ ⊂D⊃ ⊂E⊃
62 ⊂A⊃ ⊂B⊃ ⊂C⊃ ⊂D⊃ ⊂E⊃
63 ⊂A⊃ ⊂B⊃ ⊂C⊃ ⊂D⊃ ⊂E⊃
64 ⊂A⊃ ⊂B⊃ ⊂C⊃ ⊂D⊃ ⊂E⊃
65 ⊂A⊃ ⊂B⊃ ⊂C⊃ ⊂D⊃ ⊂E⊃
66 ⊂A⊃ ⊂B⊃ ⊂C⊃ ⊂D⊃ ⊂E⊃
67 ⊂A⊃ ⊂B⊃ ⊂C⊃ ⊂D⊃ ⊂E⊃
68 ⊂A⊃ ⊂B⊃ ⊂C⊃ ⊂D⊃ ⊂E⊃
69 ⊂A⊃ ⊂B⊃ ⊂C⊃ ⊂D⊃ ⊂E⊃

Part B

	I		II		CE
101	⊂T⊃ ⊂F⊃		⊂T⊃ ⊂F⊃		⊂ ⊃
102	⊂T⊃ ⊂F⊃		⊂T⊃ ⊂F⊃		⊂ ⊃
103	⊂T⊃ ⊂F⊃		⊂T⊃ ⊂F⊃		⊂ ⊃
104	⊂T⊃ ⊂F⊃		⊂T⊃ ⊂F⊃		⊂ ⊃
105	⊂T⊃ ⊂F⊃		⊂T⊃ ⊂F⊃		⊂ ⊃
106	⊂T⊃ ⊂F⊃		⊂T⊃ ⊂F⊃		⊂ ⊃
107	⊂T⊃ ⊂F⊃		⊂T⊃ ⊂F⊃		⊂ ⊃
108	⊂T⊃ ⊂F⊃		⊂T⊃ ⊂F⊃		⊂ ⊃
109	⊂T⊃ ⊂F⊃		⊂T⊃ ⊂F⊃		⊂ ⊃
110	⊂T⊃ ⊂F⊃		⊂T⊃ ⊂F⊃		⊂ ⊃
111	⊂T⊃ ⊂F⊃		⊂T⊃ ⊂F⊃		⊂ ⊃
112	⊂T⊃ ⊂F⊃		⊂T⊃ ⊂F⊃		⊂ ⊃
113	⊂T⊃ ⊂F⊃		⊂T⊃ ⊂F⊃		⊂ ⊃
114	⊂T⊃ ⊂F⊃		⊂T⊃ ⊂F⊃		⊂ ⊃
115	⊂T⊃ ⊂F⊃		⊂T⊃ ⊂F⊃		⊂ ⊃
116	⊂T⊃ ⊂F⊃		⊂T⊃ ⊂F⊃		⊂ ⊃

The Princeton Review

1.

YOUR NAME: _____
(Print)   Last   First   M.I.

SIGNATURE: _____ DATE: __/__/__

HOME ADDRESS: _____
(Print)   Number and Street

_____
City   State   Zip Code

PHONE NO.: _____
(Print)

IMPORTANT: Please fill in these boxes exactly as shown on the back cover of your test book.

2. TEST FORM

_____

6. DATE OF BIRTH

Month		Day		Year	
⊂ ⊃ JAN					
⊂ ⊃ FEB					
⊂ ⊃ MAR	⊂0⊃	⊂0⊃	⊂0⊃	⊂0⊃
⊂ ⊃ APR	⊂1⊃	⊂1⊃	⊂1⊃	⊂1⊃
⊂ ⊃ MAY	⊂2⊃	⊂2⊃	⊂2⊃	⊂2⊃
⊂ ⊃ JUN	⊂3⊃	⊂3⊃	⊂3⊃	⊂3⊃
⊂ ⊃ JUL		⊂4⊃	⊂4⊃	⊂4⊃
⊂ ⊃ AUG		⊂5⊃	⊂5⊃	⊂5⊃
⊂ ⊃ SEP		⊂6⊃	⊂6⊃	⊂6⊃
⊂ ⊃ OCT		⊂7⊃	⊂7⊃	⊂7⊃
⊂ ⊃ NOV		⊂8⊃	⊂8⊃	⊂8⊃
⊂ ⊃ DEC		⊂9⊃	⊂9⊃	⊂9⊃

3. TEST CODE

⊂0⊃	⊂A⊃	⊂0⊃	⊂0⊃	⊂0⊃
⊂1⊃	⊂B⊃	⊂1⊃	⊂1⊃	⊂1⊃
⊂2⊃	⊂C⊃	⊂2⊃	⊂2⊃	⊂2⊃
⊂3⊃	⊂D⊃	⊂3⊃	⊂3⊃	⊂3⊃
⊂4⊃	⊂E⊃	⊂4⊃	⊂4⊃	⊂4⊃
⊂5⊃	⊂F⊃	⊂5⊃	⊂5⊃	⊂5⊃
⊂6⊃	⊂G⊃	⊂6⊃	⊂6⊃	⊂6⊃
⊂7⊃		⊂7⊃	⊂7⊃	⊂7⊃
⊂8⊃		⊂8⊃	⊂8⊃	⊂8⊃
⊂9⊃		⊂9⊃	⊂9⊃	⊂9⊃

4. REGISTRATION NUMBER

⊂0⊃	⊂0⊃	⊂0⊃	⊂0⊃	⊂0⊃	⊂0⊃
⊂1⊃	⊂1⊃	⊂1⊃	⊂1⊃	⊂1⊃	⊂1⊃
⊂2⊃	⊂2⊃	⊂2⊃	⊂2⊃	⊂2⊃	⊂2⊃
⊂3⊃	⊂3⊃	⊂3⊃	⊂3⊃	⊂3⊃	⊂3⊃
⊂4⊃	⊂4⊃	⊂4⊃	⊂4⊃	⊂4⊃	⊂4⊃
⊂5⊃	⊂5⊃	⊂5⊃	⊂5⊃	⊂5⊃	⊂5⊃
⊂6⊃	⊂6⊃	⊂6⊃	⊂6⊃	⊂6⊃	⊂6⊃
⊂7⊃	⊂7⊃	⊂7⊃	⊂7⊃	⊂7⊃	⊂7⊃
⊂8⊃	⊂8⊃	⊂8⊃	⊂8⊃	⊂8⊃	⊂8⊃
⊂9⊃	⊂9⊃	⊂9⊃	⊂9⊃	⊂9⊃	⊂9⊃

7. SEX
⊂ ⊃ MALE
⊂ ⊃ FEMALE

The Princeton Review

5. YOUR NAME

First 4 letters of last name				FIRST INIT	MID INIT
⊂A⊃	⊂A⊃	⊂A⊃	⊂A⊃	⊂A⊃	⊂A⊃
⊂B⊃	⊂B⊃	⊂B⊃	⊂B⊃	⊂B⊃	⊂B⊃
⊂C⊃	⊂C⊃	⊂C⊃	⊂C⊃	⊂C⊃	⊂C⊃
⊂D⊃	⊂D⊃	⊂D⊃	⊂D⊃	⊂D⊃	⊂D⊃
⊂E⊃	⊂E⊃	⊂E⊃	⊂E⊃	⊂E⊃	⊂E⊃
⊂F⊃	⊂F⊃	⊂F⊃	⊂F⊃	⊂F⊃	⊂F⊃
⊂G⊃	⊂G⊃	⊂G⊃	⊂G⊃	⊂G⊃	⊂G⊃
⊂H⊃	⊂H⊃	⊂H⊃	⊂H⊃	⊂H⊃	⊂H⊃
⊂I⊃	⊂I⊃	⊂I⊃	⊂I⊃	⊂I⊃	⊂I⊃
⊂J⊃	⊂J⊃	⊂J⊃	⊂J⊃	⊂J⊃	⊂J⊃
⊂K⊃	⊂K⊃	⊂K⊃	⊂K⊃	⊂K⊃	⊂K⊃
⊂L⊃	⊂L⊃	⊂L⊃	⊂L⊃	⊂L⊃	⊂L⊃
⊂M⊃	⊂M⊃	⊂M⊃	⊂M⊃	⊂M⊃	⊂M⊃
⊂N⊃	⊂N⊃	⊂N⊃	⊂N⊃	⊂N⊃	⊂N⊃
⊂O⊃	⊂O⊃	⊂O⊃	⊂O⊃	⊂O⊃	⊂O⊃
⊂P⊃	⊂P⊃	⊂P⊃	⊂P⊃	⊂P⊃	⊂P⊃
⊂Q⊃	⊂Q⊃	⊂Q⊃	⊂Q⊃	⊂Q⊃	⊂Q⊃
⊂R⊃	⊂R⊃	⊂R⊃	⊂R⊃	⊂R⊃	⊂R⊃
⊂S⊃	⊂S⊃	⊂S⊃	⊂S⊃	⊂S⊃	⊂S⊃
⊂T⊃	⊂T⊃	⊂T⊃	⊂T⊃	⊂T⊃	⊂T⊃
⊂U⊃	⊂U⊃	⊂U⊃	⊂U⊃	⊂U⊃	⊂U⊃
⊂V⊃	⊂V⊃	⊂V⊃	⊂V⊃	⊂V⊃	⊂V⊃
⊂W⊃	⊂W⊃	⊂W⊃	⊂W⊃	⊂W⊃	⊂W⊃
⊂X⊃	⊂X⊃	⊂X⊃	⊂X⊃	⊂X⊃	⊂X⊃
⊂Y⊃	⊂Y⊃	⊂Y⊃	⊂Y⊃	⊂Y⊃	⊂Y⊃
⊂Z⊃	⊂Z⊃	⊂Z⊃	⊂Z⊃	⊂Z⊃	⊂Z⊃

---

1 ⊂A⊃ ⊂B⊃ ⊂C⊃ ⊂D⊃ ⊂E⊃
2 ⊂A⊃ ⊂B⊃ ⊂C⊃ ⊂D⊃ ⊂E⊃
3 ⊂A⊃ ⊂B⊃ ⊂C⊃ ⊂D⊃ ⊂E⊃
4 ⊂A⊃ ⊂B⊃ ⊂C⊃ ⊂D⊃ ⊂E⊃
5 ⊂A⊃ ⊂B⊃ ⊂C⊃ ⊂D⊃ ⊂E⊃
6 ⊂A⊃ ⊂B⊃ ⊂C⊃ ⊂D⊃ ⊂E⊃
7 ⊂A⊃ ⊂B⊃ ⊂C⊃ ⊂D⊃ ⊂E⊃
8 ⊂A⊃ ⊂B⊃ ⊂C⊃ ⊂D⊃ ⊂E⊃
9 ⊂A⊃ ⊂B⊃ ⊂C⊃ ⊂D⊃ ⊂E⊃
10 ⊂A⊃ ⊂B⊃ ⊂C⊃ ⊂D⊃ ⊂E⊃
11 ⊂A⊃ ⊂B⊃ ⊂C⊃ ⊂D⊃ ⊂E⊃
12 ⊂A⊃ ⊂B⊃ ⊂C⊃ ⊂D⊃ ⊂E⊃
13 ⊂A⊃ ⊂B⊃ ⊂C⊃ ⊂D⊃ ⊂E⊃
14 ⊂A⊃ ⊂B⊃ ⊂C⊃ ⊂D⊃ ⊂E⊃
15 ⊂A⊃ ⊂B⊃ ⊂C⊃ ⊂D⊃ ⊂E⊃
16 ⊂A⊃ ⊂B⊃ ⊂C⊃ ⊂D⊃ ⊂E⊃
17 ⊂A⊃ ⊂B⊃ ⊂C⊃ ⊂D⊃ ⊂E⊃
18 ⊂A⊃ ⊂B⊃ ⊂C⊃ ⊂D⊃ ⊂E⊃
19 ⊂A⊃ ⊂B⊃ ⊂C⊃ ⊂D⊃ ⊂E⊃
20 ⊂A⊃ ⊂B⊃ ⊂C⊃ ⊂D⊃ ⊂E⊃
21 ⊂A⊃ ⊂B⊃ ⊂C⊃ ⊂D⊃ ⊂E⊃
22 ⊂A⊃ ⊂B⊃ ⊂C⊃ ⊂D⊃ ⊂E⊃
23 ⊂A⊃ ⊂B⊃ ⊂C⊃ ⊂D⊃ ⊂E⊃

24 ⊂A⊃ ⊂B⊃ ⊂C⊃ ⊂D⊃ ⊂E⊃
25 ⊂A⊃ ⊂B⊃ ⊂C⊃ ⊂D⊃ ⊂E⊃
26 ⊂A⊃ ⊂B⊃ ⊂C⊃ ⊂D⊃ ⊂E⊃
27 ⊂A⊃ ⊂B⊃ ⊂C⊃ ⊂D⊃ ⊂E⊃
28 ⊂A⊃ ⊂B⊃ ⊂C⊃ ⊂D⊃ ⊂E⊃
29 ⊂A⊃ ⊂B⊃ ⊂C⊃ ⊂D⊃ ⊂E⊃
30 ⊂A⊃ ⊂B⊃ ⊂C⊃ ⊂D⊃ ⊂E⊃
31 ⊂A⊃ ⊂B⊃ ⊂C⊃ ⊂D⊃ ⊂E⊃
32 ⊂A⊃ ⊂B⊃ ⊂C⊃ ⊂D⊃ ⊂E⊃
33 ⊂A⊃ ⊂B⊃ ⊂C⊃ ⊂D⊃ ⊂E⊃
34 ⊂A⊃ ⊂B⊃ ⊂C⊃ ⊂D⊃ ⊂E⊃
35 ⊂A⊃ ⊂B⊃ ⊂C⊃ ⊂D⊃ ⊂E⊃
36 ⊂A⊃ ⊂B⊃ ⊂C⊃ ⊂D⊃ ⊂E⊃
37 ⊂A⊃ ⊂B⊃ ⊂C⊃ ⊂D⊃ ⊂E⊃
38 ⊂A⊃ ⊂B⊃ ⊂C⊃ ⊂D⊃ ⊂E⊃
39 ⊂A⊃ ⊂B⊃ ⊂C⊃ ⊂D⊃ ⊂E⊃
40 ⊂A⊃ ⊂B⊃ ⊂C⊃ ⊂D⊃ ⊂E⊃
41 ⊂A⊃ ⊂B⊃ ⊂C⊃ ⊂D⊃ ⊂E⊃
42 ⊂A⊃ ⊂B⊃ ⊂C⊃ ⊂D⊃ ⊂E⊃
43 ⊂A⊃ ⊂B⊃ ⊂C⊃ ⊂D⊃ ⊂E⊃
44 ⊂A⊃ ⊂B⊃ ⊂C⊃ ⊂D⊃ ⊂E⊃
45 ⊂A⊃ ⊂B⊃ ⊂C⊃ ⊂D⊃ ⊂E⊃
46 ⊂A⊃ ⊂B⊃ ⊂C⊃ ⊂D⊃ ⊂E⊃

47 ⊂A⊃ ⊂B⊃ ⊂C⊃ ⊂D⊃ ⊂E⊃
48 ⊂A⊃ ⊂B⊃ ⊂C⊃ ⊂D⊃ ⊂E⊃
49 ⊂A⊃ ⊂B⊃ ⊂C⊃ ⊂D⊃ ⊂E⊃
50 ⊂A⊃ ⊂B⊃ ⊂C⊃ ⊂D⊃ ⊂E⊃
51 ⊂A⊃ B ⊂C⊃ ⊂D⊃ ⊂E⊃
52 ⊂A⊃ ⊂B⊃ ⊂C⊃ ⊂D⊃ ⊂E⊃
53 ⊂A⊃ ⊂B⊃ ⊂C⊃ ⊂D⊃ ⊂E⊃
54 ⊂A⊃ ⊂B⊃ ⊂C⊃ ⊂D⊃ ⊂E⊃
55 ⊂A⊃ ⊂B⊃ ⊂C⊃ ⊂D⊃ ⊂E⊃
56 ⊂A⊃ ⊂B⊃ ⊂C⊃ ⊂D⊃ ⊂E⊃
57 ⊂A⊃ ⊂B⊃ ⊂C⊃ ⊂D⊃ ⊂E⊃
58 ⊂A⊃ ⊂B⊃ ⊂C⊃ ⊂D⊃ ⊂E⊃
59 ⊂A⊃ ⊂B⊃ ⊂C⊃ ⊂D⊃ ⊂E⊃
60 ⊂A⊃ ⊂B⊃ ⊂C⊃ ⊂D⊃ ⊂E⊃
61 ⊂A⊃ ⊂B⊃ ⊂C⊃ ⊂D⊃ ⊂E⊃
62 ⊂A⊃ ⊂B⊃ ⊂C⊃ ⊂D⊃ ⊂E⊃
63 ⊂A⊃ ⊂B⊃ ⊂C⊃ ⊂D⊃ ⊂E⊃
64 ⊂A⊃ ⊂B⊃ ⊂C⊃ ⊂D⊃ ⊂E⊃
65 ⊂A⊃ ⊂B⊃ ⊂C⊃ ⊂D⊃ ⊂E⊃
66 ⊂A⊃ ⊂B⊃ ⊂C⊃ ⊂D⊃ ⊂E⊃
67 ⊂A⊃ ⊂B⊃ ⊂C⊃ ⊂D⊃ ⊂E⊃
68 ⊂A⊃ ⊂B⊃ ⊂C⊃ ⊂D⊃ ⊂E⊃
69 ⊂A⊃ ⊂B⊃ ⊂C⊃ ⊂D⊃ ⊂E⊃

Part B

	I	II	CE
101	⊂T⊃ ⊂F⊃	⊂T⊃ ⊂F⊃	⊂ ⊃
102	⊂T⊃ ⊂F⊃	⊂T⊃ ⊂F⊃	⊂ ⊃
103	⊂T⊃ ⊂F⊃	⊂T⊃ ⊂F⊃	⊂ ⊃
104	⊂T⊃ ⊂F⊃	⊂T⊃ ⊂F⊃	⊂ ⊃
105	⊂T⊃ ⊂F⊃	⊂T⊃ ⊂F⊃	⊂ ⊃
106	⊂T⊃ ⊂F⊃	⊂T⊃ ⊂F⊃	⊂ ⊃
107	⊂T⊃ ⊂F⊃	⊂T⊃ ⊂F⊃	⊂ ⊃
108	⊂T⊃ ⊂F⊃	⊂T⊃ ⊂F⊃	⊂ ⊃
109	⊂T⊃ ⊂F⊃	⊂T⊃ ⊂F⊃	⊂ ⊃
110	⊂T⊃ ⊂F⊃	⊂T⊃ ⊂F⊃	⊂ ⊃
111	⊂T⊃ ⊂F⊃	⊂T⊃ ⊂F⊃	⊂ ⊃
112	⊂T⊃ ⊂F⊃	⊂T⊃ ⊂F⊃	⊂ ⊃
113	⊂T⊃ ⊂F⊃	⊂T⊃ ⊂F⊃	⊂ ⊃
114	⊂T⊃ ⊂F⊃	⊂T⊃ ⊂F⊃	⊂ ⊃
115	⊂T⊃ ⊂F⊃	⊂T⊃ ⊂F⊃	⊂ ⊃
116	⊂T⊃ ⊂F⊃	⊂T⊃ ⊂F⊃	⊂ ⊃

NOTES

NOTES

NOTES

NOTES

NOTES

AP Exams

Cracking the AP Biology Exam,
2004–2005 Edition
0-375-76393-7 • $18.00/C$27.00

Cracking the AP Calculus AB & BC Exam,
2004–2005 Edition
0-375-76381-3 • $19.00/C$28.50

Cracking the AP Chemistry Exam,
2004–2005 Edition
0-375-76382-1• $18.00/C$27.00

**Cracking the AP Computer Science
A & AB Exam ,** 2004-2005 Edition
0-375-76383-X • $19.00/C$28.50

**Cracking the AP Economics (Macro &
Micro) Exam,** 2004-2005 Edition
0-375-76384-8 • $18.00/C$27.00

Cracking the AP English Literature Exam,
2004–2005 Edition
0-375-76385-6 • $18.00/C$27.00

Cracking the AP European History Exam,
2004–2005 Edition
0-375-76386-4 • $18.00/C$27.00

Cracking the AP Physics B & C Exam,
2004–2005 Edition
0-375-76387-2 • $19.00/C$28.50

Cracking the AP Psychology Exam,
2004–2005 Edition
0-375-76388-0 • $18.00/C$27.00

Cracking the AP Spanish Exam,
2004–2005 Edition
0-375-76389-9 • $18.00/C$27.00

Cracking the AP Statistics Exam,
2004–2005 Edition
0-375-76390-2 • $19.00/C$28.50

**Cracking the AP U.S. Government
and Politics Exam,** 2004–2005 Edition
0-375-76391-0 • $18.00/C$27.00

Cracking the AP U.S. History Exam,
2004–2005 Edition
0-375-76392-9 • $18.00/C$27.00

Cracking the AP World History Exam,
2004–2005 Edition
0-375-76380-5 • $18.00/C$27.00

SAT Subject Tests

Cracking the SAT Biology E/M Subject Test,
2005-2006 Edition
0-375-76447-X • $19.00/C$27.00

Cracking the SAT Chemistry Subject Test,
2005-2006 Edition
0-375-76448-8 • $18.00/C$26.00

Cracking the SAT French Subject Test,
2005-2006 Edition
0-375-76449-6 • $18.00/C$26.00

Cracking the SAT Literature Subject Test,
2005-2006 Edition
0-375-76446-1 • $18.00/C$26.00

**Cracking the SAT Math 1 and 2
Subject Tests,** 2005-2006 Edition
0-375-76451-8 • $19.00/C$27.00

Cracking the SAT Physics Subject Test,
2005-2006 Edition
0-375-76452-6 • $19.00/C$27.00

Cracking the SAT Spanish Subject Test,
2005-2006 Edition
0-375-76453-4 • $18.00/C$26.00

**Cracking the SAT U.S. & World History
Subject Tests,** 2005-2006 Edition
0-375-76450-X • $19.00/C$27.00

Available at Bookstores Everywhere
PrincetonReview.com

Need More?

If you want to learn more about how to excel on the SAT Subject Test in Chemistry, you're in the right place. Our expertise extends far beyond just this test. But this isn't about us, it's about getting you into the college of your choice.

One way to increase the number of fat envelopes you receive is to have strong test scores. So, if you're still nervous—relax. Consider all of your options.

We consistently improve students' scores through our books, classroom courses, private tutoring and online courses. Call 800-2Review or visit *PrincetonReview.com*.

If you like our *Cracking the SAT Chemistry Subject Test*, check out:

- *The Best 357 Colleges*
- *Cracking the New SAT*
- *11 Practice Tests for the New SAT and PSAT*
- *Cracking the AP Chemistry Exam*
- *Cracking the SAT Biology Subject Test*
- *Cracking the SAT Physics Subject Test*